Conceptual Landscapes

Conceptual Landscapes explores the dilemma faced in the early moments of design thinking through a gradient of work in landscape and environmental design media by both emerging and well-established designers and educators of landscape architecture. It questions where and, more importantly, how the process of design starts.

The book deconstructs the steps of conceptualizing design in order to reignite pedagogical discussions about timing and design fundamentals, and to reveal how the spark of an idea happens – from a range of unique perspectives. Through a careful arrangement of visual essays that integrate analog, digital, and mixed-media works and processes, the book highlights differences between diverse techniques and triggers debate between design, representation, technology, and creative culture in the field.

Taken together, the book's visual investigation of the conceptual design process serves as a learning tool for aspiring designers and seasoned professionals alike. By situating student work alongside that of experienced teachers and landscape architects, the book also demystifies outdated notions of individual genius and sheds new light on the nearly universally messy process of discovery, bridged across years and diverse creative vocabularies in the conceptual design process. Lavishly illustrated with over 210 full color images, this book is a must-read for students and instructors in landscape architecture.

Simon M. Bussiere is Assistant Professor of Landscape Architecture and Urban Ecological Design at the University of Hawai'i at Mānoa. His research explores intersections of ecological urbanism, design communication, and pedagogy.

Conceptual Landscapes

Fundamentals in the Beginning
Design Process

Edited by
Simon M. Bussiere

LONDON AND NEW YORK

Designed cover image: Simon M. Bussiere

First published 2023
by Routledge
4 Park Square, Milton Park, Abingdon, Oxon OX14 4RN

and by Routledge
605 Third Avenue, New York, NY 10158

Routledge is an imprint of the Taylor & Francis Group, an informa business

British Library Cataloguing-in-Publication Data
A catalogue record for this book is available from the British Library

Library of Congress Cataloging-in-Publication Data
Names: Bussiere, Simon M., editor.
Title: Conceptual landscapes: fundamentals in the beginning design process / edited by Simon M. Bussiere.
Description: Abingdon, Oxon; New York, NY: Routledge, 2023. | Includes bibliographical references and index. | Identifiers: LCCN 2022047136 (print) | LCCN 2022047137 (ebook) | ISBN 9780367513030 (hbk) | ISBN 9780367513047 (pbk) | ISBN 9781003053255 (ebk)
Subjects: LCSH: Landscape design. | Sustainability.
Classification: LCC SB472.45 .C638 2023 (print) | LCC SB472.45 (ebook) | DDC 712—dc23/eng/20221118
LC record available at https://lccn.loc.gov/2022047136
LC ebook record available at https://lccn.loc.gov/2022047137

ISBN: 9780367513030 (hbk)
ISBN: 9780367513047 (pbk)
ISBN: 9781003053255 (ebk)

DOI: 10.4324/9781003053255

Typeset in Helvetica Neue
by codeMantra

Contents

Notes on Contributors

Aidan Ackerman is Assistant Professor of Landscape Architecture at the State University of New York College of Environmental Science and Forestry. His research investigates methods of computationally simulating and visualizing landscape ecology, with a focus on information-driven environmental modeling. He teaches courses in landscape visualization, parametric modeling, and computational landscape design, building information modeling (BIM) for landscape architecture, and undergraduate as well as graduate design studios. Ackerman develops cultural and historic landscape visualization projects through the ESF Center for Cultural Landscape Preservation and the Olmsted Center for Landscape Preservation. Visualization projects include Liberty Island, New York, NY; Flight 93 National Memorial, Shanksville, PA; Home of Franklin D. Roosevelt National Historic Site, Hyde Park, NY; and Martin Van Buren National Historic Site, Kinderhook, NY. He also researches tools for computational modeling, simulation, and visualization of large-scale forest sites using immersive virtual reality technology, creating immersive forest visualizations as part of the Climate and Applied Forest Research Institute (CAFRI).

Simon M. Bussiere is a licensed landscape architect and assistant professor of landscape architecture and urban ecological design at the University of Hawai'i at Mānoa. His teaching and research is centered on ecological design practice, communication, and pedagogy. Trained at the University of Massachusetts Amherst (BSLA, 2005) and Harvard University (MLA, 2009), Bussiere's professional experience ranges from design-build work in New England, to large-scale landscape, architecture, and urban design with EDAW/AECOM Australia, to architectural research, design, and construction with Estudio Teddy Cruz in Nicaragua, and most recently through the University of Hawai'i Community Design Center (UHCDC). Simon has held academic positions at Ball State University, the University of Nagasaki, the University of Utah Asia Campus in Seoul, and Tongji University in Shanghai through the UH Global Track Program. He is Second Vice-President of the Council of Educators in Landscape Architecture and is a Past-President of the American Society of Landscape Architects, Hawai'i.

Leonard Grosch is a landscape architect. He grew up in Munich, completed his training as a perennial plant gardener there. Thereafter, he studied at the TU Dresden, the Royal Danish Academy of Fine Arts in Copenhagen, and the TU Berlin. He has been managing the competition department at Atelier Loidl since 2003 and been a partner in Atelier Loidl Landscape Architects since 2007. With his team, he has won numerous competitions and realized the projects that developed from them (for detailed information, please see www.atelier-loidl.de). Parallel to his work as a landscape architect Leonard works as a photographer and artist. Leonard lives in Berlin.

Richard L. Hindle is a designer, innovator, and educator. He teaches courses in ecological technology, planting design, and site design studios. Professor Hindle's research focuses on technology in the urban and regional landscape with an emphasis on material processes, innovation, and patents. His current research explores innovation in landscape-related technologies across a range of scales, from large-scale mappings of riverine and coastal patents to detailed historical studies on the antecedents of vegetated architectural systems. A recurring theme in Hindle's work is the tandem history, and future, of technology, city, and landscape. His writing and making explore environmental futurism as chronicled in patent documents and the potential of new technological narratives and material processes to reframe theory, practice, and the production of landscape. Richard has worked as a consultant and designer, specializing in the design of advanced horticultural and building systems, from green roofs and facades to large-scale urban landscapes.

Rob Holmes is an associate professor and chair of the Undergraduate Landscape Architecture Program at Auburn University. His research and creative work centers on infrastructure design and landscape change, with a particular focus on sediment as a link between infrastructure, people, and landscapes. He is also cofounder of the Dredge Research Collaborative, an independent nonprofit organization that seeks to improve sediment systems through design research, building public knowledge, and facilitating transdisciplinary conversation. His DRC projects include participating in the Resilient By Design Bay Area Challenge as part of the Public Sediment team, organizing the DredgeFest event series, collaboration with the US Army Corps of Engineers' Engineering With Nature program, and study of landscape infrastructure designs for coastal communities in Mobile Bay, funded by NOAA's Effects of Sea Level Rise program.

Justine Holzman is a landscape researcher, designer, and educator with a background in landscape architecture, and a member of the Dredge Research Collaborative. Holzman is currently training as an historian of science at Princeton University where her doctoral work focuses on how knowledge is produced about environments and how landscapes are designed and transformed for scientific research. Holzman has previously taught in departments of Landscape Architecture, Architecture, and Urban Design at Columbia University, the University of Toronto, the University of Tennessee, and Louisiana State University. At LSU, Holzman worked as a research fellow with the LSU Coastal Sustainability Studio, a transdisciplinary research studio with scientists, engineers, and designers working on coastal issues in Louisiana. Holzman is coauthor of *Responsive Landscapes: Strategies for Responsive Technologies in Landscape Architecture* (2016) and received an MLA from LSU and a BA in Landscape Architecture from UC Berkeley.

Zaneta Hong is an Assistant Professor in Landscape Architecture. Trained as a landscape architect and industrial designer, her teaching and research focuses on material ecologies, landscape technologies, and sustainable practices. Prior to her arrival at Cornell University, she worked at the Harvard Graduate School of Design, University of Virginia, and University of Texas in Austin. Her work has been recognized by the Graham Foundation and Environmental Design Research Association, and she has been awarded the Garden Club of America Rome Prize Fellowship, MacDowell Fellowship, and Certificate of Teaching Excellence by the Harvard Derek Bok Center. Along with teaching, Zaneta is Co-Director of the Design + Culture Lab and Research + Design Consultant for GA Collaborative.

Yun Hye Hwang is an accredited landscape architect in Singapore and Associate Professor of Landscape Architecture at the School of Design and Environment, NUS, currently serving as Programme Director of the Bachelor's program. Her research, teaching, and professional activities speculate on emerging demands in fast-growing Asian cities by exploring ecological design and management versus manicured greenery and the multifunctional role of everyday landscapes. She focuses on transferring knowledge of urban ecology from academia to practice through active interdisciplinary and transdisciplinary collaborations.

Sara Jacobs is Assistant Professor of Landscape Architecture at the University of British Columbia, where she is grateful to live and work on the unceded traditional territories of the Musqueam, Squamish, and Tsleil-Waututh Nations. Through transdisciplinary methods that connect across her experience in landscape architecture, environmental history, and geography, Sara writes and draws about how practices of care and socio-ecological relations become legible through landscape histories to rethink dominant environmental knowledge within contested landscapes. Recent work has been supported by the Graham Foundation and the Center for Land Use Interpretation, and published in the *Journal of Landscape Architecture*, *Journal of the Society of Architectural Historians, Journal of Architectural Education,* and *SITE Magazine.*

Forbes Lipschitz is Associate Professor of Landscape Architecture at the Knowlton School. As a faculty affiliate for the Initiative in Food and AgriCultural Transformation, her current research investigates the potential of design to reframe and reshape conventional working landscapes. Through public installations and participatory workshops, she explores ways for design to help communities better understand and engage with agricultural systems. Her research has been published nationally and internationally and her creative work has been featured in Landscape Architecture Magazine, Metropolis Magazine, and Smithsonian Magazine. She has been awarded funding from the Foundation for Food and Agricultural Research, the Graham Foundation for Fine Arts, and the Van Alen Institute. She received her Master's in Landscape Architecture from the Harvard Graduate School of Design, and a Bachelors of the Arts from Pomona College in Claremont, California.

Kees Lokman teaches design studios in the landscape architecture program at UBC. Before joining SALA in 2014, he taught at Washington University in St. Louis, the Illinois Institute of Technology, and at Archeworks, a hands-on, alternative design school in Chicago. Kees has practiced landscape architecture at the offices of plantsman Piet Oudolf in the Netherlands and at Terry Guen Design Associates in Chicago and is the founder of Parallax Landscape. The collaborative and interdisciplinary design and research platform explore design challenges related to water and food shortages, depleting energy resources, climate change, and ongoing urbanization. The work focuses on urban strategies that have the capacity to link each site's unique character to ecologies, infrastructures, and economies on larger scales. Parallax Landscape is the recipient of numerous design awards and recognition, including first prize in the "Transiting Cities – Low Carbon Futures" design competition in 2012, and in 2013 finalist in the international ideas competition "Infill Philadelphia – Soak it Up!" and winner of the International Garden Festival in Allariz, Spain. In 2014, Kees was shortlisted in the Netherlands for the Prix de Rome. His writing and academic research, focused on the relationships between geography, economy, ecology, and infrastructure, have been published in various journals, including MONU Magazine and Landscape Architecture Frontiers.

Ferdinand Ludwig's research is focused on architectural concepts in which plants play a central role. Integrating plants – both functionally and creatively – into construction designs not only provides answers to some of today's most pressing ecological issues, such as the adaptation to climate change. It also presents a methodological challenge, encouraging exploration into ways of dealing with aspects of growth and decay, chance and probability in architecture and landscape design. Ferdinand Ludwig studied architecture and completed his doctorate studies at the University of Stuttgart with a dissertation entitled "The Botanical Fundamentals of Baubotanik and their Application in Design". In 2007, he founded the research group "Baubotanik" at the University of Stuttgart's Institute of Architectural Theory and Design (IGMA), and he headed this group as a research associate until 2017. Professor Ludwig applies the botanical-constructive approach to architecture, urban planning, and landscape design in the office collaboration "ludwig.schönle: Baubotanik – Architecture – Urbanism", which he founded with Daniel Schönle in 2010.

Karen Lutsky is an assistant professor of landscape architecture at the University of Minnesota and director of the Great Lakes Design Labs. Karen has held teaching and research positions in landscape architecture at a number of institutions including the University of Pennsylvania, the Illinois Institute of Technology, Penn State University, and the Ohio State University. Her design research and work focus on how landscape architects and designers might better design 'with' changing landscapes be they shorelines of the Great Lakes Basin or southern boreal forests. She is the coauthor of the forthcoming book *Five Bay Landscapes; Curious Explorations of the Great Lakes Basin* being published by the University of Pittsburgh Press and also has writings and work that can be found in publications such as Places Journal, Scenario Journal, Landscape Architecture Magazine, LUNCH, and *The Third Coast Atlas*. She holds a master's degree in Landscape Architecture from the University of Pennsylvania and a bachelors' degree in 'Environment and Society' from Brandeis University.

Fadi Masoud is Assistant Professor of Landscape Architecture and Urbanism at the University of Toronto and the Director of the Centre for Landscape Research. His research and teaching focus on the relationships between environmental systems, multiscalar design, and instrumental planning policy tools. Masoud currently leads projects on climate adaptive urbanism, novel resilient urban codes, and the design of inclusive and resilient public open space. Prior to joining the University of Toronto, Masoud held teaching and research appointments at the Massachusetts Institute of Technology and was trained and practiced as a planner, landscape architect, and urban designer. Masoud currently sits on Waterfront Toronto's Design Review Panel and was a member of the City of Toronto's Urban Flooding Working Group.

Mary Pat McGuire is a landscape architect and associate professor at the University of Illinois Urbana-Champaign, where she also directs the design research studio Water Lab in Chicago. Her research and teaching focus on the histories and transformation of urban land, rainwater design, climate adaptation design, and surface design strategies including depaving. McGuire is the coeditor of *Fresh Water: Design Research* *for Inland Water Territories* (AR+D) and has published research in the *Journal of Landscape Architecture, Landscape Journal, Plan Journal, Environmental Research: Infrastructure and Sustainability, Topos, Next City, and Grist*. Her research has been supported by US-EPA, National Sea Grant (NOAA), Wright Ingraham Institute, Walder Foundation, and Landscape Architecture Foundation among others. McGuire previously taught at IIT and practiced with Peter Walker & Partners and Conservation Design Forum. McGuire has a Master's in Landscape Architecture from the University of Virginia and was recently awarded the President's Award from the Council of Educators in Landscape Architecture.

Scott Jennings Melbourne is a designer, teacher, and founding principal of MxM Landscape Architecture. He is dedicated to designing-inspired landscapes that bring communities together while strengthening ties between individuals and their environment. During the past two decades, he has contributed toward a range of park, university, urban mixed-use, and hospitality projects for public and private clients alike. His award-winning teaching has explored the potential for design to inform decision-making in developing regions of Southeast Asia, with a particular focus on Yangon, Myanmar and East Java, Indonesia. Melbourne holds a Master's in Landscape Architecture with distinction from Harvard University and is the author of *Refining Nature: The Landscape Architecture of Peter Walker*, published by Birkhäuser.

Emma Mendel is a practicing landscape designer, researching and writing on topics pertaining to sociocultural materiality, infrastructure, and representation. Mendel's project Access to safe drinking water for First Nations Communities in Ontario was published in the *Ontario Association of Landscape Architects Journal* which featured her sculptural pieces that captured mutable boundaries between materials. Her design was recognized in the Canadian wide competition, Future Legacies, that offered perspectives on the role of legacy as a driving force in the creation of a nation. She is a Graham Foundation grantee for her project Ephemeral Material Infrastructures: Expanding Intuitive Knowledge of Hydrological Systems. Her publications include the *Princeton Architectural Journal*, *Kerb Landscape Architecture Journal*, and the winning project (Coastal Paradox) published in the University of Pennsylvania's *LA+* journal. Mendel previously taught at the University of Virginia in the Department of Landscape Architecture. She holds a bachelors from Rhode Island School of Design, a Master's in Landscape Architecture from the University of Toronto, and a Master's in Design at the Harvard Graduate School of Design in Cambridge, MA, where she currently resides.

Elizabeth Mossop is Dean of the UTS School of Design, Architecture, and Building and a landscape architect and urbanist with wide-ranging experience in both landscape design and urban planning. Elizabeth is a founding principal of Spackman Mossop & Michaels landscape architects based in Sydney and New Orleans. Her professional practice concentrates on urban infrastructure and open space projects such as the multiple award-winning Bowen Place Crossing in Canberra, Press Street Gardens in New Orleans, and Sydney's Cook and Phillip Park. She has also been involved in many aspects of the post-hurricane reconstruction of New Orleans and the Gulf Coast and the ongoing revitalization of Detroit. With an academic career spanning 25 years, Elizabeth has held key roles at universities in both the United States and Australia. Before joining UTS, she was Professor of Landscape Architecture and Director of the Robert Reich School of Landscape Architecture at Louisiana State University, one of the highest ranked landscape architecture programs in the United States. Previously, she was the Director of the Masters of Landscape Architecture program at the Harvard Graduate School of Design.

Sergio Sanna is a landscape architect and Professor for Urban and Territorial Interventions at the Academy of Fine Arts of Palermo. He is also the cofounder of Ground Action, a collective engaged in environmental performances which promotes maintenance as a form of design and reuse as act of transformation in spatial and social process. His research focuses on the operational workshop methodology that was specifically developed with associations such as Landworks in Sardinia, Topografia del Trauma and Giardini in Campo in Sicily, and during Manifesta 12 The Planetary Garden in Palermo. Sanna studied Architecture in Palermo (Italy) and Mendrisio (Switzerland) with Elia Zenghelis, then completed a Master's in Landscape Architecture at the UPC (Polytechnic University of Catalonia), where he worked at the Urban Planning Department. He has been researcher at the Iuav University of Venice and adjunct professor for Territorial Analysis and Landscape Design at the Academy of Fine Arts of Catania.

Emily Vogler is a landscape architect whose research, design, and teaching investigate social–ecological systems surrounding water infrastructure, sense of place, and climate uncertainty. She has ongoing research projects looking at the irrigation ditches in New Mexico, aging dam infrastructure in New England, and coastal adaptation strategies in Narragansett Bay. In her research and design practice, she investigates methods to address regional environmental and cultural issues at the site and material scale; novel approaches to engaging the public in the design and decision-making process; and strategies for strengthening the collaboration and communication between designers, artists, and scientists. Vogler is an associate professor at the Rhode Island School of Design where she served as department head from 2017–19. Prior to teaching at RISD, she was a senior project manager at Michael Van Valkenburgh Associates and the 2010 National Olmsted Scholar.

Acknowledgments

Many people deserve credit for the content that follows, most notably the chapter authors themselves, for their patience, generosity, and willingness to put their work on these pages for you, the reader. I'm incredibly thankful to Megha Patel, the book's editorial assistant, who along with her team at Routledge was instrumental in seeing this project come together. Louise Baird-Smith, Grace Harrison, and Sadé Lee shepherded the project along before her with aplomb. And without you – the student, the emerging professional landscape architect, the seasoned academic, the practice leader – the audience for this book, I would have no idea how to frame this topic and present it to you for consideration. I'm grateful for all your criticism, time, and attention in reading these essays and their arguments for and around innovations in conceptual landscape design. I hope some seeds of new, provocative, and insightful concepts begin to form as you find connections between these thinkers and yourself; their ideas and yours.

In 2015, Quilian Riano, Dustin Headley, and I cocurated thinkfast, a traveling exhibition that compiled early conceptual design work from a range of emerging and established researchers and practitioners in architecture, landscape architecture, urban design, and industrial design. With funding from Ball State University, Kansas State University, and Parsons School of Design Strategies, the interdisciplinary exhibition resulted in encouraging reviews. The dialog of prospective curiosity that grew out of thinkfast was fundamental to this book's inception. My efforts to refocus the idea and publish it for a landscape architecture audience came later at the advice of two of my closest mentors, Meg Calkins and Jody Rosenblatt-Naderi.

I owe my ability to piece together complex ideas about landscape to my teachers Richard Forman, Michael Van Valkenburg, John Stilgoe, Jack Ahern, Tim O'loan, Jon Shinkfield, and Teddy Cruz. And, I credit my many colleagues, including Harry Eggink, Lance Walters, Jason Selley, Hunter Heavilin, Ara Laylo, Ben George, Joe Blalock, Loren Deeg, Sean Burns, Dave Ferguson, Andrew Wit, Michel Mounayar, Phoebe White, Karla Sierralta, Cathi Ho Schar, Laura McGuire, Wendy Meguro, Kevin Nute, Bundit Kanisthakhon, David Rockwood, Andy Kaufman, Clark Llewellyn, Martin Despang, and Judith Stilgenbauer, for pushing me as a designer and educator. Guillermo Vásquez de Velasco, Daniel Friedman, and Bill Chapman have made it possible for me to do the research for this book, kindly aligning my teaching and scholarship over the last decade with courses focused largely on beginning design and design research.

I'm greatly indebted to my University of Hawai'i 'Ohana for their constant aloha and generous guidance. And none of my work would be possible without the love and support of my family and my partner Carmela Arcenas. My mom, despite having raised three boys on her own, convinced me from an early age that everyone had an innate talent for something. Some find passion in it and excel, others aren't able to realize theirs, but none start without some imaginative potential. I hold hope in that fragile idea, in beginning design education, and more broadly, in each of our capacities to make something productive out of that nascent potential, and for the betterment of humanity. I hope this book's readers find their unique place in the field, and realize as I have, that each of our perspectives is valuable, and all our contributions hold promise in expanding the discourse. While we as individuals benefit from the study and application of our own ideas, the field itself advances from the outcomes of those works. Hypothetical or physically tested, the work once made and lived out builds forward as a conglomerating envelope that is ever-redefining the boundaries of what this discipline, profession, and artform can be. The better we leverage our talents, in short, the stronger landscape architecture becomes.

Introduction

Simon M. Bussiere

Designers have the capacity to transform ideas into reality. *But how* does the process of design start? How do those first fragile steps taken bring an idea out of obscurity and into a form where it can be tested and somehow communicated to others? *How* are those earliest critical factors framed and formed to determine whether an idea about the landscape first manifests? On paper, as a model, a sketch, a phrase? And in the transitioning from our own education to the future of the larger field, *how* will conceptual design in landscape architecture likely continue to evolve as it has for decades? *(Centuries?)* This book asks and presents critical positions from experts in landscape architecture and design from across the globe to reveal a small but significant cross-section of attitudes and approaches to this key question and to offer a set of unique contemporary perspectives advancing the body of knowledge in this field.

As an undergraduate student, I became intensely interested in the process of finding ways to conceive of and communicate new ideas in physical space. I was obsessed with mapping and making, framing and forming, tinkering with tools and processes, criticizing historical practices and furtively attempting to develop a voice and a strategic means of speaking it aloud. Surrounded by seemingly endless sources of inspiration in school, my extraordinary peers, professors, libraries, and the broader intellectual community in my orbit, I was drawn into the search for the foundations of those creative stimuli. And although I was aware that those innumerable conceptive forces were often layered and simultaneous, the tangible or literal birth of ideas and the methods of their construction as critical artifacts of understanding largely remained a mystery. My classmates at the time and my students today seem to share in that same experience of paradoxically exciting uncertainty.

As a professor, I see my students excited by the prospect of articulating a new idea, but nearly always struggling with the ambiguous origins of each new project. While they recognize that some struggle comes as a matter of course, this *beginning* is nevertheless a typically furtive or surreptitious endeavor, to say the least. Further complicating things for students, their instructors inevitably imbue their teaching with their individuality, rich in the diverse methods and biases that have shaped them as humans and designers.

Competent teachers do their best to understand outcomes and standards; they review the appropriate texts and prepare lessons that optimize the learning process toward those outcomes. Especially good ones recognize that students are individuals as well, and they tailor much of their teaching to meet students where they are individually. But until a student progresses far enough through a program of study, to the point where they realize that each project, each problem, and each design grows from a unique set of perspectives, they might very well believe there are right and wrong ways of starting. It is clear in having done the research for this book, there are not.

When I started my academic career, and by that I mean when I first became a teacher, I was fresh out of practice as they say, and that wasn't too long after grad school. My first appointment as Instructor was in 2011 and I was 26 years old. I was capable and confident to work on about any design project as a designer, but as a new teacher, I was impatient and inconsistent. I was often younger and admittedly less mature than some of my graduate students (still am, sometimes) and back when I started I had a lot to learn about how to *teach* design (and still do). I can see now as I look back, that my initial teaching approach was tied too closely to the way I was taught, and my expectations, particularly of professional students, were set in what must have appeared to them as an outdated paradigm. I say all this because often it is the teachers who students rely on to teach design. That's at least a third of their job after all. But, I maintain that while design can be learned, obviously, the act of design, the urgency and intention to make the world anew, that is, to design it (to develop a process by which design manifests) is very difficult to teach. That said, there are certainly ways of going about it that make a lot of sense, and some arguably less effective approaches that can always use some updating. The Council of Landscape Architecture Annual Conference reaffirms that assertion in my view each and every year.

In light of the reciprocity required between students and a teacher, or a teacher and their students, the contemporary design studio itself, by necessity, has to be treated as a design problem. Each one – every semester. And while students might think that all design faculty take this view, that isn't always the case. Students should, however, be at least somewhat aware that teachers are under immense pressure to formulate their methods toward achieving standardized outcomes. Adjunct instructors to a lesser degree, and tenure-track faculty especially. Teaching performance is carefully recorded and governed by department, school, college, university, and national oversight and accrediting bodies. Professionally accredited programs must equip their graduates with the tools and methods of the profession, and their policies are inherently aimed at preparing emerging designers for licensure and practice. The standards, while critical for ensuring minimal competency across graduate cohorts, can seem restrictive, particularly for new faculty aiming to make their mark. Teachers scan pages and make lectures, we redraw important diagrams and charts, we organize a sequence of exercises suitable for a given curriculum and pedagogy, and we adhere to official learning objectives/outcomes set before us by accrediting bodies. If we come to understand the limits of such formal models of "transmitting knowledge", we might start integrating more interactive or otherwise discursive (or otherwise collaborative or messy) elements into the process. We might, therefore, observe how students are able to learn from one another and even encourage more interface and collaboration. Delivery of content, absorption, discussion, application, critique, and revision – these phases are all scaffolded by performance and accreditation standards to ensure quality education is being delivered. In short, teaching design presents an intrinsic challenge of both creative and organizational dimensions. Despite the external influence of uniformity and stability, it takes on a variety of nuanced forms, rhythms, and modalities, with profound and beautiful inconsistencies resulting in equally varied vocabularies, approaches, and outcomes. It's only in looking back on the totality of one's education, however, that students can possibly comprehend that everyone approaches, teaches, and learns to design a bit differently.

And so, as contemporary students take on each new design challenge, they often face a predicamental position somewhere between total uncertainty about how to begin their work, on the one hand, or find themselves under overly prescriptive and seemingly myopic or parochial constraints, on the other hand. Perceptions of both extremes can be stifling at that critical moment at the root of the messy and recursive process of design. Having taught design in a range of learning environments for more than a decade, I have become acutely aware that there is a need for an inspirational and accessible resource for students of the environmental design disciplines who are *beginning* the design process – one that is dedicated solely to issues concerned with *conceptual landscape design* and one that helps springboard visual-thinking across multiple histories, scales, techniques, and areas of academic and disciplinary focus. That critical need is the inspiration and justification for this book.

The collection of work in the following pages explores the common dilemma faced in the early moments of conceptual design through a gradient of work in landscape media by both emerging and well-established teachers and practitioners of landscape architecture. These chapters and the diverse perspectives within are not intended to offer formulae, nor exact prescriptions to follow toward "success", but rather some small assurance that within the vast array of possible trajectories in conceptual landscape design, no two paths follow the same course. The book offers exposure to multiple points of view, illustrating a range of approaches and foci, and thereby deconstructing the elemental components of the early process of conceptual thinking. The book takes on an expository tack, revealing concepts in design through the lens of each chapter's author – their oeuvre, biases, region, students, and other creative and technical aspirations in order to reignite pedagogical discussions about timing, technique, fundamentals, and also to reveal how the *spark of an idea* happens from a given range of unique experiences. Through a careful arrangement of heavily visual essays that integrate theoretical positions with supporting analogue, digital and mixed-media works, and processes, the book highlights differences between diverse practices and argues for more meaningful debate between design, representation, technology, and creative culture in the field.

In Chapter 2, Emma Mendel asks her readers to embrace "obsession" or the rapt state of the obsédé, as a precursor to meaningful concept development. Mary Pat McGuire in Chapter 11 examines "grounding" and site-dependence as a means of rationalizing materiality and working processes. Emily Vogler discusses cross-pollinating potentials in the interface between site-scale artful interventions and their broader implications for regional landscapes in Chapter 7. And Fadi Masoud in Chapter 16 takes his readers through the origins of the rendered image as the quintessential means for designers and their clients to communicate change in the environment to mass audiences, enhancing our understanding of such visual creations as critical tools for engaging reaction, to name a few. Many others still explore practical constraints that guide decision-making, data filtering, information indexing, and a host of other possibilities in the early acts of making a concept come into being.

Taken together, the book's visual investigation of the conceptual design process serves as a learning tool for aspiring designers and seasoned professionals alike. By situating student work alongside that of experienced teachers and landscape architects, the book also aims to demystify outdated absurd notions of individual genius and sheds new light on the nearly universally messy and collaborative process of conceptual landscape discovery. Much of the message in the words and pictures which follow herein are reserved for the offices and classrooms which house these writers and their teams. Bridged across years, geographies, and diverse creative vocabularies, this book is a hopeful and prospective tribute to their work, their working methods, and the dissemination of those unique and profoundly varied agendas to all of us in landscape architecture hoping to broaden and yet define our boundaries and capacities for making landscapes and thereby evolving the field and discipline of landscape architecture.

Who Is This Book For?

This book is primarily a tool for students in professional landscape architecture programs and those preparing to or having recently entered into the landscape architecture profession. It contains high-quality images and descriptions of exemplary work and provocative supporting theory and argument, structured in a way to help deconstruct a range of possible conceptual design approaches. While some of the text may at first appear aimed at a more experienced audience, the intention of the collection overall is to serve all levels of readers concerned with making their own design process more rigorous, clear, and deliberate. I edited this book, wrote this introduction, and curated these chapters together with beginning BLA and MLA students in mind, but anyone with a keen eye and a curiosity for finding deeper meaning in the conception and conceptualization of their own work will find inspiration within. New and emerging professional landscape architects especially need this book, along with so many other sources of information, to help them form new connections between their unique values and experiences and the powerful, stimulating, and ever-evolving vocabularies and models of working in the broader discourse. The written words when read with intention string together and form novel arguments about our histories and about the nature of how things continue to change. And, new designers need exposure to both these formulated theories and practical applications of thought most of all. Their words and images will, in fact, undoubtedly shape key aspects of the future/yet-to-be-formed world around us all. Communicating ideas beyond the board room or the ivory tower is central to landscape architects' role as mediators between communities, stakeholders, clients, and other agents of change. With that, the nature and intent of the designer, along with his or her particular tools and processes are, indeed, applied to a given set of conditions, but more importantly, when innovative, those new ideas have the capacity to expand and redefine the boundaries of the profession and discipline itself.

It is evident that the burgeoning field of landscape architecture continues to simultaneously evade precise definition and constraint. Much in the same way it has since its inception in common language and thought, landscape and its conceptualization as a practice is highly multifaceted. It has to be, as a tool that has evolved in reaction to, and more recently in anticipation of so many different situations. In every conceivable situation, the practice of landscape is a tool for modifying physical environments such that they might achieve outcomes deemed somehow greater, more legible or durable according to a given philosophy or set of agendas. At its simplest, perhaps. But as a contemporary artform and simultaneously a mode of research and practice, landscape holds nearly limitless accommodation. Beginning with assumptions brought about to create a perception of societal order, the land, at least in much of Western thought, was divided up into abstract legal parcels. These are the administrative and spatial constructs upon which designers base their propositions. In that inherited context, the most competent landscape architects focus on the problems and conditions of the given site, or situation, while never losing sight of the wider and interconnected ecological view. The coarse-grain regional or even global implications of designs are embedded into more practical localized schema. This process necessitates an understanding of both needs and limitations across scales and layers of temporality. And, a novel approach requires that the argument be made in conversation with established terms of art and existing modes of research and practice. In other words, new ideas do not simply spring to life, they more often grow up and out, in fits and spurts, from a very small gap in the existing body of knowledge.

Where that gap precisely is, eludes even the sharpest observer. It may also be true that experience and time factor in more significantly than we might recognize early in our careers. It could be argued that some of the most well-recognized architects in history did their best work well in their eighties. The theories get tested again and again, the tools and technologies improve version after version, and the gaps become more evident. We also learn in university that there are key theoretical building-blocks to house and foster our own interpretations. The aesthetic, picturesque, scenic, or cinematographic, the purely formal, the enthusiastically ecological, the empathically therapeutic, the energetically community-based, the historical preservation agenda, too many to list, yes, yet all windows into the same space. It would seem logical that many if not all of us have asked ourselves about the purpose of these and other theoretical lenses, just as we do with the tools and approaches deployed, and far more importantly of the lasting capacity of the profession itself. What after all, does this post-post-(post?!) modern period that we're in today mean for the work we do? For us? It would seem that virtually anything goes when it comes to conceptual design today, so long as it is deliberate, thoughtful, well-communicated, and ostensibly rigorous. The principles, theoretical positions, materials, and formal patterns can shift, provided the designs emerge as the consequence of a process. So, the question, "how has the seminal work of the field shaped our own attitudes and processes?" is an interesting one. A bit backward looking admittedly. But more interestingly, I like to wonder, "how will the next generation of designers conceive of authentic and original work to shape attitudes and values in the future?"

New technologies abound, new economies, currencies, fusions of novel cultures and ecologies, and yet all remain loosely tied to the known canon of fundamental positions. For better or worse, even without being comprehensive, learning to understand the value of the corpus is as much a right-of-passage as burning a model after a final review or pulling an all-nighter the night before. But with new ideas, new work, both in the ideation, testing and physical making of landscapes, designers incrementally move the discipline, theory, and its practice ever forward. This at first seemingly slow evolution of the field offers numerous instrumental foundations of landscape as concept, both in terms of science and of art. Once learned, or at the very least appreciated, the synthesis of what at first appears as separate, reductive, and divergent concepts begin to overlap and possible avenues for production and combine together to reveal open and terrifying territory ahead. Brownfields, infrastructure, waterfronts, the metaverse ... To put that more clearly, what we do with this wonderful fertile field is up to us. The simultaneous and varied absorption, acceptance, negotiation, and rejection of some facets of our intuitions and learned perspectives compel us to *invent* and construct both places and practices according to our best tactical judgment and articulation of vision.

I'm reminded of the purpose of the academy itself as a safe, open, and nurturing place where we go to learn, read, think, and speak. But why does anyone go to design school in the first place? I've asked hundreds of students that question, and I believe on reflection that we first enter design programs, in part, at least because we have a voice, a dream, a passion, maybe a mission, but regardless of intent, we may not yet possess the vocabulary or the skills to confidently convey that voice to influence positive change for ourselves or for the benefit of others. All the data we could ever desire exist mostly for free outside of the university campus, all the tools and texts can be obtained without paying formal tuition. And yet, the schools remain. In fact, they're growing in strength and numbers, multiplying in large and small villages all around the world. Despite the perceived isolation of the post-pandemic digital age, something persists about our desire to learn from one another, by example or by inspiration, by mimicry or through osmosis, from our peers and those a few years ahead of us. The durable incubator of the academy continues to drive and motivate students of design by enabling close and urgent proximity to the production and inspiration of the work of others. The flurry of activity and creative agency of the design studio, for example, promotes productive critique and collaboration among peers, but it also reinforces the broader argument for a multitude of possible approaches to design.

Modernist and situationist landscape architect Garret Eckbo wrote in the very first lines of *Landscapes for Living*, that "every book must justify itself". The justification for this book, therefore, is to provide a broad, current, and critical lens for understanding how conceptual landscape designs first come to be. It's less about answers, and not intended as a technical reference or as a comprehensive textbook per se, but rather as a curated view into provocative and contemporary works in the field; the burgeoning, complex, and evolving discipline and profession of landscape architecture. It is my hope that having substantially engaged with this book, readers will feel more confident and more at home with the questions themselves, more comfortable with the ephemeral, abstract, sporadic, recursive, and bewildering nature of the creative process. I expect more questions will be raised than answers offered. Yet I'm reassured, despite so much uncertainty, by a powerful quote from the bohemian poet Rainer Maria Rilke (1875–1926) who wrote in a 1903 letter to his protégé. Rilke wrote,

I want to beg you, as much as I can, dear sir, to be patient toward all that is unsolved in your heart and to try to love the questions themselves like locked rooms and like books that are written in a very foreign tongue. Do not now seek the answers, which cannot be given you because you would not be able to live them. And the point is, to live everything. Live the questions now. Perhaps you will then gradually, without noticing it, live along some distant day into the answer.

Concepts and the Conceptual

Ideas can spring into being with the speed of bold and limitless imaginations. They can also come on slowly, in fits and spurts over periods of reflection and contemplation. They can form quite suddenly or through intellectual strain and dedicated rigorous experimentation and study. According to Liane Gabora, a professor of psychology at the University of British Columbia, "it is widely assumed that this process of initial conceptualization involves searching through memory and/or selecting amongst a set of predefined candidate ideas". In her mind – like that of many creatives – the creative process is inherently heuristic. An approach in other words, to problem solving or to self-discovery that navigates through somewhat practical but less than optimal methods or techniques. So in effect when we design, we're recalling aspects of our own lived experiences – feelings and emotions brought on by environmental cues – and transmitting the character of those memories into new representational adaptations. Results in design are hardly perfect, nor are they typically expected to achieve perfection, but it *is* often expected that a conceptual design process will unfold with a relative degree of structure and a hint of determinism. In the absence of sufficient core memory, however, or lived experience, Gabora argues that new ideas also require the injection of external influence. Once a line of inquiry is set out, multiple trajectories become apparent and divergent thinking tends to find its way into the process. In general psychology, there is much evidence for, and discussion of, the role of divergent thinking in creativity.

Divergent thinking involves the often simultaneous generation of multiple, often unconventional possibilities. Exercises such as the "mash-up," made popular through creative offices like IDEO, the charrette, group-think, or brainstorm, or in communications exercises like the composite collages in Karen Lutsky's studios, explored in Chapter 3, all elicit divergence and multiplicity in ideation, yet from familiar sources. In the 21st century, it has become exceedingly rare for a singular idea born of a single mind to generate work that reaches a large audience or offers a social, cultural, or ecologically significant impact. The astoundingly interconnected nature and complexity of so many design problems necessitates multiple-authorship and sincere, genuine and deliberate acts of collaboration. But what is a concept? How is that term defined? And does it matter who is asking the question?

Concepts by definition are new; concepted, conceived, contrived, concatenated, and conveyed. But what about our understanding of the word concept itself? How do we understand the word concept in and of itself as a symbol and a map for meaning? Before exploring concepts specifically, it is important to understand the word which we often casually use to describe these powerful ideas and phenomena. For clarity and efficiency, we can split this beautiful word into two parts – "con" first and "cept" second. The prefix or root word "**con**" in Latin which **means** "with" or "thoroughly" appears in several English vocabulary words, for example: connect, convey, construct, conclude, and consensus. The **root** word **cept** means "taken". Cept as a **root** gives rise to numerous English words, including except or accept, interception or deception. Consider what happens when you have *accepted* something as a helpful way to remember the underlying Latin meaning, you have "taken" it in closer toward yourself. Concept then is about taking in something novel, and understanding it within a given situation or context.

To help demonstrate the power of the *con* root, take the compound word concatenation: con·cat·e·na·tion – kən͵katnˈāSH(ə)n, a *noun* meaning a series of seemingly disparate yet wholly interconnected things or events. I learned this word in graduate school from historian and cultural observer John Stilgoe, who uses it to build complex metaphorical networks of issues and provocations which more often than not contained a range of seemingly dissimilar topics which he intended for his students to hold together in newer richer spaces of thought. How many students I wondered, upon learning that word, thought of it in the same way I did? Was there some room left for interpretation? Where exactly were the bounds drawn? I assumed we at least, in principle, agreed on the meaning of the word, yet we each by necessity drew our own sense of a given application for it. I recall imagining the infinite reactive and proactive possibilities. The wildly different patterns we each saw connecting vastly different elements or topics together – constellations or contraptions of so many sources and distributions of energy and meaning, and in so many forms. Just as a landscape is at once a perceived place, an arrangement and juxtaposition of people, materials, and uses, *concatenation* when used as a term of art, and through an admittedly fair amount of conjecture, offers a framework to help organize looser or more informal fragments into a more unified whole. Taken, and with. With, and taken. The parts of a whole, and farther tesselations made possible by the understanding that each piece was connected to the structure, habits, patterns, and systems at play.

A working definition of the word *landscape* is a bit trickier. As a noun landscape is defined in Webster's Dictionary as follows: land·scape, ˈlan(d)͵skāp/. Noun. 1. "All the visible features of an area of countryside or land, often considered in terms of their aesthetic appeal … *The giant cacti that dominate this landscape*". And 2. "Of a page, book, or illustration, or the manner in which it is set or printed, wider than it is high." And that's the standard dictionary definition of the second key term of this text. The content in this book argues compellingly that such a definition is far too reductive. Landscape is abundantly richer and more nuanced than this nearly purely aesthetic or compositional designation. That simplistic object-level reduction of the landscape to economic efficiency and visual beauty alone has deep roots, and lives on in practice largely from our love of and appreciation for images of the landscape, describing, on the one hand, the use and utility of the land, and, on the other, its ethereal and enchanting qualities. The tradition of landscape painting for example, from Roman frescos to scenes like Qu Ding's *Summer Mountains*, Constable's *Stour Valley*, or our own personal views from the window of a train or the car or the feeds on Instagram today, is an inherited tradition of flattening the rich complex terrain into precious imagery. This limited view also grows from the myth that recognizing *landscapes as image* is a modern phenomenon born of contemporary practice. As outlined by Vittoria Di Palma in *Is Landscape …?,* it can be said that the orientation to the visual or representative qualities of landscape are not as unique to the modern traditions as previously or perhaps nostalgically believed. Palma presents this argument in her chapter, *"Is Landscape Painting"*, demonstrating a biased adherence to the notion that the landscape-as-image was born of more historical and classical roots. Many landscape designers instinctively know this connection, between land and imagery as going back much farther, and, therefore, feel it deserves a deeper classification. Humans have been making images to understand, represent, and communicate every conceivable manner of life with one another for millennia. We can perhaps trace the long and continuous line of progress in visualization as far back as the first humans of the late paleolithic epoch when our ancestors first inscribed two-dimensional symbols and abstractions into cave walls. The image of the land is in our DNA.

A more descriptive, but still partial definition is offered here to better frame what exactly a conceptual landscape might be. But before attempting to achieve any certainty, a careful reading of John Stilgoe's *What is Landscape?* offers a powerful lexicon to draw from. He and many others have filled libraries on this subject alone. Landscapes in an objective sense, can be observed and described as lived and living, accruing, self-regulating, dynamic, connecting, integrated systems, composed of fundamental patterns, collections, and distributions of energy, occupied by life, by symbiosis, and organic forms and organisms. Experientially, or perceived as the interactive, tangible, and shapeable surface of the earth, the landscape is bewildering, systematic, repetitive, layered, and sublime. And with that, you likely have the functional and necessary information to understand the intention of the book's title.

Possibilities in Representation

Nature creates landscapes in powerful ways; change over time at a geological pace erupts, deposits, and erodes the land across regions, shaping the terrain in every possible form. Whereas people more often mold the land for uses across a short- to medium-term timeframe. Ideas about landscapes, therefore, concepts and associated images spring to life in myriad forms and are directly influenced by the surrounding milieu of a given place and time. Largely because the making of actual landscapes is a collaborative act that takes place over generations, the origin stories, ceremonies and images, maintenance regimes, management, administration, and social and cultural impacts often take on unique communal and regional identity. Individuals with varied goals as diverse as the land itself, and agendas from a range of geographies, ideologies, and perspectives bring their own biases, agendas, and priorities to the making of landscapes. The methods and media brought to bear in its conception are equally as rich and varied across space and time.

In as far as the landscape itself is highly diverse and heterogeneous, so too is the body of possible methods and approaches to/for its genesis and creation; to its imagination, ideation, communication, production, and manufacture. A sketch can translate an idea from nothing more than loose lines or rough marks on a page where traces have been made to describe the laying or carving of materials. Sketches come with an ambiguity ripe with potential and flexibility. In physical modeling where raw, or "pure" media like clay can nonrepresentationally depict landform, for example, we can often see an effort to make direct links between material and storytelling about the performance, beauty and function of the materials that comprise the ground plane. A model, according to Richard T.T. Forman, is "the simplification of complex systems to gain understanding". You can, however, start the process of design anywhere – the possibilities are limited only by your imagination.

So, do not fear. Provided you are conscientious and alert, your concept will emerge. Other concepts will come too. They build on one another just as the tools and processes become more familiar and trusted. Start working through sources of inspiration. Talk to your friends. Recall meaningful memory, sketch out possibilities in plan, section, oblique, and perspective. Draw deeper meaning as you make important connections. Diagram the organizational structure that holds it together. Make models at different scales. Test your initial assumptions against the constraints of site and situation. And on and on. As the first decisions about your designs galvanize, focus only on the most critical factors, and go engage in the material world, in the site, in the available technology. Explore by asking questions and arguing through debate. Push beyond what you previously thought was impossible and look ahead to creative moments that shape your ideas. As we've seen, there is no right or wrong way to begin, so just begin.

Part 1

The Spark of an Idea

1

EXCAVATING IDEAS

Elizabeth Mossop

Being forced to articulate how our projects originate or how they come into being initially required an excavation of our first processes in design. As you would expect, we are inventive and we generate a plethora of ideas (of varying quality). We use the early design process to develop and test the ideas to discover their relevance and their significance, and to better understand our own preferences. We invest in this phase of the process, which is often slow, as we believe the quality of the ideas underpinning any project will largely determine the quality of the finished product. In our work, we are not precious about the artefacts of design.

Ideas do not always take shape visually initially. In our studios, we use a variety of means to tease out ideas: in the beginning, there is a robust discussion that continues throughout the process, and early images, diagrams, and sketches that describe first ideas and site reflection. These are followed by project and precedent research and analysis, modeling of three-dimensional ideas both physically and digitally, and extensive iterative drawing, all of which are used to develop the concept, in the project's early stages.

The project scale determines how many people are involved, but the process is most often a collaborative one. Design principals control the product that leaves the studio, but the generative process is fluid and open to the broader team. Organizationally, clear design responsibility rests with one person on each project so that decision-making is accountable.

The strength of a design concept is crucial to our ability to hold on to design integrity throughout the process of development and implementation. Collectively, we are committed to an idea of design quality that takes precedence over individual egos or expedience. Clear articulation of the concept becomes a project touchstone that guides decision-making throughout. The origin of the concept can be many different things: a site response, a conversation with a community member, an idea of how something might operate, or some characteristic of local culture. The conceptual spark can be a formal strategy, a social or political idea, an ecological process, or something else, any of which the design process translates into a site strategy. It is the bringing together of the more abstract with the more gestural

DOI: 10.4324/9781003053255-2

and physical that provides the landscape concept for a project. Collectively, we are always looking for integrity between the ideas, the formal approach, and the values that drive the practice.

Naturally, we all bring to this process our underlying preoccupations and preconceptions, such as a love of the richness of flowering meadows, a desire to see more urban canopy, fascination with particular water effects, and so on. Some of these are enduring and some are more cyclical, but they are not unexamined. We are collectively fascinated with plant material, both ecologically and aesthetically, and seeking to harness its dynamic qualities in service of design ideas. Conceptually, we are seeking a clarity of spatial structure and the means to strip away ideas to their essential components. Collectively, our underlying ambition is always to drive better and more equitable outcomes for people that support a healthy planet. We are looking for authenticity and integrity between formal expression, materials, and cultural ideas. These ideas and values are part of the conversation around projects and design approaches, and we try to reflect on and tease them out in design conversations and to be self-aware in the process.

For every project, there are a series of processes that we always go through. The ordering to some extent is determined by the context, and sometimes the activities happen in parallel, but they are all necessary to the conceptual process. The breadth and rigor of the process both allows for, and disposes of, the tyranny of inspiration. It is also useful as a mechanism for forcing us to keeping open minds and also to employ a range of different types of thinking in approaching the problem.

Critical site analysis is shaped by the nature of the site and problem. We use a broad range of tools to describe and analyze the existing site and problem: field work, photographs, sketches, maps, diagrams, notes and key words, site responses, and precedents.

Listening to people; clients, publics, interest groups, etc. As much of our work is in the public domain, we use a vast array of techniques in consultation.

Ideation; ideas come through conversation, argument, drawing, the *parti* describes an organizing idea, and ideas are sparked by reference to other landscapes, artworks, buildings, and so on.

The landscape concept which draws from all three earlier phases in differing amounts describes the ideas in relationship to the place or site, creating an integrated foundation for the design solution.

Bowen Place Canberra Australia

The concept for this project was developed as a design competition entry, and so, the process was very fast and resulted from a collaborative conversation with architects Lahz Nimmo. This is a long-standing design collaboration and, thus, allowed some shorthand conversations through response to site and precedents that developed the idea quickly.

Figure 1.1 Bowen Place's overall form responds to the cloverleaf geometry. Spackman Mossop Michaels.

The simplicity of the functional brief (for a pedestrian/cycle under-pass) belies the complexity of the three-dimensional problem to be solved. The idea that drives this project is a desire to bring together the planar geometry of Walter Burley Griffin and Marion Mahoney's original city plan with the three-dimensional puzzle of the complex multi-modal intersection to create a purely sculptural landscape. To solve the form, the idea was immediately modelled to test its validity. The overall form and organization respond to the cloverleaf geometry of Bowen Place with an integrated wall/path/earthwork as a unified element (Figure 1.1).

The 'deferential' concrete wall responds to Canberra's modernist civic architecture (such as the adjacent High Court; Figure 1.2), set against a green lawn. Christo's *Running Fence* and Jeffrey Smart's painting *Cahill Expressway* were also generative with the idea of the wall as a white slice through the manicured green landscape of the lake edge (Figure 1.3). The Australian plant materials refer to the National Gallery Sculpture Garden (Figure 1.4) and reinforce the indigenous landscape identity.

Miller Park, Chattanooga, Tennessee, USA

The concept for Miller Park in Chattanooga was driven by a long series of conversations with different groups of people in the city. As with any significant public space, there were lots of community workshops, interviews, and conversations, and as always happens, many interesting and unexpected findings (Figure 1.5).

Figure 1.2 The High
Court of Australia.
Elizabeth Mossop.

Figure 1.3 At Bowen Place, the white wall slices through the green landscape. Spackman Mossop
Michaels.

Figure 1.4 The indigenous landscape of the National Gallery of Australia Sculpture Garden. Elizabeth Mossop.

Figure 1.5 Broad community engagement informed the conceptual design of the park. Spackman Mossop Michaels.

In Chattanooga, there was a startling consensus about how much people loved and appreciated the city, they shared the narrative of the city's comeback from the 'dirtiest city in America', and there was great consistency across a wide range of socio-economic and racial differences. While there were certainly social differences and divisions, there was a universal aspiration for a place where the city could 'come together'.

This led us to a big, central embracing space at a city scale, easy to access and open to all. We also felt it important for the space to symbolize this inclusion by expressing a single dominant form. There are two major components to this, one is the new ground plane created by the grading, which brings the park up close to street level, including an encircling perimeter which allows for terraces, slopes, ramps, and so on, to bring a disparate set of street edge conditions and levels, to meet the edge of the lawn. The second is the planar form of the central lawn, a large organic unified shape held by broad curving terrace steps, symbolizing the public heart of the city (Figure 1.6).

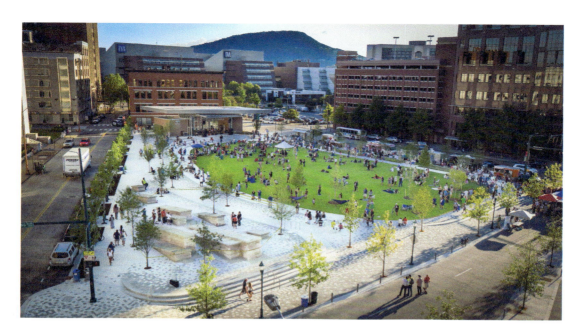

Figure 1.6 Miller Park's central lawn is embraced by terraced steps connecting to the street edges. Spackman Mossop Michaels.

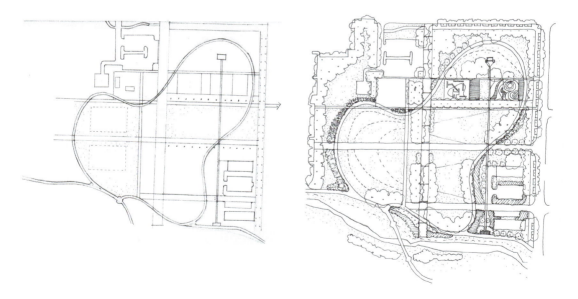

Figure 1.7 Pre-existing park elements persist into the new design. Spackman Mossop Michaels.

Luther George Park, Springdale, Arkansas, USA

The design for this 14-acre park is underpinned by an idea of resourcefulness. This comes from both a site-driven idea and a cultural idea. The project involves a reimagining of an existing park within a constrained budget, so the imperative is there to somehow

Figure 1.8 The landscape quilt of the new Luther George Park. Spackman Mossop Michaels.

use the elements of the existing landscape to create something new. So, first ideas look at what exists in the landscape and the elements that might persist to a new incarnation (Figure 1.7).

The same idea is echoed in a response to the local communities. These include communities from the Marshall Islands, from Hispanic cultures, and from traditional southern community practices of making art from necessities, as expressed in textile arts and quilt-making. These practices are often a cooperative community effort and exemplify the bringing together of what is available to create beauty and utility. If we look at some of the local examples, we see also an idea of layering where we have the quilt texture created by the sewing techniques of its fabrication, and also the graphic pattern-making through the use of color overlaid on the texture. The design concept brings these ideas together in a new structure for the park that reflects the site response in the idea of a landscape quilt (Figure 1.8).

2

OBSESSIONS

Emma Mendel

Obsessions as Needed

As Susan Sontag once wrote in her drafting notations

> The writer must be four people: …1) the nut, the obsédé, 2) the moron, 3) the stylist, 4) the critic … 1) supplies the material, 2) lets it come out, 3) is taste, 4) is intelligence. A great writer has all 4- but you can still be a good writer with only 1) and 2).[1]

In agreement with the political activist, writer and filmmaker, I believe the obsédé (the obsessed), although understood in our everyday lives as unhealthy or at worst a burden, is at its core very innately and necessarily, a part of the act of design.

In fact, scientists have hypothesized that Darwin may very well have suffered from Obsessive-Compulsive Disorder. Darwin wrote about various obsessional thoughts and his inability to get away from them. In a letter dated in 1859, the year the Origin of Species was published, the scientist wrote to a friend, "I could not sleep and whatever I did in the day haunted me at night with vivid and most wearing repetition."[2]

Although a crippling disorder, one can argue that the Origin of Species could not have been developed without Darwin's obsession with the living world. Moreover, the scientist at one point mentions his own condition in the process of developing his body of work. In the Autobiography of Charles Darwin, Barlow quotes, "Even ill-health, though it has annihilated several years of my life, has saved me from the distractions of society and amusement."[3] In a similar sense, today's advancements in string theory and the piecing together of the universe holds similar obsessive trials and errors. As described by physicist and astronomer, Clifford V. Johnson in his graphic novel 'The Dialogues,' "It's like solving a jigsaw puzzle. But one of those, you know, 10,000-piece ones, of a vast landscape with large areas of subtly changing features. And just to be clear. This puzzle comes with no picture of what is printed on the box."[4]

This is not an advocation to become ill with obsession but to celebrate, in the act of design, the necessity of the practice of obsession. In that, for design to make a landing on the grounds of a

DOI: 10.4324/9781003053255-3

given reality, we must turn over every puzzle piece, refute no option without proof of error, question ourselves and our logic in order to find a pattern in the fragmented, where information precedes data. As landscape architects and designers, it is at this juncture that we reinterpret ideas, where design process slows down and site begins to rearrange, push back and explicate preconceived predictions. It is also at a point in which the designed outcome warps its way through a slurry of forms, reacting to data, inspired thought and articulated forms in time and space.

The Practice of Obsession

Considering the many ways in which obsession necessitates itself in the education of landscape architecture, one method is taught in the second week of the Summer Design Institute at the University of Virginia. The Summer Design Institute is a four-week-long program, taught by four faculty members in architecture and landscape architecture before the fall semester begins. The summer program was specifically developed for incoming Master of Landscape Architecture and Master of Architecture students, international students coming into the Masters of Landscape Architecture program as well as Urban Planning students pursuing an Urban Design Certificate. Its purpose to introduce incoming students to methodologies, theories and techniques to be successful in design studios. A long-standing program at the university, a number of faculty members such as Leena Cho and Tat Bonvehi-Rosich have been testing and iterating on the content and methodology of the program. The past two years, the program has been taken on by myself, Bradley Cantrell and Anthony Averbeck, with Jorge Pizzaro joining us in the first year and Katie Stranix in the second year. Each week introduces essential concepts for incoming design students.

In the four weeks, students were tasked to research case studies, distill and articulate site, extract elements and reorganize systems and select and emphasize site processes through space and time. For the students, each week gave birth to its own set of unwarranted obstacles, set on unfamiliar paths in the pursuit of a designed idea. The first week focuses on abstracting case studies through rigorous research in order to develop a series of graphic representations that penetrate beyond the apparent form of the project. The second week focuses on the observation and articulation of site in order to distil inventory into a notational system, a base plan and a stepped topographic model. Week three focuses on extracting and defining elements from case studies and sites visited from weeks two and three, in order to translate and iterate on spatial and formal relationships. Week four focuses on site selection with the emphasis of designing with time, space and site processes to refine and evolve geometries preconceived in week three's spatial and formal relationships. Students in each week produced and curated completed work which was reviewed and discussed with invited and internal faculty. Within the weeks, invited lectures were organized as well as readings, rigorous workshops, pin ups and discussions.

Dialling back to week two, the practice of obsession was introduced as a necessary process to complete the week's exercise.
This was broken down into four branches: obsession in observation, obsession in relation, obsession in description and obsession
in craft. In the first approach, obsession is explored in the act of
observation. For many, the introduction of a site visit can be an
overwhelmingly sensorial experience and, oftentimes, a return to
site with a focused lens on what to observe, record and reinterpret
is needed. Beginning by activating obsessions through what the
observer sees, senses and gathers, initial impressions were to be
developed into one analogue drawing done by hand. A physical
copy of a base plan, a sketchbook, along with quantitative meas-
uring and sensing tools were carried to the site prior to its introduction. Initial introductions to the site are concentrated on creating
an impression on the observer, allowing the observer to reinterpret
what lenses to focus on before returning to the site (Figures 2.1
and 2.2).

"Landscape, by contrast [to geography] is that space revealed
by sensation," as philosopher, feminist theorist and professor,
Elizabeth Grosz describes, "which has no fixed coordinates but
transforms and moves as a body passes through it."[5] Working in
teams, students are encouraged to collect, record, abstract and
capture as much as possible. In the process of reinterpreting an
experience into a representational function, obsession in observation lends itself to ask questions pertaining to the relationship
of description and site; How would one catalogue, group, draw
conclusions, map, trace or abstract a set of site characters and
qualities? To reinterpret, is to "interpret (something) in a new or
different way."[6] As defined in the Oxford English Dictionary. Representational tools were explored with the goal of consistency, but
also evocative of site. How does one layer of information connect
to different scales of data and, thus, how does this reinterpretation
necessitates a new representational language and system? This is

Carytown Tobacco

Violet Crown movie theater

26

27

Figure 2.1 Summer Design Institute, University of Virginia 2018. Week 02, Obsession in
observation. Pen in sketchbook. Jane Lee.

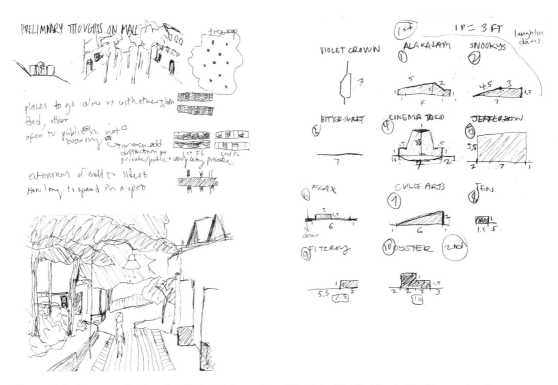

Figure 2.2 Summer Design Institute, University of Virginia 2018. Week 02, Obsession in observation. Pen on paper. Jane Lee and Taro Matsuno.
Lee and Matsuno reinterpret site with informed, historical, material studies and impressions of enclosures, entryways and entrances to focus on concepts of arrival throughout the downtown mall in Charlottesville.

not a conventional representation created by layering data on top of one another, but rather reworking each layer and obsessing on how different forms of data begin to respond to one-another powerfully symbolic of space and time (Figures 2.3–2.5).

To consider the role of obsession in craft, the second exercise asks students to collectively laser cut and hand glue a stepped topography model. In this, the art of crafting and executing a collective model is crucial in the process of concentrating a set of tasks into a series of steps. Herein, craft derives itself in the nuanced ways of planning and thinking on the designers' part. Obsession in making and remaking transfers itself into a final reinterpreted, individualized method of construction. No model is made equal but rather re-informs heuristic methods in making (Figures 2.6 and 2.7).

Focusing obsession in description, the third exercise asked each team to update and articulate the AutoCAD base plan provided of the site by identifying blind spots to be created as new layers of data. In this instance, blind spots exist because the data used to generate the initial plans are derived from remote sensing and general surveys. The site visit reveals that sites themselves are much

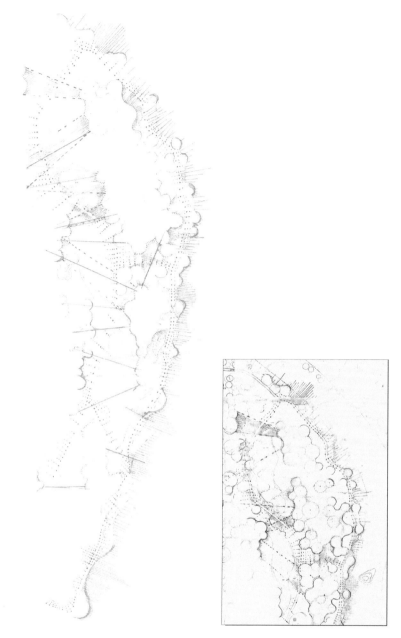

Figure 2.3 Summer Design Institute, University of Virginia 2019. Week 02, Obsession in relation: plant distribution and sound. Pen on vellum. Meng Chao and Zihe Ye.

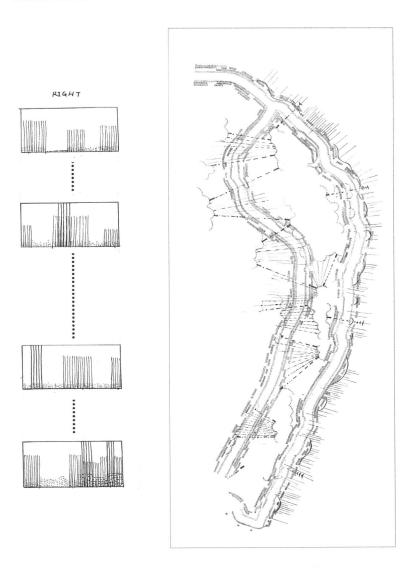

Figure 2.4 Summer Design Institute, University of Virginia 2019. Week 02, Obsession in relation: vegetation massing heights and interstitial space. Pen on vellum. Meng Chao and Zihe Ye.

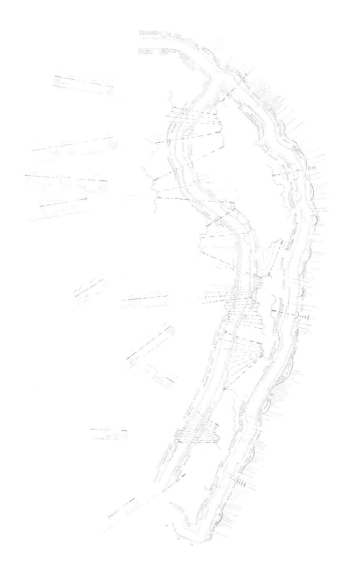

19

**Figure 2.5 Summer Design Institute, University of Virginia 2019. Week
02, Obsession in relation: final analogue plan drawing. Pen on vellum.
Meng Chao and Zihe Ye.**
Chao and Ye obsess over the relationship between the anatomy of the
human body and site phenomena. Through layered complexities and
iterations the notational plan is refined into a palimpsest of relationships
between the observer, scale and time.

Figure 2.6 Summer Design Institute, University of Virginia 2018. Week 02, Obsession in craft: collective laser-cut model. Photographed by Daniel Hoogenboom.

more complex and the layers provided in the current AutoCAD plans are not enough to describe these environments. Moreover, taking into account the agency of representation in Corner's recognition that

> representation provides neither a mirror reflection of things nor a simple objective inventory … a mirror copy of the world- or a description that is so precise and truthful as to be identical to the object it describes- is simply an impossible illusion and that the ontological presence of the representation itself is unavoidable.[7]

Figure 2.7 Summer Design Institute, University of Virginia 2018. Week 03, Object translate: process model. Daniel Hoogenboom.
Hoogenboom utilizes lessons learnt from week 02's model to develop further conceptualize special organizations of site in week 03 of the Summer Design Institute.

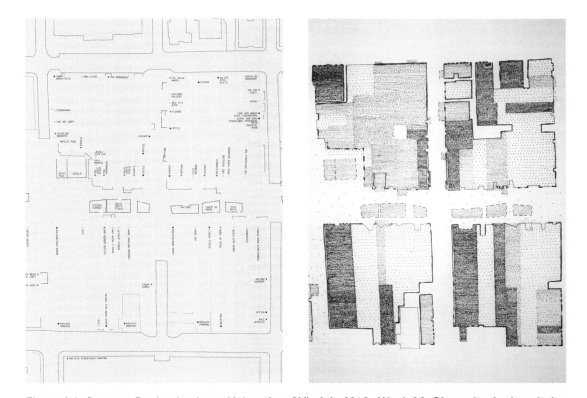

Figure 2.8 Summer Design Institute, University of Virginia 2018. Week 02, Obsession in description. Digital print on paper (left), Pen on vellum (right). Jane Lee and Taro Matsuno.
Matsuno and Lee obsess in the description and sequence of the Downtown Mall in Charlottesville through abstraction of walls and enclosures to blur definitions between indoor and outdoor typologies.

Therefore, the description of the site is highly dependent on the students' identification of blind spots. New layers were needed to further articulate the base plan with the intent of meticulous description and translation into linework. Conventions are developed to perpetuate consistency in graphic standards between team members to create a well-crafted, consistently executed plan that elicits the complexity of site (Figure 2.8).

What is revealed in the practice of obsession are abilities to reinterpret and refine in methods previously unimaginable and unrealized. Obsession allows charges, reactions and responses to emerge from standardizations, generalizations and predictions (Figures 2.9–2.12).

At this fragile stage, where layers can make or break the course of design, obsession must keep atrophy at bay. The puzzle doesn't fall into place, it requires patience, reiteration, meticulous obsession in flipping over puzzle pieces. "Sometimes you're lucky and a few pieces that have been turned over can be seen to fit together," the character in 'The Dialogues' says. "Or one piece simply leads you to find another piece."[4]

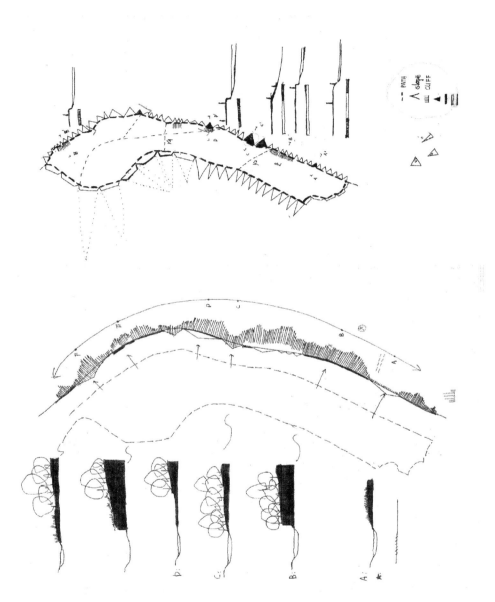

Figure 2.9 Summer Design Institute, University of Virginia 2018. Week 02, Obsessions inform reinterpretations: topography. Pen on paper. Binyu Yang and Jingyi Hu.

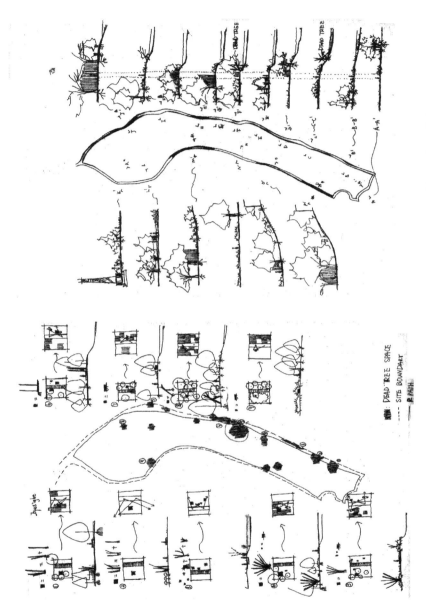

Figure 2.10 Summer Design Institute, University of Virginia 2018. Week 02, Obsessions inform reinterpretations: spatial organizations, light and shadow. Pen on paper. Binyu Yang and Jingyi Hu.

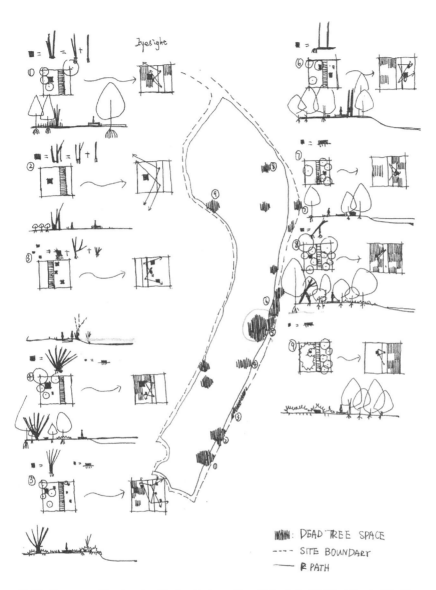

Figure 2.11 Summer Design Institute, University of Virginia 2018. Week 02, Obsessions inform reinterpretations: draft analogue plan drawing. Pen on vellum. Binyu Yang and Jingyi Hu.

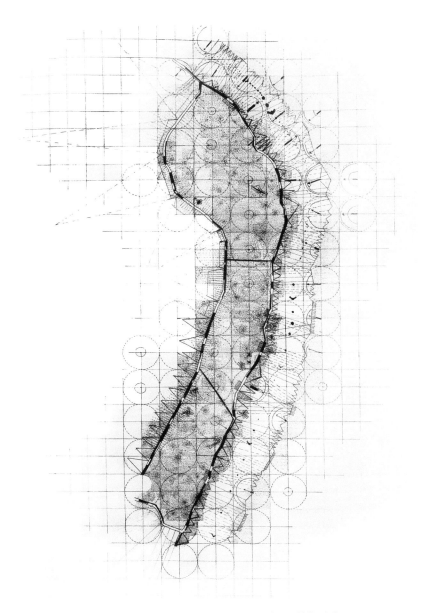

Figure 2.12 Summer Design Institute, University of Virginia 2018. Week 02, Obsessions inform reinterpretations: draft analogue plan drawing. Pen on vellum. Binyu Yang and Jingyi Hu.
Yang and Hu obsess, reinterpret and refine multi-scalar documentations of the Rivanna River in Charlottesville. Preconceived in personal mnemonics along with the standardization of the grid, Yang and Hu develop notational tests of vegetation, boundaries, topography, light and shadow. Obsession in representational clarity and information complexity dissolve the plan into an abstraction of site, with collapsed and overlaid data.

Bibliography

1. Sontag, Susan, and David Rieff. *Reborn: Early Diaries, 1947–1963*. London: Penguin, 2012.
2. Darwin Correspondence Project, "Letter no. 2615," accessed on 27 August 2019, http://www.darwinproject.ac.uk/DCP-LETT-2615.
3. Darwin, Charles, and Nora Barlow. *The Autobiography of Charles Darwin, 1809–1882: With Original Omissions Restored*. New York: Norton, 1969. 28.
4. Livni, Ephrat, "A physicist ponders the universe's most mysterious questions- in a comic book," qz.com. accessed on 27 August 2019, https://qz.com/1308481/a-physicist-ponders-the-universes-most-mysterious-questions-in-a-comic-book/.
5. Grosz, Elizabeth, *Chaos, Territory, Art: Deleuze and the Framing of the Earth*. New York: Columbia University Press, 2008. 72.
6. Oxford Dictionaries, s.v. "reinterpret," accessed on 29 August 2019, https://www.lexico.com/en/definition/reinterpret.
7. Corner, James, "Aerial Representation and the Making of Landscape," in *Taking Measures across the American Landscape*, by James Corner and Alex S. Mclean. New Haven, CT: Yale University Press, 1996. 15–20.

3

COMPOSITE DRAWINGS + LANDSCAPE IDEATIONS

Karen Lutsky

As popular culture often represents the design process, more often than not, it follows the sequence of (1) a 'problem' or 'purpose' is identified; (2) the designer has a 'good idea' as a response; and *then* (3) they represent it, and build it. The process is discussed as a linear endeavor with a great deal of emphasis resting on the strength of that fully formed, 'good idea' to drive the design progress. As most practicing in the design, creative, and experimental fields acknowledge though, this is not the typical sequence. Rather, the process is much more cyclical and tumultuous, or 'storm-like' as the architecture professor, Kyna Leski, recounts in her book, *The Storm of Creativity*.[1] As Leski, and others have noted, design generally progresses through phases of contextualization and recontextualization (what Leski calls 'gathering'[2] and I have in previous writings called 'probing')[3] of information coupled with and guided by methods of representation such as drawings and composites, photographs, models, diagrams, etc., where the project takes shape and ideas, forms, and relationships are tested, developed, improved, and expanded. Within the process of early contextualization, where knowledge and information are being collected and ideas are just forming, I have found both in my practice and teaching of landscape architecture that the representational method of composite drawing has been particularly fruitful. Composite drawing, also commonly referred to as 'collage', 'montage', 'photomontage', or 'assemblage',[4] is more broadly defined in this essay as a collection of separate elements, mainly two-dimensional such as photographs, sketches, magazine clippings, bits of material, etc., recontextualized to and with each other within a singular composition. These elements may be found or created individually, but what makes them particularly unique is the way that they meet upon the page and the exploration developed through their making.

In landscape architecture, these elements, the contexts of our projects, are comprised of and influenced by a vast variety of scales. From weather patterns and climate shifts to earthworms and edging, our projects must take in considerations large and small, fast and slow. Typically, these contexts, when studied and measured,

[1] Kyna Leski, et al. *The Storm of Creativity*. The MIT Press, 2015.
[2] Kyna Leski, et al. *The Storm of Creativity*. The MIT Press, 2015. Pg. 49.
[3] Karen Lutsky and Sean Burkholder, "Curious Methods," *Places Journal*, May 2017. Accessed 20 Aug 2019. https://doi.org/10.22269/170523
[4] There are important distinctions among these terms and in the field of art, architecture, and landscape architecture they each have a history and relevancy.

DOI: 10.4324/9781003053255-4

are siloed for clarity and control, but in the framework of the physical landscape, these elements and forces will always be intertwined and influencing one another. The composite drawing, particularly in the beginning phases of design, significant in that it releases the need for 'clarity' or 'control' in exchange for the discovery and testing of relationships between the variant scales of context such as region and site, second and century, human and vegetal. As the designer orients, crops, copies, erases, and folds the pieces, they begin to mingle and inform each other; coaxing new patterns and forms into conversations.

In the practice of landscape architecture, many have long heralded this critical importance of composite drawings in the early stages of the design process, maybe most notably James Corner in his essay, 'Eidetic Operations and New Landscapes'. In the essay, which continues to be republished and appears as a main staple in the canon of landscape architecture, Corner strongly advocates for the need of 'eidetic operations', or thoughtful, intuitive methods of drawing including composite drawings such as the 'Ideogram', to be developed and advanced within the practice.[5] He notes the importance of these methods of 'imaging' to free the potentials and projective possibilities of the multiple scales of material, system, influence, and time inherent in landscapes. This essay was recently reprinted and bolstered by a compilation and exhibition titled, '*Composite Landscapes*', by Charles Waldheim and Andrea Hansen which focuses solely on the usage of the composite throughout the field's history. Echoing Corner in their opening pages, they too reflect on the strengths of composite drawing in the design process, noting that it 'has long been valued for its unique capacity to efficiently and effectively represent a complex range of landscape interventions with an economy of visual means' and 'has been privileged for its ease of use and accessible visual language'.[6] The volume also features an essay titled 'Structuring Relations: From Montage to Model in Composite Imaging' by landscape architecture professor, Karen M'Closkey, in which she notes that the current 'convention' of using the digital composite drawing to develop photorealistic perspectives (a practice currently popular across landscape firms including Corner's own firm) has 'transform[ed] the role of montage from image making that is critical to one that is conciliatory'. But as she notes, digital composites, like the earlier analog-based composites, could, in their own right, be used in investigative and exploratory methods.[7] This shift though, she reflects, must approach the digital programs as a medium, a tool, and an element that lends itself to knowledge development and the finding of relationships. Like all composite drawings, the addition of the digital medium must still support the subjective explorations to be helpful in ideation.

Along similar lines, landscape architecture professor, Valerio Morabito, in his essay and his teaching exercise 'The Extended Representation of the Landscape' discusses the use of a hybrid

[5] James Corner and Alan Balfour, *Recovering Landscape: Essays in Contemporary Landscape Architecture*. Princeton Architectural Press, 1999. Pg. 166–167.
[6] Charles Waldheim, et al., *Composite Landscapes: Photomontage and Landscape Architecture*. Hatje Cantz Verlag, 2014. Pg. 16.
[7] Charles Waldheim, et al., *Composite Landscapes: Photomontage and Landscape Architecture*. Hatje Cantz Verlag, 2014. Pg. 127–128.

analog/digital composite drawing technique that brings together hand sketches and photographs as a method of exploring 'space in the landscape'.[8] This specific composite method, which I also teach my students and should be recognizable in some of the following examples, is not about depicting a 'beautiful image' but rather supports imagination and playfulness through experimentation and 'extension' of pattern, scale, material, and memory. As Morabito notes, the sketch recognizes and celebrates the subjective hand, while the photographs bring 'reality' into the drawing[9] so that no matter how it is manipulated and 'extended', the composite is inherently rooted in elements that are both of the landscape and of the designer. Of course, whether a composite includes elements of hand rendering, or perhaps very intentionally taken photographs, the production of the composite, from the selection of components to their organization, will always reflect the decisions of the designer.

That said, I find composite drawings and their collection of non-hand-drawn elements equally helpful in the development of one's practice of seeing and exploring the many facets and scales of landscape and dispelling the notions of the need for a singular 'good idea' before embarking on a project's representation. Such notions tend to be intentionally, or unintentionally, supported by methods of hand drawing often pursued by students, in which they try to first formulate the design in their minds and *then* draw from the beacon of their 'idea'. Such approaches are not surprising, particularly in new students who lack confidence in their representational techniques and fear 'wasting time' representing their project – wishing to be only 'efficient' in their process. But alas, the method largely fails in that it requires the designer to know

[8] Valerio Morabito, "The Extended Representation of the Landscape". *Paisea* 014. Pg. 21.
[9] Valerio Morabito, "The Extended Representation of the Landscape". *Paisea* 014. Pg. 24.

Figure 3.1 A composite of site investigation. Images of movement through the site, materiality, and change over time are overlaid and sequenced in photoshop. Bria Fast, University of Minnesota, MLA, Spring 2018.

Figure 3.2 Developed in a hybrid method of Photoshop alterations, printed material, and then hand cut and pasted, this composite explores the early ideation of a design of a stand of poplar trees. Kyle Franta, University of Minnesota, MLA, Spring 2019.

Figure 3.3 This hybrid composite method brings hand sketches of physical models together with a limited material palette in Photoshop in an exercise to explore how simple alterations of scale, form, and material may be used to invent compelling imaginative landscapes. Bria Fast, University of Minnesota, MLA, Spring 2018.

Figure 3.4 This hybrid composite method brings hand sketches of physical models together with a limited material palette in Photoshop in an exercise to explore how simple alterations of scale, form, and material may be used to invent compelling imaginative landscapes. Anna Bride, University of Minnesota, MLA, Spring 2019.

Figure 3.5 David Hedding, University of Minnesota, MLA, Spring 2019.
This pair of composites were developed in Photoshop using images mainly obtained on site as part of the beginning phase of designing a 'climate-adaption' forest path. They explore materiality (top) along with the sequence of movement and the quality of edges (bottom).

Figure 3.6 This was a quick analog composite developed in the beginning phase of a studio design along the Minnesota River exploring the material and spatial potentials of an altered edge condition. Alexandra Boese, University of Minnesota, MLA, Spring 2017.

Figure 3.7 This composite brings together mud texture and mark making collected on site to explore form, pattern, and material. It is composed and altered in Photoshop. Sydney Shea, University of Minnesota, MLA, Spring 2018.

Figure 3.8 This analog composite includes hand drawing, collected on site material 'mud marks', photographs, and found images. This drawing was later developed in the ideation of the project depicted in Figure 3.7. Sydney Shea, University of Minnesota, MLA, Spring 2019.

Figure 3.9 This digital composite produced in Photoshop uses site photos and found images to explore the spatial, material, and temporal conditions of red maple trees. Yiyuan Shao, University of Minnesota, MLA, Spring 2019.

Figures 3.10/3.11/3.12 This series of composites explore the spatial, material, political, and infrastructural relationships surrounding the invasive species of Asian Carp, Zebra Mussels, and Phragmites. (They may be best displayed together.)Bria Fast, University of Minnesota, MLA, Spring 2018.

Figures 3.10/3.11/ 3.12 Continued.

Figures 3.10/3.11/ 3.12 Continued.

Figure 3.13 This hybrid composite method brings hand sketches of physical models together with a limited material palette in Photoshop in an exercise to explore how simple alterations of scale, form, and material may be used to invent compelling imaginative landscapes. Bria Fast, University of Minnesota, MLA, Spring 2018.

beforehand what they are designing and inhibits the process of knowledge growth and development surrounding the specifics of any project. I would argue that particularly beginning designers, with their nascent knowledge of landscape and often underdeveloped abilities, are often much better served and successful in ideation and project development when releasing themselves from misplaced expectations and embracing the explorations and findings brought forth from the making of a composite drawing. With the inclusion of external materials and information into the drawing and making process, the design storm 'gathers' its strength and direction, and ideation begins to take form not from confines of a singular perspective but, like landscape, through a convergence of materials, scales, forces, and time (Figures 3.1–3.13).

4

PICTORIAL CARTOGRAPHY AND DIGITAL PRINTMAKING

Experiments in Representing the Working Landscape

Forbes Lipschitz

As landscape architects have shown an increasing interest in territorial design, including the spaces of agricultural commodity production known as working landscapes, maps and aerial images have gained renewed importance as design and representation tools. While mapping and aerial imagery can convey scale and territorial relationships, they fail to capture the unique qualities and experiential eccentricities of the working landscape. Territorial maps effectively other the working landscape, defining it as a space to be experienced and understood from afar. Moreover, such representational techniques pose the risk of homogenizing local space and identity, often defining the rural landscape as either an ecological repository or urban-industrial staging ground. This reinforces a disciplinary blindness to the nuances of working landscapes, as evidenced in the persistent use of the term "hinterland." From the German *hinter* "behind" land, the 19th-century term refers to uncharted territories or the areas "surrounding a town or port and served by it" or "an area lying beyond what is visible or known."[1] The term, therefore, defines such landscapes either in relation to city or something which is so far beyond sight that it has become unknowable.

To move beyond the vagaries of the "hinterland," landscape architects must develop new tools in order to more effectively describe and design within the working landscape. The work highlighted in this chapter explores the potential of pictorial cartography and digital printmaking to answer this call.

In Defense of Subjectivity

Throughout the 20th century, manual mapping methods were the primary means by which researchers and designers studied and communicated territorial landscapes. The overlay mapping techniques popularized by Ian McHarg laid the groundwork for the

[1] Oxford Dictionaries, s.v. "hinterland," accessed July 1, 2019, www.oxforddictionaries.com/definition/english/hinterland.

DOI: 10.4324/9781003053255-5

Geographic Information Systems (GIS) software that emerged in the 1980s and became popular throughout professional design and planning practices soon thereafter. Overlay maps allowed McHarg to approach the working landscape primarily through the lens of environmental suitability. His work highlighted large-scale agriculture as a primary driver of landscape change and lamented the loss of farmland to urban and suburban development. McHargian maps and their GIS derivatives largely privileged the physiographic conditions of landscapes over social, historical, or experiential qualities.

As McHarg's *Design with Nature* celebrates its 50th anniversary, the map continues to be primary representational medium through which contemporary landscape architects engage the working landscape. In their text *Taking Measures Across the American Landscape*, James Corner and Alex S. Maclean employ aerial photographs and composite map diagrams to examine how technologies for surveying and developing the Midwest, the Great Plains, and the Mississippi River have shaped the landscape. Alan Berger's *Drosscape* similarly observes American working landscapes through aerial perspective. Employing a more graphically evocative approach to cartography, the silkscreen prints and maps of Mathur and da Cunha's *Mississippi Floods* reveal that the way the river was drawn and mapped influenced how it was subsequently designed, engineered, and controlled. More recently, Richard Misrach and Kate Orff couple a photographic record of Louisiana's industrial landscape with speculative maps in In *Petrochemical America*, creating an "Ecological Atlas" of the region.

Though their cartographic styles are varied, from the dispassionately technocratic diagrams of Corner and Berger to the expressive and speculative maps of Mathur and da Cunha, the work of these designers can be understood as explicit rejections of the pictorialization of landscape practice. Julia Czerniak writes that "pictorialism biases how a landscape appears as a *picture*, a retinal image, over how it works as a *process*."[2] She argues that the "synpotic" aerial imaging and mapping techniques used in *Taking Measures Across the American Landscape* "challenge the tyranny of the pictorial embedded in landscape production."[3] But need the representation of the landscape as a framed picture necessarily preclude its understanding as a process? Could pictorial imaging be combined with map-making in order to communicate both scale and character, landscape and narrative?

By embedding a map with image and text, the pictorial map tells a visual story that highlights a sense of place. Such maps are not scientific and technocratic visualizations of geospatial data, but rather artistic interpretations of places, landscapes, and regions. As quoted in *Picturing America: The Golden Age of Pictorial Maps*, by Stephen J. Hornsby, map maker Jac Atherton noted in the 1930s that "through a wealth of illustration and a reasonable degree of geographic accuracy, [decorative maps] reveal intimately

[2] Czerniak, Julia. (1997). "Challenging the Pictorial: Recent Landscape Practice" *Assemblage*, no. 34. Cambridge: The MIT Press, p. 110.
[3] Ibid.

the innermost character of a country, incorporating subtly the charm and romance of the past with a vivid picture of the present."[4] Though the emergence of scientific cartography and Geographic Information Systems has facilitated the decline of pictorial mapping as an artform, the following conceptual work seeks to revive the method as a speculative design medium particularly well suited to territorial design projects. The work also investigates strategies for integrating hybrid digital and analog printmaking techniques into such an approach.

Preliminary Experiments in Pictorial Cartography

In the Spring of 2019, an upper level graduate and undergraduate design studio in the landscape architecture section of the Knowlton School at the Ohio State University experimented with new ways to represent the working landscape. The class worked collaboratively to reenvision the productive landscapes of the Great Plains in the face of climate change. The territorial scale of the project site necessarily required mapping as the primary design tool. Comprised of four Level II terrestrial ecoregions, the site covered three countries and 13 states, extending from the Canadian edge of the Temperate Prairies to the southern border of the Tamaulipas-Texas Semi-Arid Plain in Mexico. Yet, the fundamental challenge of studio was how to develop a territorial design strategy that highlighted the regions many unique eco-cultural identities.

Seeking to balance the scale of such a territorial design project with the cultural realities on the ground, the class turned to the age-old technique of pictorial cartography. Though the history of pictorial cartography is long, closely following the history of mapmaking in general, the art form experienced a golden era in 20th-century America. American pictorial maps were vibrant, colorful, and, at times, cartoonish artifacts of popular culture. Pictorial cartographers embraced the techniques of commercial artists, incorporating speech, bubbles, serial comic strips, and panoramas into their maps. By avoiding overly abstract graphic notations, such maps could easily be read and understood by a wide audience. Agricultural companies often employed pictorial maps often promoted the productive landscapes of the United States. The 1960s promotional map from the meatpacking conglomerate Armour & Company, for example, proclaims that "the greatness of the United States is founded on Agriculture." The map uses pictorial symbols to highlight the primary agricultural commodities of American regions, as well as identify the location of Armour's 34 meatpacking plants (Figure 4.1). Ultimately, pictorial cartography lost favor to the scientific mapping methods that emerged toward the end of the 20th century, the playful maps largely tossed aside as "the flotsam and jetsam of an enormous sea of popular culture."[5]

The course also experimented with strategies in woodcut printing – the process of printing an image from the raised portion of a carved or etched wood block. Woodcut printing is one of the oldest forms

4 Hornsby, Stephen J., and Ralph E. Ehrenberg. (2017). *Picturing America: The golden age of pictorial maps*. Chicago: University of Chicago Press, p. 4.

5 Ibid., p. 9.

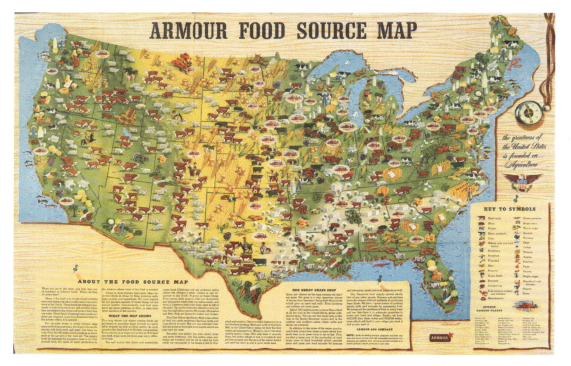

Figure 4.1 Armour Food Source Map, Cornell University – PJ Mode Collection of Persuasive Cartography.

of printmaking and has a strong history in rural landscapes, where it was an early, low-cost form of mass production. More modern intaglio and lithograph printmaking techniques required harsh chemicals, special materials, and expensive presses, all of which were readily available in metropolitan areas, but difficult to find in rural America. The only thing a rural artist needed to create an original print was a plank, some rudimentary cutting tools, ink, paper, and a wooden spoon. The artform gained renewed significance the 1930s when the Works Progress Administration commissioned thousands of artists to create posters and prints as part of the Federal Arts Program (FAP). Many FAP artists sought to depict uniquely American scenes, creating works that reflected the moment's social, economic, and environmental turmoil in addition to visions of what might be (Figure 4.2).[6] Inspired by this history, the students worked together to create a speculative pictorial map of the Great Plains using digital and analog relief printing techniques.

The studio began with data collection and analysis. As a combined studio, students built a collective understanding of the past, present, and future of agricultural ecosystems in the Great Plains. Students then developed a typological toolkit of historic and contemporary climate adaptation strategies that could be theoretically applicable to the future climate of the Great Plains. Each student was then assigned a Level III ecoregion. Following further research into their specific ecoregion, students identified which design

[6] Gamble, Antje K. and Martin T. Michael. (2016). "Art for the People: WPA Prints and Textiles from the Permanent Collection". Faculty & Staff Research and Creative Activity. 17. Accessed on July 1 2019. https:// digitalcommons.murray-state.edu/faculty/17

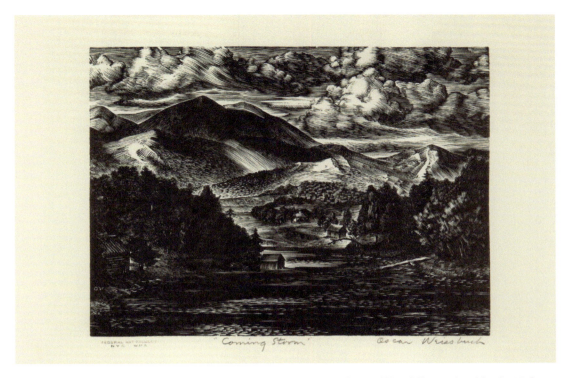

Figure 4.2 Oscar Weissbuch, American, born 1904 Coming Storm Wood Engraving block: 15.2 x 20.2 cm. (6 x 7 15/16 in.) sheet: 22.1 x 29 cm. (8 11/16 x 11 7/16 in.) Federal Art Project, W.P.A. Loan x1941-58.

typologies would be best suited to the productive, cultural, and ecological conditions of their site. With site analyzed and strategies identified, students then began the difficult task of developing relief prints and pictorial maps of their design proposals.

Each student developed a basemap depicting major hydrology, infrastructure, regional labels, and cities. Students then developed original pictorial symbols and hatches to communicate their territorial design proposals (Figure 4.3). In addition, each student was instructed to create a perspectival vector vignette to incorporate into the final map (Figure 4.4). Reviews and pinups were used to develop a cohesive visual style across the class. Students collaboratively selected typefaces, text bubbles, and hatches to share across the class.

With drafts of their pictorial maps created, the class experimented then with different approaches to digital relief printing. Digital drawings were first composed in Adobe Illustrator or AutoCAD (Figure 4.5). The drawings were then prepped for either the laser cutter or CNC router, where they would be etched or milled, respectively (Figure 4.6). Printing ink was rolled onto the etched or milled block before pressing paper into the ink (Figure 4.7).

Block material experiments included balsa wood, plywood, and MDF. The laser cutter accommodated finely detailed digital

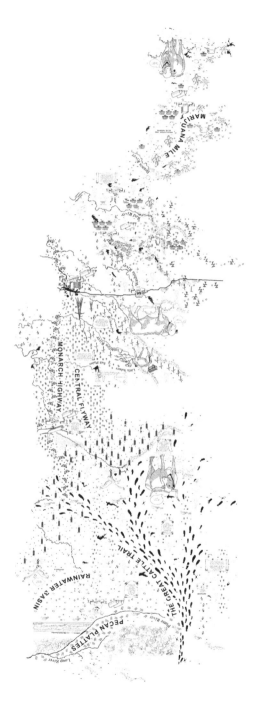

Figure 4.3 Pictorial map of the Central Great Plains ecoregion.

Figure 4.4 Embedded vignette, Central Great Plains ecoregion.

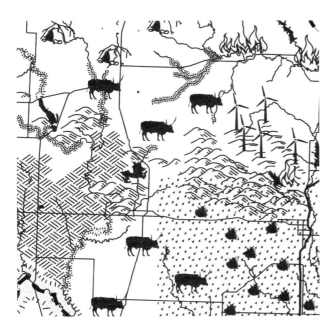

Figure 4.5 Digital drawing.

Figure 4.6 Milled woodblock.

Figure 4.7 Woodcut print on paper.

drawings, while the bit-size of the CNC router required that the digital drawings employ relatively thick 3pt minimum line weights. Because cutting and milling the drawings proved to be a lengthy endeavor, with a single 12×12" drawing taking over an hour to fabricate, students also developed stamps that could be used as hatches in the final prints (Figure 4.8). Finally, each student created multiple prints from each block, experimenting with different materials, inks, and stamping techniques (Figures 4.9–4.12).

Figure 4.8 Stamps.

Figure 4.9 Lasercut block print tests on paper and fabric.

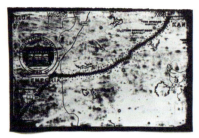

Figure 4.10 Milled block print tests on paper and fabric.

Figure 4.11 Milled block print test on paper.

Figure 4.12 Milled block print test on paper.

Figure 4.13 Digitally printed pictorial map.

Results

The results of the printing experiments were varied. Contrasting ink and paper colors highlighted the underlying textures and grains of the carved block. The smooth texture of printing paper was well suited to both etched and milled blocks. Though the woodcuts were particularly well suited for mapping large landscape features like rivers and roads, the finely grained details of the vector pictorial maps were often lost in the final print. Ultimately, the complexities of the pictorial maps proved too difficult to reconcile with the technical constraints of the digital woodcut blocks. For the final installation, students printed their pictorial maps using a conventional digital printer (Figure 4.13) and opted to create multicolor woodcut prints of smaller promotional posters.

The mapping and printing experiments discussed herein are far from comprehensive and should be considered springboards for further design investigation. The studio employed simple black and white vector drawing techniques to both ensure graphic consistency across the class and provide a simple interface with digital printmaking tools. Future work in pictorial cartography could potentially explore the use of color and photomontage as way to add more visual interest to the map. Though the maps created herein were also drawn manually in Adobe Illustrator and AutoCAD, future designers could consider developing new tools in ArcGIS to automate this process and tie it more seamlessly into geospatial datasets. Finally, landscape architecture students and practitioners should explore further opportunities for digital printmaking techniques. The studio used traditional drill bits in the CNC machine. Future work could include the creation of new drill or drawing bits that could be employed either on the block before it is printed or as a form of post-production on the resulting print. Such future work would challenge the technocratic nature of contemporary mapping methods and allow for more nuanced and expressive modes of representing the working landscape.

5

MATERIALITY AS INQUIRY

Environmental Histories for Enacting New Worlds

Sara Jacobs

How might designers think and act relationally? As climate change destabilizes how land is known through edges, borders, and properties, landscape can be increasingly understood as a relational process. Geographer Doreen Massey describes relationality as the coalescing of space in relation to other subjects and structures co-constituted through complex power relations.[1] Similarly, post-colonial poet and theorist Édouard Glissant suggests that relationality names the visible and invisible "relation[s] between different people, places, animate and inanimate objects, visible and invisible forces, the air, the water, the fire, the vegetation, animals and humans" to shape "worldmentalities" outside neoliberal and globalizing capital accumulation.[2] In the earliest stages of design, a combination of historical research and embodied practice can make visible the ways socio-ecological entanglements are assembled and layered relationally through landscape to envision these worlds.

Designed landscapes are representative of human–nature relationships. At the same time, they *are* human–nature relationships. Extending Massey and Glissant's thinking to the ways landscapes are relational, visual representation becomes a key way of interpreting, challenging, and rebuilding asymmetrical historical relations between place and power. Grounding design inquiries within historical processes foregrounds how issues such as climate change, racial violence, and ongoing colonial dispossession are rooted in specific, structural contexts with real, material traces. Visual representation helps illustrate these contexts and how contemporary spatial processes are co-constituted through human and more-than-human relations shaped over time. Naming and drawing these relations—often the ways social contexts produce physical, material traces—begins to reveal how alternative systems can be dreamed and imagined.

Combined with methods of representation, historical inquiry can challenge past ideas while producing new ways of seeing, and

[1] Massey, Doreen. *For Space*. London, Thousand Oaks, CA: SAGE, 2005.

[2] Édouard Glissant quoted in Manthia Diawara, "Édouard Glissant's Worldmentality: An Introduction to One World in Relation." https://www.documenta14.de/en/south/34_edouard_glissant_s_worldmentality_an_introduction_to_one_world_in_relation. Accessed November 2019.

DOI: 10.4324/9781003053255-6

by extension, thinking, to imagine transformative, collective, and more just socio-ecological futures. Future worlds begin to be realized the moment a drawing or model is made and shared. Visual representation, therefore, becomes a key link between historical interpretation and speculative design.[3] In the conceptual stages of design, this work may take many several forms. Drawing, counter-cartography, and collage can be used to understand how landscapes are entangled with flows of time and space, while physical models can understand how materials extend across spatial and temporal boundaries, record the accumulation and decomposition of historic layers on a site, and connect how materials of landscape assembly extend to spaces of extraction. Two positions ground the importance of history and representation (Figures 5.1 and 5.2).

First, urban environmental histories are central allies of landscape architecture that are capable of illustrating how social, political, and scientific histories are deeply bound with environmental relations.[4] Urban environmental histories trace the specific materials, processes, and systems of a place, revealing how historical causation, similar to landscape, is not linear or one-directional.[5] Urban environmental histories reveal how the production of urban nature is also deeply political in ways that are often overlooked because of how uneven power relations can obscure environmental conditions. Tracing the material assembly of roads, garbage dumps, canals, electric grids, and other infrastructure that are often seen in contrast to urban nature can reveal underlying dominant social and political contexts. As landscape architect Jane Hutton describes, tracing these objects and artefacts can reveal an "entanglement of materials, effects, and affect," or the material life of landscape relations.[6] Collage and photo ideograms, in particular, are an effective means of combining archival material with site observations to trace how past, present, and future assembles of air, water, and land have shaped communities experiencing environmental injustices today and how climate change might be experienced into the future (Figure 5.3).

Second, visual representation itself can enact new worlds, ideas, and spaces. While historical inquiry grounds and contextualizes, acts of drawing produce new possibilities and implications of landscape. Yet, drawing, models, and maps are deeply reflective of their maker and are always situated and positioned relative to lived experience.[7] Visual representations are, therefore, not stand-ins for yet to be scenarios as they can also reproduce the status quo. Ideas, spaces, and lives represented in design concepts, however dreamy they may seem, start to be realized the moment they are put into the world, akin to speculative fiction. Visual representation is therefore never trivial but a powerful force for social change with the ability to engender shifts in how landscapes are designed and for whom.

Bringing together visual representation and environmental histories to produce new narratives of material life is perhaps best

[3] Rose, Gillian. "Rethinking the Geographies of Cultural 'Objects' through Digital Technologies." *Progress in Human Geography* 40, no. 3 (2016): 334–351.

[4] Pritchard, Sara B. *Confluence: The Nature of Technology and the Remaking of the Rhône.* Cambridge, MA: Harvard University Press, 2011; Gandy, Matthew. "Marginalia: Aesthetics, Ecology, and Urban Wastelands." *Annals of the Association of American Geographers* 103, no. 6 (2013): 1301–1316; Heynen, Nik. "Urban Political Ecology I." *Progress in Human Geography* 38, no. 4 (2014): 598–604.

[5] Duempelmann, Sonja. "Taking Turns: Landscape and Environmental History at the Crossroads." *Landscape Research* 36, no. 6 (2011): 625–640; Tarr, Joel. *The Material Basis of Urban Environmental History.* 744–746. Oxford: Oxford University Press, 2005.

[6] Hutton, Jane. *Material Culture: Assembling and Disassembling Landscapes.* Landscript; 5. Berlin: Jovis Verlag GmbH, 2017.

[7] Haraway, Donna. "Situated Knowledges: The Science Question in Feminism and the Privilege of Partial Perspective." *Feminist Studies* 14, no. 3 (1988): 575–599.

Figures 5.1 and 5.2 Ideogram collage and clay model examining histories of sedimented racial violence and the potential of unmaking racialized topographies in Charlottesville, Virginia (Colleen Brennen).

Figure 5.3 Still from animation combining archival records, site photos, and collage imagines past, present, and future relations between air, water, and land in Seattle, Washington (Rich Desanto, Asya Snejnevski, Lauren Wong).

illustrated through counter-cartographies. Cartography is often wielded as a form of power steeped in rational and positivist world-views and used to maintain dominant power structures.[8] Counter-cartography uses the tools of cartography but treats maps and drawings as situated, relational, and reflective of the maker's positionality. When combined with material studies from environmental history, counter-cartography can produce new spatial relationships by illustrating how sites bounded by abstract property lines have social, cultural, and political consequences that extend to untold spatial and temporal limits. Recognizing the material life of landscape opens the possibility of reworking the materiality of the past and future by recognizing that one cannot disentangle the present from past or future worlds.[9] (Figure 5.4)

Finally, site is central to the possibilities that exploring historical processes and visual representation create. Tracing the material life of a site includes following patterns created by soil, water, animals, or geology; social practices such as spaces of cultural mediations with nature and economic processes like the extraction and movement of goods. In tracing the material life of a site, representation becomes a method of research, where ecological traces may emerge as cultural memories through documents, maps, and images. Alternatively, stories, communities, and timelines that

[8] Cosgrove, Denis E. *Geography and Vision Seeing, Imagining and Representing the World*. London: I.B. Tauris, 2008; Harley, J. B. *The New Nature of Maps: Essays in the History of Cartography*. Baltimore, MD: Johns Hopkins University Press, 2001; Kurgan, Laura. *Close up at a Distance: Mapping, Technology, and Politics*. First hardcover edition. Brooklyn, NY: Zone Books, 2013.

[9] Barad, Karen. "Nature's Queer Performativity." *Qui Parle: Critical Humanities and Social Sciences* 19, no. 2 (2011): 121–158: 150.

Figure 5.4 Photogram illustrating entanglements of air pollution, highway infrastructure, and embodied experience in Seattle, Washington (Lauren Wong).

otherwise may be missing or erased through normative mapping become known. Organic materials, such as coal, sediment, or rubble, might be recorded and recast to reflect processes of social precarity, or fabric might be used to explore the instability of geologic time (Figure 5.5).

The entanglements that these materials form with their urban and regional histories reveal the forces and flows of the world, reflecting both lived experience (how one comes to know a place) and structural processes (how one exists within broader systems of power).[10] With this awareness comes a responsibility to recognize who has and who has not historically been able produce or control knowledge about landscape. Working between historical inquiries and visual representations allows for the plurality and multiplicity of site to emerge.

Enacting new worlds that are livable, just, and liberatory begins with representing the worlds we each want to live in. The co-production of histories and visual representation create practices of design inquiry that can conceptualize current environmental and social processes within historical contexts to challenge and reshape the contemporary designed landscape. Through the material life of environmental histories, landscape representation becomes a

[10] Ingold, Tim. "Toward an Ecology of Materials." *Annual Review of Anthropology* 41 (2012): 427–442.

Figure 5.5 Fabric model examining how highway infrastructure has fragmented community health in Seattle, Washington (Lauren Wong).

process of revealing underrepresented stories, places, and narratives. This approach grounds broader societal and political questions to create knowledge about landscape that is specific and situated in time and place. In this way, the earliest design concepts have the power to subvert and rearticulate historic narratives while bringing forth new ways of being and living.

6

DEVELOPING CONCEPTS

Scott Jennings Melbourne

Before preparing a conceptual design, identifying program requirements, conducting site analysis, confirming objectives, or signing contracts, there are questions to ask: what is the role of the designer—the role of *design*—in this given place and time?

These foundational considerations are relevant in any context, but within regions experiencing significant urban change, the questions are that much more essential. During phases of rapid economic development, critical decisions are being made regarding infrastructure and land uses, and with that there is a hope that a relatively modest influence on these forces can carry an outsized effect with lasting consequences. At the same time, disciplinary roles are less likely to have been clarified and there is greater risk in proposals failing to gain traction or result in meaningful impact. What then might be methods for better equipping designers to provide their skills and insights in ways that help inform decision-making?

This question has been at the heart of a seven-year teaching effort that engages the forces of urban change and helps prepare young designers for an increasingly dynamic world. Studio work has focused primarily on Yangon, Myanmar (Rangoon, Burma), and East Java, Indonesia. Reflections on these experiences may be helpful for those seeking to apply design thinking in other developing regions.

Yangon is the economic capital of Myanmar, a metropolitan region[1] of more than 7 million and growing as increased industrialization and nascent professional services in the city attract workers from the country's still largely rural population. Built upon an alluvial plain with a historic colonial city core, bounding river to the south and sprawling development to the north, this city faces severe urban challenges of transportation, basic sanitation, and debilitating seasonal flooding. All the while risks of natural disasters including cyclones and even earthquakes linger.

In the "desakota"[2] region of East Java, Indonesia, an interplay of roadside urban development and still largely small-scaled agricultural land uses overlay a dramatic natural landscape punctuated by active volcanos. Challenges revolve around how this urban fabric will scale up to hold a growing population during the next

[1] For a concise review of the city's geography, see Morley, Ian. "Rangoon." *Cities* 31 (2013): 601–614.
[2] For more regarding this urban growth pattern see McGee, Terry. "The spatiality of Urbanization: the policy challenges of Mega-urban and Desakota Regions of Southeast Asia" UNU-IAS Working Paper No. 161 (2009).

DOI: 10.4324/9781003053255-7

stages of industrialization, while also allowing communities to be safely responsive to natural disasters including those triggered by the volcanos.

A pedagogy of engagement in these regions has affirmed the distinct value of tools and methods available during each stage of the design process. This includes initial desktop research, to be sure—helping establish the historic, economic, and environmental context of the place while making use of information resources that may not be available within the region itself. Meanwhile, investigations into related disciplinary concepts help expand the realm of conceptual thinking beyond the conventional purview of landscape design.

Next and most critically, there is significant time spent on the ground (in our case, typically at least a week) in which students gain a visceral understanding of conditions and issues, experienced in person and collected through the full range of senses. Often, there are surprises to be had in how the *vibe* of the place is different than suggested through the preceding studies. This also is a time to meet directly with community members, local experts, and others who can provide insight that no amount of online searching would ever produce. Knowing that design proposals will ultimately benefit from a high degree of specificity (mind, distinct from the degree of adaptiveness within the proposal itself), observations made through looking critically during these study trips often provide the spark of inspiration. Sketching out the first notions of a concept *in situ* jumpstarts the design process and allows for immediate feedback from conversations with local partners, often conducted in a structured but informal manner that helps course-correct these initial ideas.

Returning to studio offers a helpful degree of detachment as concepts are iterated upon, visualized, tested, and ultimately committed to. During this phase, students find themselves somewhat between worlds, on the one hand, pulled toward familiar forms of design discourse while, at the same time, recognizing how ineffective such terminology and framing might be in communicating ideas with local parties. Discussing the same idea in different ways nurtures a high level of criticality and, even better, some will successfully develop a more unified means of clearly communicating their ideas to a diverse audience. In this context, a concept is only as valuable as much as it is understood—something made apparent during final reviews when a range of critics including local experts and representatives participate.

The process outlined above may sound simple enough, but it is filled with challenges. For all involved, there is a high degree of uncertainty to be navigated in everything from logistics, cultural norms of communication, on to how effectively core issues will be identified. Students are called upon to embrace a sense of adventure in a way that previous life experiences (let alone schooling)

Figure 6.1 Students learning about conditions of volcanic Mount Bromo, East Java through discussions with local experts and in-person explorations.

Figure 6.2 Gaining insight on functions and context of small scale plantations being transformed to eco-tourism destinations within East Java.

Figure 6.3 Small-scaled agricultural resources such as this tea plantation in the Batu Valley are being integrated to urban growth plans.

Figure 6.4 Presenting observations and initial design concepts during site trips allows for immediate feedback from local partners at Yangon Technological University.

Figure 6.5 Working with local students to explore potential for linking public space improvements with infrastructure works in downtown Yangon.

may not have prepared them for. Administrators are asked to be supportive or at least turn something of a blind eye to a process that is inherently less safe than standard practice. And, instructors must play even more roles than with a typical design studio—not just teacher, but also travel agent, diplomat, and adventurer.

These difficulties are overcome in the service of establishing conditions within which a concept may spark, not in isolation, but rather as a design-driven link between critical observation and the expressed concerns of local communities. Proposals include the familiar elements of site plans, phasing diagrams and the like, but more than anything, these concepts are suggestive more than declarative, identifying a point of entry for designers. In this way, the process functions as a kind of prelude for the "necessary collaboration" described by Carl Steinitz[3] within the geodesign framework for facilitating decision-making amongst varied parties on complex spatial problems.

[3] A valuable synthetization many decades' worth of design teaching can be found in Steinitz, Carl. *A Framework for Geodesign: Changing Geography by Design*. Redlands, CA: Esri, 2012.

Figure 6.6 Students presenting background studies and learning from city planners at Yangon City Hall.

Figure 6.7 Identifying critical regional issues with students at the University of Brawijaya in Malang, East Java, Indonesia.

Figure 6.8 Learning from former residents of a village destroyed by the "human made disaster" at Sidoarjo, East Java, Indonesia.

Figure 6.9 Presenting design concepts at the University of Hong Kong.

Early, during our time in Yangon, we were told a perhaps apocryphal story. "In Myanmar we once had two landscape architects: then one retired, and the other became a monk." Jumping forward to the present day and seeing work produced by students in landscape studios being led by some of the very individuals we collaborated with on our first visits, it is clear that the number of practitioners is in the process of changing (Figures 6.1–6.9).

7

CRITICAL MAKING

Emily Vogler

Critical Making is a practice that combines the analytical, evaluative, and reflective aspects of critical thinking with the material, iterative and embodied aspects of making.[1] At RISD, this approach guides studio work and emphasizes the importance of the formation of ideas through hands-on practices. Rosanne Somerson, the President of RISD from 2015 to 2021, wrote: "The artistic mind relies on 'making' as a critical activity, one that informs a particular kind of deep intelligence that cannot be learned without real material manipulation and sensory, embodied experience."[2] At the core of critical making is a focus on embodied knowledge, material explorations, and the iterative creative process.

At RISD, the landscape architecture department exists alongside other arts and design disciplines including sculpture, industrial design, ceramics, glass, textiles, and furniture design, to name just a few. Each of these departments has a unique relationship with the craft and materials of their discipline. They work directly with the final objects and develop in-depth knowledge of the opportunities and limitations of their materials. Unlike these disciplines, landscape architects work with large complex sites and systems and rarely have the opportunity to physically construct their final designs.[3] Despite this, I would like to argue that the core principles of critical making: embodied knowledge, material explorations, and the iterative creative process, are fundamental important to the way that landscape architects ideate and practice and yet it is currently lacking from many academic institutions and design practices.

Embodied Knowledge –Ideation Through Experience

Embodied knowledge is a direct result of engaging with real materials and real scale. Our contemporary digital culture has led to the disconnect of people from the material physical reality of this world. We increasingly interact virtually across the Internet, we rely on Google Earth for site data, and we design remotely through computer programs. There is a need for a radical reorienting within landscape architecture to value the embodied physical, spatial, temporal, and material knowledge that comes from spending time interacting with real materials, physical landscapes, and actual people. Whether that is spending time in the field observing the

[1] Rosanne Somerson. *The Art of Critical Making: Rhode Island School of Design on Creative Practice*. Edited by Rosanne Somerson and Mara Hermano. 1st edition (Hoboken, NJ: Wiley, 2013).
[2] Somerson. *The Art of Critical Making*.
[3] James Corner. "Representation and Landscape." In *Theory in Landscape Architecture: A Reader*. Edited by Simon Swaffield (Philadelphia, PA: Penn Studies in Landscape Architecture, 2002).

DOI: 10.4324/9781003053255-8

Figure 7.1 Students gaining an embodied experience of a deep section soil profile. Photo credit – RISD Landscape Architecture Department.

spatial and experiential qualities of different types of landscapes, carving wood to understand its inherent material properties, or asking a stranger about their vision for the future of their city – each of these experiences, builds a deeper understanding of the spaces and communities we operate within. The interrogation of this embodied experience can be the method through which design ideas are formed and helps move beyond the abstract into the material (Figure 7.1).

Material Practices – Ideation Through Material Exploration

As landscape architects, our artistic media are soil, plants, wood, metal, concrete, stone, water, light, sound, buildings, ecosystems, processes, cities, and regions. In many landscape architecture schools and design practices, materials are relegated to technical specifications and the reliance on off the shelf prefabricated materials rather than seeing the tactile materials as a source of creativity and inspiration for design. By understanding these materials through an embodied and deep understanding of their elemental properties, designers can understand how they can be composed to form meaning and unique places that are transformative for those who experience them. Through these experiences, materials become something we work with rather than a passive substance that we work on (Figure 7.2).

Iterative Process – Ideation Through Iteration

While landscape architects benefit from gaining an embodied understanding of landscapes and materials, the profession still requires scaled drawings and models to mediate between design

Figure 7.2 Visiting
a granite quarry,
students learn
about the extraction
process and material
properties of granite.
Photo credit –
RISD Landscape
Architecture
Department.

[4] Somerson. *The Art of Critical Making*.

ideas and the physical transformation of landscapes.[3] When working in the studio, the iterative design process is a key to critical making. The iterative design process includes the interplay between thinking, modeling, drawing, and writing.[4] It is an approach that values models and drawing as a creative process of ideation rather than just a final product. This includes shifting from thinking of models as something we laser cut after the design is complete, to understanding models as a critical three-dimensional sketching tool to develop spatial and conceptual understanding of a project. Through this iterative approach, drawings and models become the tools that we have as designers to discover, invent, explore, test, and reflect. In addition, it is where the distinctive and emotionally rich forms of creative expression and individual voice can emerge (Figure 7.3).

As Department Chair of the Landscape Architecture Program at RISD from 2017 to 2019, one of my goals was to strengthen how we incorporated these principles of critical making into our core curriculum. One example of this was the reworking of our "Material Thinking" course sequence to include more opportunities for our students to gain hands-on experience working directly with materials. There are three materials courses in the sequence; "*Material Logic*," "*Materials Experiments*," and "*Material Assemblies.*" These courses build in complexity from understanding the elemental properties of materials, to learning how to experiment with them through digital fabrication tools and culminating in the understanding of how multiple materials come together to construct complex physical landscapes. In addition, there are three additional classes in the sequence focused on plants, ecology and hydrology. Students spend extensive time in the field studying plant communities, in the lab looking at plants under the microscopes and in the

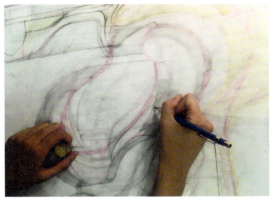

Figure 7.3 In the Landscape Architecture studios students work iteratively through models and grading plans. Photo credit – RISD Landscape Architecture Department.

studio learning how plants are used by designers to shape space. Each of the classes in this sequence has been adapted to provide more immersive, embodied experiences for students to interact and learn from the physical materials of our discipline.

Coming out of our core curriculum, our advanced elective studios provide the opportunity to explore the productive overlap that exists when we bring the site-based questions from landscape architecture together with the material-based explorations of the fine arts disciplines. These interdisciplinary studios provide a way to investigate the boundaries of landscape architecture and explore new artistic means of making and understanding the world and landscapes that surround us.

In 2017 and 2018, I designed and led two interdisciplinary studios between landscape architecture and ceramics. I co-taught the class with a colleague, David Katz, a sculptor and installation artist working primarily with ceramics and unfired clay. In these studios, we looked at how interdisciplinary practices can support new approaches to the design and management of the dynamic edge between land and water. For the past century, the design of the water's edge has been dominated by engineering approaches that favor large-scale, top-down, single purpose infrastructure. The simplification of the gradient from water to land into a hard edge has led to the loss of the ecological and hydrological complexity of these dynamic landscapes. Through the studios, we sought to challenge these conventions and to develop an approach that explored the gradient from wet to dry, water to land, and aquatic to terrestrial ecologies.

In 2017, the studio was titled *"Acequias: Infrastructural Logic| Material Logic"* and focused on the network of irrigation ditches (known locally as acequias) of the Middle Rio Grande Valley in New Mexico. Although the ditches were originally constructed solely as irrigation infrastructure to water agricultural fields, as the city of

Albuquerque grew around them, they became an integral part of the region's ecological, hydrological, recreational, and transportation network. Unlike most urban water infrastructure which is buried underground or sealed in concrete, the irrigation ditches of the Middle Rio Grande Valley are earthen and can function as living systems that engage with dynamic ecological and hydrological processes. The "leaky" irrigation ditches serve to recharge the aquifer and maintain the region's riparian habitat by spreading the water and associated ecologies across the river valley, essentially reengineering the original broad floodplain without flooding people's houses. However, every year as the water flows in the earthen channels, it slowly erodes at the clay soils along the ditch banks. Over time, this has led to severe erosion along many of the ditches. The city responds to the erosion by lining the ditches with shotcrete. This treatment impairs the hydrological, ecological, and aesthetic functions of the ditches and often leads to worse erosion.

In this studio, students were asked to design a system made out of ceramic modules that could help reduce erosion while supporting and strengthening the ecology, hydrology, and of the water's edge. The modular approach was intended to allow students to develop proposals at a scale that they could fabricate in the studio but to understand the opportunity for their proposals to scale up and have a systemic impact at an infrastructural scale. Some of the material, formal, performative, and infrastructural questions we asked in the studio were: How does the module aggregate and disperse to respond to different site conditions? Can the module provide slope stabilization and pockets for planting to support the range of aquatic species along the ditches? Can the module enhance the human use and aesthetic experience of the space? How long should the materials persist? Could they degrade overtime once the plant roots stabilize the banks? Could the modules be constructed by community groups along the ditch?

The first phase of the studio was a time of in-depth material investigation. The students gained hands-on experience working with clay and familiarizing themselves with it as a creative medium (Figure 7.4). In the ceramic studio, David taught the students about the inherent opportunities and limitations of clay and led workshops on slab construction, coil building, and slip casting (Figure 7.5). During this phase, students deepened their understanding of clay as an elemental medium through ceramic research methods. Students studied the effect of different clay mixes, various additives, and different firing temperatures. This research provided the students with a better understanding of the variables that could be manipulated depending on the student's intentions for how the material would perform and degrade overtime.

Following this phase of material immersion, we focused on the unique physical, ecological, and cultural landscapes of New Mexico. During a five-day site visit, students spent time walking the ditches, operating irrigation gates, making adobes, and collecting

Figure 7.4 Student's familiarize themselves with the materiality of clay through a series of exercises in the ceramic studio. Photo credit – Author.

samples of soil and vegetation from along the river (Figure 7.6). On the first day visiting the ditches, one of the ceramics students reached down and picked up a handful of dirt. Squeezing the soil between her fingers, she said; "this soil is pure clay." As a result of this observation, the students flew back to Providence with duffle bags full of soil to experiment with in the studio.

After gaining an understanding of materials and site conditions, we shifted to focus on the design and construction of the module. Students started by researching patents to understand how others have addressed issues of erosion in the past. Building on this research, the students developed a series of study models in three distinct materials: paper, clay, and digital models. Through this iterative modeling process, the students had the opportunity to understand the formal limitations of the different modeling materials. As the designs became more finalized, the students 3D printed

Figure 7.5 Students in the ceramic studio learning slab construction techniques. Photo credit – Author.

Figure 7.6 During the field trip to New Mexico students explored the irrigation ditches, operated the gates to lower and raise the water levels in the ditches, and made adobe bricks. Photo credits – Author.

their modules and were able to test their designs in a stream table (Figure 7.7). The stream table provided an analog opportunity for the students to study the hydrodynamic forces in the ditches and how the module would interact with water and soil. These studies led to the refinement of the modular system, and eventually, the students had to fabricate the module at full or half scale.

There were 14 unique projects that emerged from the studio. Some of the more interesting projects came from students who connected their design proposals to advanced materials research. Xiao Chen studied erosion control mattresses during the patent

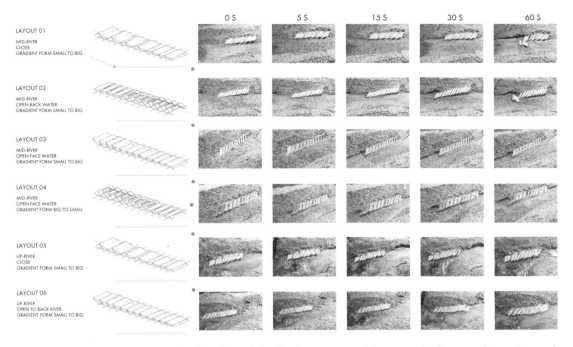

Figure 7.7 Students tested 3d printed modules in the stream table to study the way the water and sediment interacted with the modules. Image credit – Siyu Du.

research and in her project adapted the concept of the erosion control mattress to introduce a gradient of porosity through the ditch cross section. She proposed that the modules would be less porous lower down in the ditches where the water flowed continuously and more porous on the upper ditch banks where the plants could grow. In addition, she explored how the material composition could transition from a more stable material lower down to a more ephemeral material on the upper ditch banks that could degrade over time once the plants' roots stabilized the banks (Figure 7.8).

For landscape architecture student Austin Bamford, it was the historic adobe construction technique and the shared maintenance practices of the ditches that drove his design. He proposed that the modules would be constructed out of stabilized soils similar to stabilized adobes which are widely used in the region. Stabilized adobes are a combination of local soils that are mixed in different proportions with concrete. He proposed that the ratio of soil to cement would vary depending on the location of the module in relation to the areas of erosion along the ditch. The modular form itself was an elongated rectangle that is a variation on the rectangular shape of an adobe. The intention behind his simple form and material selection was that local communities could use local materials to build and install the modular system (Figure 7.9).

Given the richness of the projects that came out of the Acequias studio and the enthusiasm of the students, we were able to offer

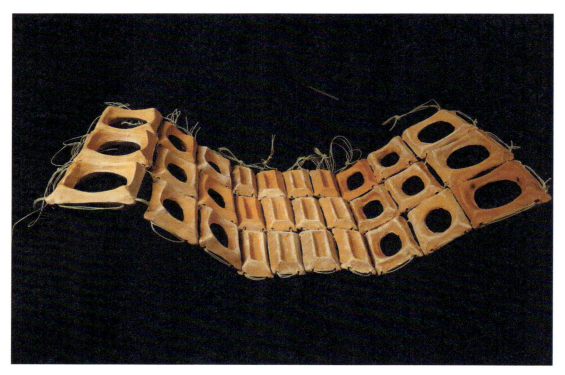

Figure 7.8 Xiao Chen's proposal included a module that was denser lower down where the water is more erosive and more porous along the ditch banks where the plants could help stabilize the soil. Image credit – Xiao Chen.

5 http://www.crmc.ri. gov/coastalresilience/ RI_Coastal_Erosion_ Adaptation.pdf. Save the Bay. *Coastal Erosion and Adaptation on the Rhode Island Coastline*. 2013.

another interdisciplinary ceramics and landscape architecture studio in 2018. The studio was titled "*Intertidal: Infrastructural Logic| Material Logic*" and focused on the intertidal zone in Narragansett Bay. There are over 400 miles of coastal edge in Narragansett Bay. In over 80% of these areas, the coastline is migrating landward as a result of sea-level rise, wave energy, and other shoreline dynamics.[5] Across the Bay, there are a range of local conditions that this migratory force is encountering. In salt marshes, the landscape is slowly and silently migrating landward as the salt marshes erode into the Bay and the high marsh retreats. In the outer Bay, the wave and storm action are actively carving away at the coastline and threatening existing buildings and infrastructure.

The Intertidal studio followed a similar structure as the first studio by beginning with deep immersion into site and materials. Through a process of territorial mapping and repeated site visits, the students mapped the range of typical conditions found within the Bay and identified the specific parameters they would work with in the studio. These typological conditions included different combinations of coastal forces, bathymetry, adjacent structures and communities (Figure 7.10). Given the range of forces in the Bay, each student was asked to determine the materials for the modules and to articulate how the material selection responded to the specific

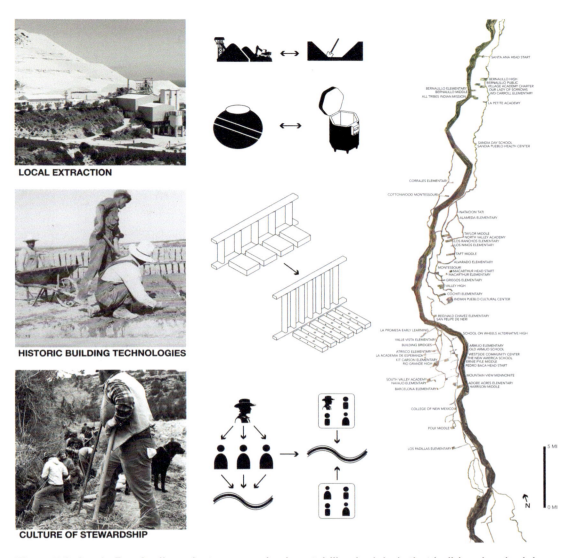

LOCAL EXTRACTION

HISTORIC BUILDING TECHNOLOGIES

CULTURE OF STEWARDSHIP

Figure 7.9 Austin Bamford's project proposed using stabilized adobe's that build on local adobe construction techniques and community stewardship of the ditches. Image credit – Austin Bamford.

site forces they were engaging. As a result, some of the students working in higher energy zones transitioned from using clay to constructing their modules out of concrete (Figure 7.11).

These experimental studios tested how critical making and interdisciplinary practices could be at the core of landscape architecture studios. They aimed to move past the speculative digital abstraction that is so common in contemporary landscape architecture programs to prioritize embodied knowledge, material explorations, and the iterative creative process. There is often the misconception that working with materials means that the projects will be small-scale rather than taking on the more significant

Figure 7.10 Evan
Davenport mapped
the relationship
between sea level
rise, development and
hardened edges to
identify the specific
conditions he was
working with in
Narragansett Bay.
Image credit – Evan
Davenport.

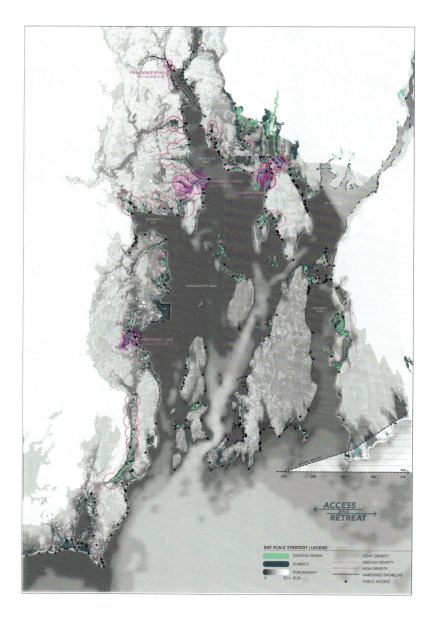

Figure 7.11 Modules from the Intertidal Studio. Image credit – Madison Murray, Xinrui Yang, and Weixin Li.

environmental, social, and urban issues that many within our field are striving to address. These interdisciplinary landscape architecture and ceramics studios are an example of how we can take on large-scale environmental and infrastructural issues that often exist at the regional scale but understand the agency that we have as designers and artists to address these issues with action-based solutions at the site and material scale. These multiscalar practices enable designers and artists to bridge from the conceptual to the material, the global to the local, and the system to the site. Ultimately, to enact physical change in this world, we will need to address the symbolic and physical aspects of landscapes, and it is through an embodied understanding of landscapes and deep material knowledge that this will be possible.

Part 2

Concept in Translation

8

MATERIALIZING ATMOSPHERES

Translating the Immaterial

Zaneta Hong

In "Landscape or the Weather-world?," from *Being Alive: Essays on Movement, Knowledge and Description*, Tim Ingold writes,

> Theories of how people perceive the world around them generally work from the assumption that this world is terrestrial. It is a world in which we can expect to find formations of the land such as hills and valleys, mountains and plains, interspersed with settlements such as villages and towns and threaded by paths, roads and waterways. To describe such a world, it is customary to use the word 'landscape'. … In reality, of course, the landscape has not already congealed from the medium. It is undergoing continuous formation, above all thanks to the immersion of its manifold surfaces in those fluxes of the medium that we call weather – in sunshine, rain, wind and so on. The ground is not the surface of materiality itself, but a textured composite of diverse materials that are grown; deposited and woven together through a dynamic interplay across the permeable interface between the medium and the substances with which it comes into contact.

We are immersed in atmospheres that envelop our bodies, we move between environments, and we interact with elements and forces, whether natural or constructed. These environments, whether exposed or enclosed, habitable or inhabitable, at the scale of the body or of the city, are subjected to climatological change – a change that directly and indirectly impacts the ways in which we understand, experience, and design for the built environment. As landscape designers, we visualize and materialize these spaces of sensory entanglement between landscape and atmosphere. In order to do so, one must first recognize that landscape architecture is an acknowledgment of designing with air and atmosphere, as it has already been well established for ground and water. Likewise, atmosphere (a scientific term) and atmospherics (a qualitative construct or expression) are interdependent terms used

DOI: 10.4324/9781003053255-10

in design. This relationship between landscape and atmosphere, while seemingly apparent and obvious is, however, rarely acknowledged or formalized as a spatial intervention. Our conventional and accustomed procedures to transform the land, a cornerstone to the practice of landscape architecture, can and should fold in the study of air, atmosphere, and its concomitant meteorological elements, i.e., light, wind, temperature, humidity, precipitation, etc., rather than be elements sidelined to the periphery of landscape design discourse.

In a foundation design studio at the University of Virginia, students were introduced to an environmental ethos that considered the holistic undertaking of atmosphere as performative space and designed conditions. Student projects investigated the challenges of integrating the dynamics of climate/weather with the design of urban landscapes that strived to provide both human comfort and landscape resiliency. With these objectives in mind, the studio served to highlight the tools and techniques that document site at particular climatic timescales, alongside the development of conceptual design ideas.

Environmental Phenomena and Site Analysis

- *To sharpen inductive and deductive skills as they apply to the observation, description, and representation of site; and to value corporeal and cognitive perceptions of space.*
- *To develop an understanding of timescales and concepts of temporality alongside landscape conditions and phenomena; and to explore various methods of recording and representing them.*
- *To advance an understanding of seasonality and materiality; and to integrate design strategies that would elicit and highlight the experiential qualities affected by diurnal and cyclical processes.*

The studio was organized by two phases, where each phase allowed students to explore various indexes and parameters relevant to microclimate and the human/landscape interface. The first phase provided students with a series of exercises that explored landscape conditions as timescales – with an emphasis on exploring phasing, intervals, and duration through cyclical and/or continuous timeframes, e.g., seasons, years, months, days, hours, minutes, and seconds. This study was articulated through the identification of the averages and extremes of four meteorological categories: **light/radiation** (sun orientation/path, view from/of sun, shadow studies, accumulated/temporary shade, accumulated solar exposure, collected solar/thermal energy, radiation of heat and surface materials, and glare); **wind** (flow, direction, speed, weathering/decay, and erosion/deposition); **perceived temperature and relative humidity/pressure** (evaporation, evapotranspiration, plant uptake, and transpiration); and **precipitation** (rain/snow, surface water flow, water percolation/seepage, drainage, flooding, drought, fog, cloud formation, erosion/deposition, pollutant/contaminant transportation, and runoff) (Figures 8.1–8.3). Each of these environmental elements was then mapped to exploit a time-based study of states, instances, or episodes visualized at two discrete scales: the *macroscopic* – the scale in which objects and/or processes are of a size that is both measurable and observable with the naked eye, and the *microscopic* – the scale in which objects and/or processes are of a size that is measurable, but only observable through augmented senses or correlated events.

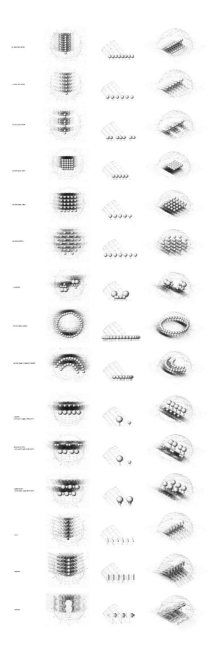

Figure 8.1 Shadow and shade study for various planting strategies and tree morphologies.
Student: Yolanda Xiang Zhao. Planted strategies represented: 10' spacing row; 15' spacing row; 10' spacing grid; 20' spacing grid; 20' quincunx; 2 groves; 10' spacing circle; 10' spacing double curve; 2 rows of 18' plants and 30' plants; hip-hop rows of 18' plants and 30' plants; 2 mixed rows of 18' plants and 30' plants. Tree morphologies represented (in order of appearance): cone, cylinder, canopy.

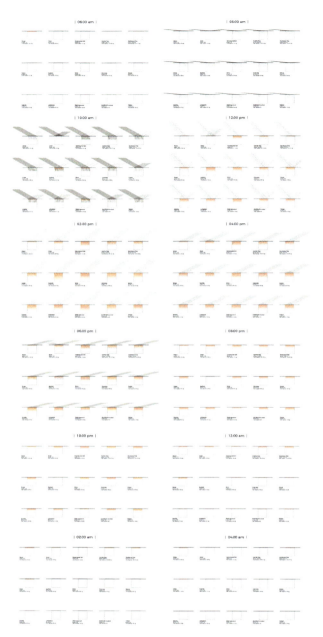

Figure 8.2 Hourly effect of light radiation for various ground materials and plants.
Student: Erica Mutschler-Nielsen.
"This research focuses on a material's interaction with the climate just above the ground, the space in which we inhabit. Each material has a different engagement and an effect on the space of air we inhabit. Each material absorbs a different amount of sunlight, reflecting the rest. As this sunlight enters the material the sun's energy is converted into heat energy. This happens as the electrons in the material have a certain frequency they like, which corresponds to a different frequency of light radiation. As the electrons in the material absorb the light rays which match their frequency they start to vibrate. This vibration is what produces heat energy. Each material has a different threshold in which it heats up, each requires a different amount of light radiation for the material to increase one degree." – Erica Mutschler-Nielsen
Materials represented (in order of appearance): water, snow, constructed soil, conifer tree, deciduous tree, grass, asphalt, brick, concrete, gravel, granite, limestone, steel (galvanized), aluminum (anodized), and timber. The matrix translates a material language for Urban Heat Island Effect.

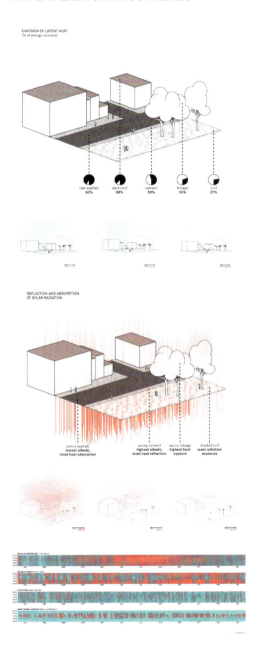

Figure 8.3 Emission of latent heat and reflection and absorption of solar radiation.
Student: Lindsey Luria. Material effects of temperature, humidity, air velocity and wind chill. Represented data correspond to average annual weather data for Washington, D.C.

The iterative study to climatic timescales allowed students to critique initial theories and to eventually proceed forward with recommended design outcomes. In addition, the representation of climate through process vignettes, systems simulations, and catalogs of atmospheric and phenomenological animations further highlighted a materiality to environmental processes, something that could be characterized as both dimensional and structural in matter (Figures 8.4 and 8.5).

Figure 8.4 Porosity airflow and porous materials.
Student: Elizabeth Camuti. Degrees of wind break porosity represented: 10%, 50%, and 90% porosity. Simulation represented with a 10' x 10' wall with 10 mph winds and 0.5 micrometer particle size.

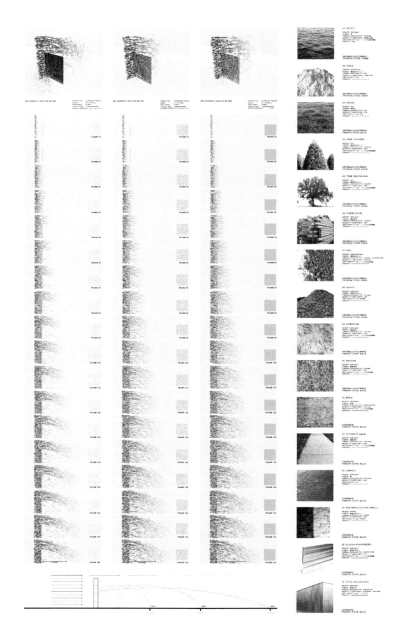

Experimentation in Design Process and Production

• *To situate design process and representation through a conceptual framework that is both flexible and adjustable, experimental and novel.*
• *To develop and refine both analog and digital representation techniques with a high level of craft; and to value experimentation and fabrication as a mode of design process and production.*

In the second phase of the studio, students furthered their design concepts through material experiments that explored landscape

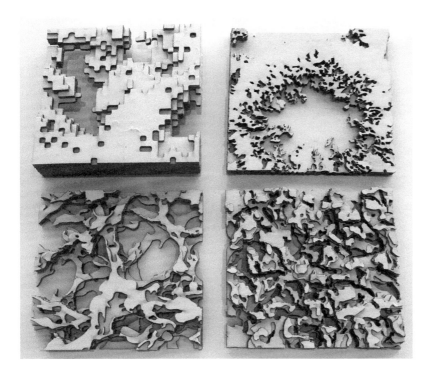

Figure 8.5 Material surficiality and porosity.
Student: Elizabeth Camuti. Translations of landscape materials undergoing various processes, e.g., expansion, contraction, growth, decay. Materials represented range from natural to synthetic.

temporality. Rather than exclusively being generative of form and appearance alone, designed space was the product of proposed landscape conditions and performance properties, most notably those induced by phenomenological and meteorological processes investigated during phase one. The content from this phase generated a series of digital and physical models that materialized the dynamic qualities of environmental phenomena (Figure 8.6).

As an extension to this phase, students were asked to explore two basic spatial conditions of human occupation – exposed and enclosed – through the formal exploration of four basic landscape typologies. These typologies included a **hill** (a hill is a raised area or mound of land; hills are formed by rock debris or sand deposited by glaciers and wind), a **berm** (a berm is a level space, shelf, or raised barrier separating two areas; berms are used to control erosion and sedimentation by reducing the rate of surface runoff, as much provide a physical, stationary barrier of some kind), **a basin or depression** (a depression in geology is a landform sunken or depressed below the surrounding area; there are many types of basins including debris basin, drainage basin, sedimentary basin, structural basin, tidal basin, etc.), and a **canal or channel** (a canal is a man-made channel of water; a body of water that connects two larger bodies of water). The landform typologies were mapped in seriality in order to delineate subtle differences accounted for in geometric transformation and material specification; but more importantly, these measured and calculated landform speculations

Figure 8.6 Wind analysis. Student: Matthew Walter.

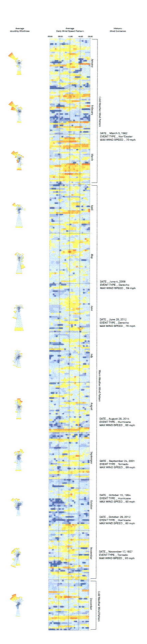

and landforming processes allowed students to further their experimentation and manipulation of particular environmental conditions and landscape performance (Figures 8.7 and 8.8).

Iteration was once again a methodology for design development – an enterprise that was facilitated in large part to the applied software and digital tools. The catalog of landformations allowed students to present multiple deployments and multiple phenomenal effects for a single site intervention (Figures 8.9 and 8.10). The simulation of selected geometric and material manipulations

Figure 8.7 Catalogue of human occupation (exposed and enclosed).
Student: Yolanda Xiang Zhao.

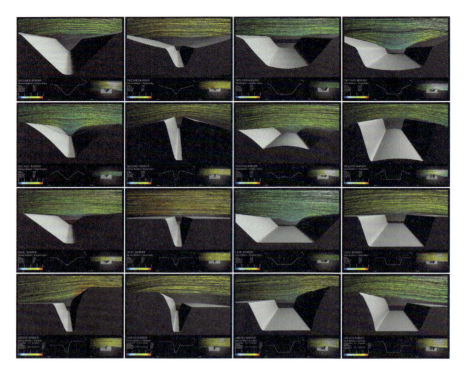

Figure 8.8 Landform and climate analysis.
Student: Matthew Walter.

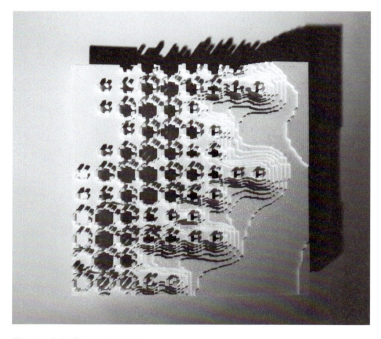

Figure 8.9 Site strategy.
Student: Elizabeth Camuti.

demonstrated specific physical relationships, e.g., patterns, varia-bilities, and irregularities that were previously researched and ani-mated during the first phase. In progressing forward, the catalog matrix provided students with a range of morphological variation and dimensional parameters, e.g., height, width, depth, elevation, slope/angle of repose, perimeter to area ratio that allowed them to exploit programmatic variations, infrastructural relationships, and diverse climatic and material qualities.

In the final projects, students continued to translate concepts of atmosphere/atmospherics by exploring, experimenting, and sim-ulating projective landscape scenarios. In applying the tools and techniques from the earlier phase, this research methodology afforded students an ability to conceptualize and design land-scapes that presented a stronger alliance between site analysis and a site's climatic futures (Figures 8.11–8.14).

Landscapes are largely registered through sensory responses that are beyond our visual domain alone. In this framework, landscapes

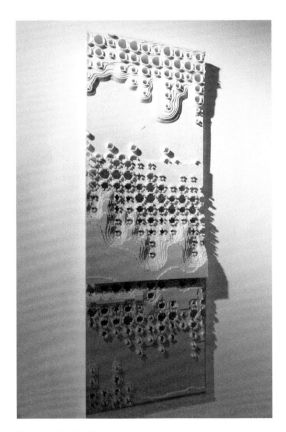

Figure 8.10 Site strategy.
Student: Elizabeth Camuti.

afford us with the physical memory and distinction of place and identity, where the human body and its corporeal qualities determine the identity and threshold of one landscape from another. The materiality induced by climate and weather play crucial roles in the ways that humans occupy these landscapes; and design considerations toward affect, comfort, and enjoyment are all a part of the media and conditions that we employ as landscape architects.

Figure 8.11 Climate and site analysis.
Student: Liza Court.
Prevailing winds and hydrological patterns for region.

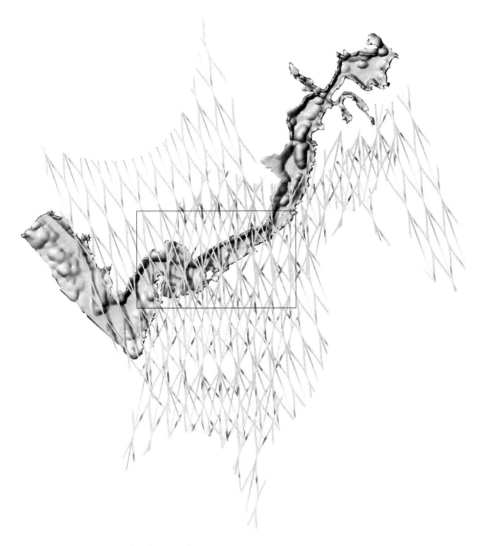

Figure 8.12 Atmospheric envelope.
Student: Liza Court.
Interpretation of a single three-dimensional site boundary (envelope) for a proposed design
intervention based on regional wind patterns and riparian surfaces.

Figure 8.13
**Atmospheric
envelopes.**
Student: Multiple.
Interpretations of
three-dimensional
site boundaries
(envelopes) for
proposed design
interventions.

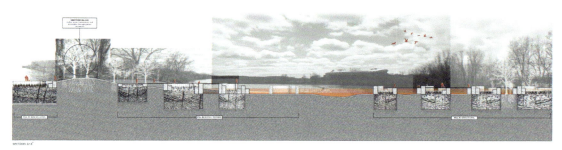

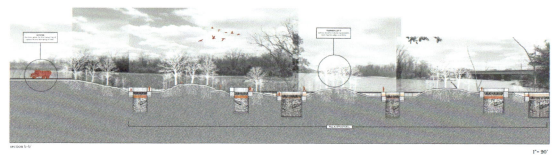

Figure 8.14 From Dredge to Detritus.

Student: Elizabeth Camuti.

"Through a process of on-site excavating, recycling and filling, the banks of the river are gradually transformed into an alternate, occupiable landfill, contrasting the present and historic use of this water body as Washington D.C.'s dumping ground. Using a series of discrete gabion structures crafted from excavated concrete and asphalt, the impervious barriers that currently keep the river in place give way to a dynamic, habitable edge over time. These modular, semi-porous collection systems not only provide unique protection against sporadic weather events and sea level rise, but also facilitate the atmospheric conversion of dredge material, litter, and sediment into durable and, at times, harvestable urban fill. This new landscape of litter, soil and sediment along the banks of the river elevates the status of materials typically considered *waste* and gives them a second life from which both humans and non-humans can derive value." –Elizabeth Camuti.

9

TACIT CONCEPTS

Ferdinand Ludwig and Sergio Sanna

Introduction

Usually, a distinction is made between the initial idea, the representation and the implementation of a project. The approach of "tacit concepts" blurs these boundaries and assumes that a concept is already given by the forces of the landscape and the skills, experiences and talents of the people involved. How this tacit or implicit concept can be made explicit – how it can become physical reality – is demonstrated by a series of ten-day workshops between 2012 and 2017. These workshops took place within the framework of LandWorks, a cultural nonprofit organization that organizes itinerant international operative workshops, welcoming each time around 100 participants – teachers, young professionals and students of landscape architecture and related disciplines from around the world, who work together intensively with local stakeholders.[1]

Approach

The starting point of any convincing landscape architectural concept is always a well-founded understanding of the place.[2] In the case of operative workshops, however, this cannot be a matter of an in-depth analysis of the landscape, its history and ecology – the ten days are far too short for that. Rather the direct experience of the place, its beauty, its peculiarities, but also its adversities, is the basis of a more direct approach, characterized by intuitive action. It is a basic intention, the first gesture to be made, which leads people to make contact with the hard consistency of thought. In fact, hands do not perform a specified disposition or instruction but they give shape to comprehension while collecting information about the spirit of the place with a sort of tactile flair.[3]

The necessity to become productive within a few days, not only by developing a concept and transferring it into a design, but also by implementing it, forces to focus on the essential: On one's own physical possibilities, on the materials and tools available, on the most pressing problems of the site and on possibilities to enter into a productive exchange with the local people, who are the custodians of history and of the relationship with the territory.

[1] https://www.landworks.site/philosophy
[2] Hensel, M., & Cordua, C. H. (2015). Relating perceptions of construction, experimental and local. Architectural Design 2015 Vol. 2 Issue 85 pp 8–15.
[3] Focillon H. In Praise of Hands (final essay) in "The Life of Forms in Art", George Kubler (translator). Zone Books, 1989, pp. 106–110.

DOI: 10.4324/9781003053255-11

In the following, the process and results of this approach will be presented on the basis of two exemplary workshops in order to elucidate the underlying methods.

Case Study Punta Rossa: The Wind as Gardener

The ruined navy fortress in Punta Rossa (Caprera/La Maddalena) was built in the XIX century in a strategic place in front of the Strait of Bonifacio between Corsica and Sardinia. Due to its position in the Mediterranean Sea, the promontory of Punta Rossa is exposed to extreme winds. Across history ships had to face the north-westerly mistral wind that strongly blows most of the year. This is reflected in the location and growth forms of the native shrubs and trees: They grow very slowly and thrive only in the lee of stones or buildings. All shoots that grow out of the lee die back. As a result, the shape of the woody plants reflects the shape of the objects that create the wind shade. They are – as formed by the hand of a gardener – precisely cut into shape. For the participants of the workshop, these forces of nature were also experienced at their own bodies: on some days, the wind was so strong that it was hardly possible to work outside. It was, therefore, obvious that wind and vegetation became the core players of the concept (Figure 9.1).

Starting from these physical experiences, the climatic and topo-graphical conditions were recorded in simple, sketchy site plans to form a base for further discussions. The concept was refined with the idea of changing the growth conditions by artificially creating wind breakers. Therefore, a particularly windy location was chosen where no woody plants had been able to thrive so far. Various options were discussed to create wind-breaking structures in a

Figure 9.1 Due to the extreme winds plants grow very slowly and thrive only in the lee of stones or buildings. Their shape reflects the shape of the objects that creates the wind shade.

quick and easily way with the materials available on site and with-out the use of complex tools or machines. Very quickly, it became clear that the only answer to this question is a technique that had been practiced on site for thousands of years: Dry stone walls. A tradition that is named by UNESCO as Intangible Heritage of Humanity. In Sardinia, the famous *nuraghe* as well as the walls of many other ancient houses are built with this technique.[4] The same way *tu'rat* are made in the dry regions of Mediterranean. These half-moon-shaped walls allow to condense the nocturnal humidity between the stones which then percolates into the soil and also protect vegetation from the wind (Figures 9.2–9.4).

In a next step, different forms of dry-walled windbreakers were developed using improvised working models. Cardboard scraps were used for the walled structures and with wool plucked from a sweater, the windshade or possible plant forms that might develop in the future were represented associatively. Parallel to these con-siderations, the dry wall technique was approached in a learning-by-doing process, with the aid of immediately available sources such as Youtube tutorials and the gratefully received advices from locals. In order to come to a decision as to which variant should be implemented, a jury consisting of the coordinators of LandWorks, other group leaders and locals was formed at short notice. Finally, a structure was chosen that represents half a pyramid on the floorplan of an arrowhead, intending that the geometry will be completed by the plant growth in the windshade and will form a complete pyramid in the future – half made of stones, half made of wind-shaped trees (Figures 9.5–9.7).

But even after this decision and with the start of the concrete structural implementation, the design process was far from being

4 Winchester, A. J. (2016). Dry stone walls: history and heritage. Amberley Publishing Limited.

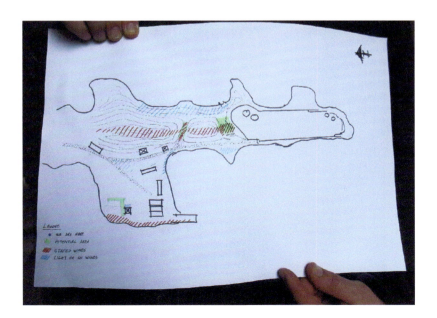

Figure 9.2 Pragmatic site plan to discuss possible locations for the intervention.

Figure 9.3 Conceptual models. The wool indicates the wind shade and thus possible future growth form.

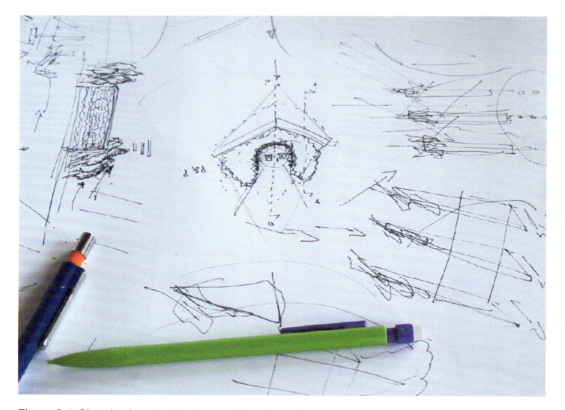

Figure 9.4 Sketch of a possible form of the dry wall structure.

Figure 9.5 Participants fighting with the wind on site – a bodily experience of the main driving forces of the concept.

Figure 9.6 First steps of implementation – as part of an ongoing design process.

completed. The design of the surface texture was developed on site: the wind determined the orientation of the structure as well as the angle of repose of the material decided the pyramid inclination. The shallower sides of the arrowhead exposed to the wind were made of smaller, loosely packed stones. The wind-protected

Figure 9.7 Wind breaker after its physical completion – the starting point of a long term developmental process of plant-wind-interaction.

5 Ludwig, F., & Schönle, D. (2018). Growth as a Concept. In Hortitecture – The power of architecture and plants (pp. 65–71). Jovis.
Ludwig, F., & Schönle, D. (2022). Growing Architecture – How to design and build with trees. Birkhäuser. https://doi.org/10.1515/9783035603392

inner sides were designed to be as even as possible, with lichen-covered stones being used exclusively on the side facing away from the sun and ungrown stones on the side facing the sun. This anticipates a possible future change of the stone surfaces and can be seen as a statement that expresses the ambivalent relationship of the approach to time and completion: The project will never be completed – in 15, 20 or 30 years the shape might come close to the designers' intention – or might not.[5] After all, the design process has not yet been completed and an important partner must not be overlooked: The wind is not just an executive agent who follows guidelines like an instructed gardener but has to be seen as an independent actor who helps shape the future of the project as a codesigner.

Case study Argentiera: We Don't Mine

The landscape around the small town of Argentiera on the west coast of Sardinia is shaped by centuries of mining. Abandoned mining towers, washeries and spoil heaps bear witness to how, until a few decades ago, materials were torn from the earth and then subdivided into "valuable" and "waste". The question of the workshop is of how this use of places and resources can be illustrated and

Figure 9.8 Careful explorations of the site.

reinterpreted against the background of the ecological crises of the 21st century: Instead of exploiting limited resources, how can we make use of what regenerates and how can we value what is usually discarded as garbage?

Against this background, the workshop began with a completely open-ended site survey. The search for suitable places and occasions led – at first somewhat surprisingly – to a field of giant reed near a spoil heap. Giant reed is generally regarded as a fragile and less durable material that can only be used for subordinate construction tasks like temporary trellises. Only the best rods can be used – a large proportion is scrap. At the same time, the reed field has a unique atmosphere. The dense structure of living and already dead sprouts forms an impermeable, introverted space, a retreat that does not allow any views to the nearby sea (Figure 9.8).

The workshop participants explored this place with childlike curiosity. At first without changing it significantly. Then, the first dead reed poles were removed. On the one hand, this created new spaces; on the other hand, it generated material for structural tests and experiments. Smaller reeds were harvested in order to explore spatial and constructive potentials in experimental models. The results were captured in sketches and photographs and gradually a clear concept emerged from the at first vague connection between the initial question and the possibilities of the site (Figures 9.9 and 9.10).

Figure 9.9 Experimental models, using material collected on site.

Figure 9.10 Sketches representing the spatial intervention – emerged out of discussion within the team.

As in mining materials were extracted from the reed field. However, only dead shoots were removed and only at places where a widening or opening of the space was intended. Apparently by chance, this process eventually was going to produce a path system due to the harvesting. Then, the extracted material was strictly sorted: Only the best shoots were used to form load-bearing bundles.[6] Unlike in mining, however, these are not exported but returned to the field where they are joined together to form a three-dimensional structure, a climbable tower that seamlessly blends into the remaining living structure, to such an extent that the structure is literally anchored to the living reeds whose roots act as foundations (Figures 9.11–9.13).

All the scrap material sorted out was not wasted but broken into small pieces and evenly distributed on the bottom of the reed field.

[6] Canyaviva Building with Cane in Fernández Nieto MA., García Carbonero M., de Lara Ruiz M., Pesqueira Calvo C. Plant Architecture, Ediciones Asimétricas, Madrid 2018, pp. 233–237.

Figure 9.11 Prototyping and physical testing – a bodily way of thinking and designing in action.

Figure 9.12 Constructing the intervention. The 1:1 implementation and the working model are closely related by using the same techniques and materials.

The result was a slippery surface where one has to walk carefully and every step causes a loud crack. When the project was presented at the end of the workshop, the visitors slowed down their steps, concentrated fully on the place and became more aware of its atmosphere. Ultimately, the material available at the site was simply restructured to open up a new function and to explore new spatial potentials. Due to the very thorough construction method, the structure, which was actually conceived as an ephemeral structure, was still in such good condition four years after completion that it could be climbed without any problems (Figures 9.14–9.17).

Conclusion

We understand these kind of workshops not as a course, where the teacher embodies the knowledge and generously shares it with his or her students. We rather see it more as a codesign process which includes the natural and the social environment too, where everyone is challenged and learns.[7]

The intense program and the ultimate purpose of the workshop – the realization – do not allow to devote too much time to representations like drawings. Nevertheless, drawing and model making are understood as basic and pragmatic tools of the project. On the one hand, they are used to get quickly to a synthesis to be shared and discussed, or they often are needed to explore specific matters in order to isolate a problem and solve the project in different

[7] Hensel M.U. Studio Mumbai. The Practice of Making. *Architectural Design*, March 2015, 85.2, pp. 8–15.

Figure 9.13 The installation blurs into the reed field were the material was sources from.

Figure 9.14 The debris was broken into small pieces and distributed on the ground. The slippery surface cracks when walked on and forces increased attention.

steps, avoiding the idea of a finished and defined design from the beginning. On the other hand, any kind of graphic material allows to report an intervention that probably might be temporary, and to verify the decisions taken during the implementation. In this case, drawings represent the *a posteriori* survey of a work never previously drawn. We could say that the reporters themselves produce an action even before they want to communicate it.[8]

Behind this approach, there also is the didactic goal of questioning and overcoming the supposed certainty that the drawing of an execution plan may suggest. The realization of a project is not simply the reproduction of a plan in another scale or material. Instead, in landscape architecture, we should always speak of the emergence of a project. Precisely, those impromptu operations are useful to test scenarios in order to build durable landscapes. They are not intended to be alternative practices but real experiences

[8] Valtorta R. editor. *Luogo e identità nella fotografia italiana contemporanea*. Piccola Biblioteca Einaudi, 2013.

Figure 9.15 The reed field after the implementation of the project. Notice the "entrance" and the bundles which look out of the reeds.

Figure 9.16 Even after four years the structure was still strong enough to carry at least three people.

Figure 9.17 Reed structure after four years, seen from the top.

that contribute to modify the common design praxis.[9] The condensation of conception, design and construction in the extremely short time of a workshop stands in strong contrast to the long-term nature that characterizes the projects resulting from it. This approach makes it possible to experience that landscape architecture never generates finished objects but is always to be thought of in ecological systems and, thus, in the context of time.[10]

[9] Zancan R. Domesticated Landscapes. Domus 964, December 2012, pp. 44–53.
[10] Noël van Dooren and Anders Busse Nielsen. The Representation of Time: Addressing a Theoretical Flaw in Landscape Architecture. *Landscape Research*, 2018, DOI: 10.1080/01426397.2018.1549655, pp. 2–5.

10

SEDIMENT IN PROCESS

Designing an Active Channel for Alameda Creek

Justine Holzman and Rob Holmes

[1] Elizabeth Meyer, "Site Citations: The Grounds of Modern Landscape Architecture," in *Site Matters: Design Concepts, Histories, and Strategies*, ed. Carol Burns and Andrea Kahn (New York: Routledge, 2005), 93–130; Christophe Girot, "Four Trace Concepts in Landscape Architecture," in *Recovering Landscape: Essays in Contemporary Landscape Architecture*, ed. James Corner (New York: Princeton Architectural Press, 1999), 58–67; George Descombes, "Shifting Sites: The Swiss Way, Geneva," in *Recovering Landscape*, 79–86.

[2] Teresa Galí-Izard, *The Same Landscapes: Ideas and Interpretations* (Barcelona: Gustavo Gili, 2005).

[3] Ian McHarg, *Design with Nature* (Garden City, NY: Published for the American Museum of Natural History [by] the Natural History Press, 1969); Wenche E. Dramstad, James D. Olson, and Richard T. T. Forman, *Landscape Ecology Principles in Landscape Architecture and Land-Use Planning* (Washington, DC: Island Press, 1996).

There are many different ways a landscape proposal might begin. By making and reacting to site readings, for instance, using procedures ably described by landscape theorists and designers like Elizabeth Meyer, Christoph Girot, and George Descombes.[1] Or by observing and deploying landscape processes: Teresa Galí-Izard's *The Same Landscapes* is one example of a catalog of such observations.[2] Both of these starting points could also be understood in more positivistic registers: Ian McHarg and his successors (or predecessors) as site readers, R.T.T. Forman and his as observers of processes.[3] Other landscape architects have, like many architects, begun their work by drawing on precedent. Catherine Dee recommends working from elemental forms, which are closely related to what Girot and colleagues at ETH would describe as topological precedents.[4] Still others begin more narrowly from typological study, such as the analysis of urban riverbanks in *River.Space. Design*.[5] Less directly, precedent is often drawn from broader cultural currents: Martha Schwartz, redeploying the themes and sensibilities of pop art, or Hargreaves Associates' early projects like Byxbee and Crissy Field, building on the earthen media and aesthetic lessons of American land art. More recently, creating and situating patterns, particularly baroque and gothic patterns produced through digital tools, have made a return to landscape practice, evidenced in surveys like Karen M'Closkey and Keith Van Der Sys's *Dynamic Patterns*, and presaged by the earlier and more analog patternings of Michel Desvigne and Christine Dalnoky's joint practice.[6] Material exploration and investigation also has a long history as a beginning point in landscape architecture and continues to be evidenced in contemporary work like the design processes documented so extensively in Alice Foxley and Günther Vogt's *Distance and Engagement*,[7] the 1:1 horticultural experimentation of Gilles Clément, or the early work of Michael Van Valkenburgh.

This proposal began differently.

DOI: 10.4324/9781003053255-12

Public Sediment

Our involvement with the work that would become Public Sediment began with a week-long event that we organized with colleagues Brett Milligan, Gena Wirth, Sean Burkholder, and Tim Maly in summer 2016, DredgeFest California. This fourth DredgeFest, hosted at the University of California, Berkeley and focused on California's Bay-Delta estuary, brought together a diverse collection of participants including local stakeholders and university experts, public agencies (such as the Bay Conservation and Development Commission, which regulates all Bay Area dredging), nonprofit organizations (such as the San Francisco Estuary Institute (SFEI), the premier Bay Area estuarine science institute, which will play a prominent role in our account of Public Sediment's design processes), private corporations, and five workshop teams of architects and landscape architects.[8] The intensive efforts of the workshop week and the months of research and study that preceded it were summarized in a book-length report issued at the end of 2016.[9] The report extracted a series of key principles from the work.

Several of these became central to the approach of the Public Sediment team. First, sediment needs to be valued as an important resource that supports both ecological and human resilience in the Bay Area. The Baylands—the marshy fringe that lies between land and water around most of the Bay—depend on the accretion of sediment to maintain elevation in the face of sea level rise, and the ambitious restoration targets already adopted by Bay governments will demand much more. Yet, the Bay today receives much less sediment than it once did. Sediment supply is declining as sediment demand is rising.

Second, the only way to address this challenge successfully is to look beyond the immediate bounds of the Bay's waters and consider the tributaries, rivers, and upland sediment sources that feed the Bay as a holistic system, or 'sedimentshed'. At the same time that the total volume of sediment received by the Bay has declined, an important shift in the geography of that supply has occurred. Historically, the majority of the Bay's sediment came from two major rivers, the Sacramento and the San Joaquin, via their delta. Today, the majority of the Bay's supply comes from the many smaller tributaries that feed directly into the Bay, such as the Napa River, Coyote Creek, Walnut Creek, and Alameda Creek (Figure 10.1).

Third, many of the obstacles to getting sediment where it is needed are social, institutional, or political. Sediment's role in sustaining ecological processes and benefiting human communities is not broadly understood; consequently, motivating people to care about or advocate for sediment is difficult. Meanwhile, policy, regulations, and environmental governance around the Bay area generally developed in an earlier period of sediment surplus, a time when sediment was a problem as opposed to a resource.

[4] Catherine Dee, *To Design Landscape: Art, Nature, and Utility and/or Form and Fabric in Landscape Architecture: A Visual Introduction* (New York: Routledge, 2012); Christophe Girot, ed. et al. *Topology: Topical Thoughts on the Contemporary Landscape*, Landscript Vol. 3 (Berlin: Jovis, 2013).

[5] Martin Prominski, Antje Stokman, Daniel Stimberg, Hinnerk Voermanek, Susanne Zeller, and Katarina Bajc, *River. Space.Design: Planning Strategies, Methods and Projects for Urban Rivers*, 2nd ed. (Basel and Boston: Birkhäuser, 2017).

[6] Karen M'Closkey and Keith Van Der Sys, *Dynamic Patterns: Visualizing Landscapes in a Digital Age* (London and New York: Routledge, 2017); Michel Desvigne and Christine Dalnoky, *Desvigne & Dalnoky: The Return of the Landscape* (New York: Whitney Library of Design, 1997).

[7] Alice Foxley and Günther Vogt, Distance and Engagement: Walking, Thinking, and Making Landscape (Zürich: Lars Müller, 2010).

[8] DredgeFest was a roving event series organized by the Dredge Research Collaborative, which both authors are members of. Between 2012 and 2016, the DRC hosted four events, one on each of the four major coasts of the continental United States: Atlantic, Gulf, Great Lakes, and Pacific.

[9] Brett Milligan, Rob Holmes, Gena Wirth, Tim Maly, Sean Burkholder, and Justine Holzman (Dredge Research Collaborative), "DredgeFest California: Key Findings and Recommendations" (2016), http://dredgeresearchcollaborative.org/works/dredgefest-california-white-paper/.

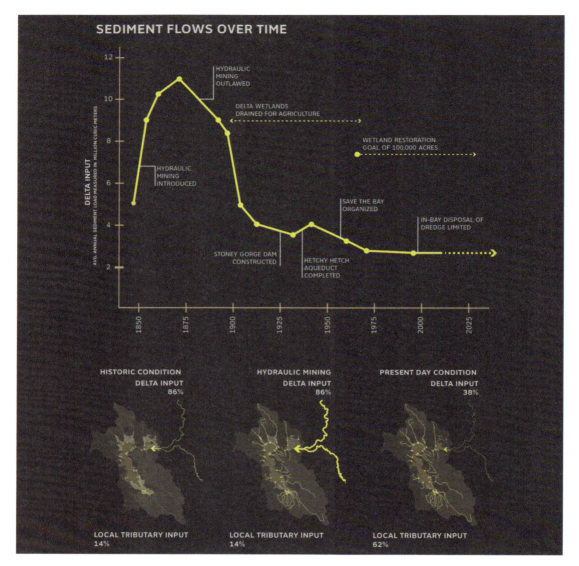

Figure 10.1 Bay sediment flows over time.

These observations became the starting point for Public Sediment. On the heels of its prominent and well-publicized competitive design process in the New York metropolitan area, the Resilient by Design organization decided to organize a second design competition for the Bay Area. This Bay Area Challenge launched in summer 2017 with a competitive RFP process. Public Sediment, our team composed of lead landscape architects SCAPE Landscape Architecture, the Dredge Research Collaborative, engineering firm

ARCADIS, faculty from the UC Davis Departments of Human Ecology and Design, local landscape architects TS Studio, the CCA-based Architectural Ecologies Lab, and artist Cy Keener, was one of ten teams selected to participate in the year-long design process.

When this team of collaborators coalesced that summer, we already knew what our work was about. Sediment would be the primary medium for our response to the challenges of human and ecological resilience in the Bay, we would look to the tributaries as a main source of sediment, and building a constituency for sediment among the public and key decision-makers would be at the core of our approach. Consequently, our design process was less about inventing a concept, and more about situating, testing, and refining an approach whose contours were already roughly defined. The mappings, sketches, and models that we have selected for this chapter reflect that.

Three Approaches

With a diverse and transdisciplinary team, the landscape as both site and design was conceptualized in a variety of ways. The work discussed here represents only a few of the deeply intertwined lines of questioning, thought, and design development that occurred during the competition. To name a few: the Architectural Ecologies Lab investigated modular form-making for engineering performance alongside habitat creation; Cy Keener and Justine Holzman (author) deployed and designed strategies for sensing and monitoring along the creek; Gena Morgis and SCAPE developed methods of calculation and visualization for spatially quantifying sediment need in context of sea level rise for the Baylands; and the UC Davis team developed a number of public outreach and participatory design events.[10]

Our focus here, however, is on three approaches to design process that the authors played lead roles in. These approaches used methods of *mapping*, *sketching*, and *modeling* to develop an *active channel* as a key component of the final "Unlock Alameda Creek" phase II proposal.

Mapping

During the first (fall) phase of the competition, each participating team was asked to identify at least three site-specific projects, with the knowledge that the competition organizers would pick one of those projects and ask the team to focus on that project for the second (spring) phase. Given that our team wanted one of our points of focus to be the potential of local tributaries to provide increased sediment supply to the Bay, identifying one tributary or a set of tributaries would be the best test case. Over several months, we produced a series of mappings (Figure 10.2) that drew

[10] Some of the most central work in the project is particularly difficult to fit into typical categories of methods for design development. Many members of team, particularly Gena Wirth (SCAPE), Brett Milligan (DRC), and Gena Morgis (SCAPE), spent a great deal of time listening to and asking questions of experts, stakeholders, and decision-makers from partners like ACFCD, SBSPR, and SFEI. These conversations were at least as instrumental in advancing the project as any design drawing, model export, or sensor mock-up was, yet they produced no immediate physical artifacts beyond meeting notes.

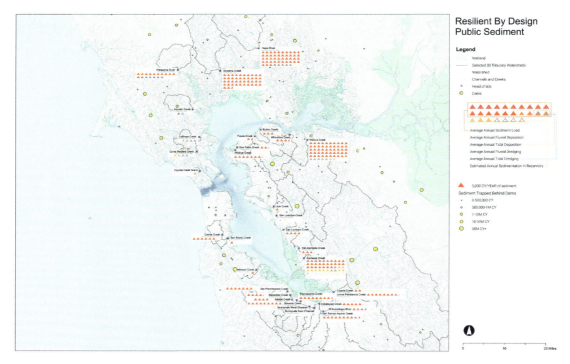

Figure 10.2 Bayscale tributary sediment holistic assessment.

on existing scientific studies of Bay sediment, particularly reports produced by SFEI. These existing studies were largely in text and spreadsheet formats, so the main purpose of the mappings was to spatialize that information and synthesize it with other relevant data so that it would be readily accessible for decision-making. With them, we sought to answer questions such as: How much sediment is stuck in the channels of local tributaries?; How much sediment is making it to the Bay from each tributary?; and "How much sediment is trapped upstream behind dams?.

The answers to these questions quickly pointed us toward a small subset of tributaries that variably appeared to have a great deal of untapped potential to supply sediment, to provide the opportunity to demonstrate the full range of geographic approaches to sediment supply we were considering (bayland, channel, and upland), and/or to pair sediment needs with social vulnerability. One tributary, Alameda Creek, emerged as the best combination of all these concerns. We proposed a project for it as one of our three site-specific projects, and were able to move into the second phase of work focused on how Alameda Creek could be redesigned to better deliver sediment to the Bay.[11]

In that second phase, mappings again played an important role. Maps focused on Alameda Creek (Figures 10.3–10.6) were created to understand channel morphology and the behavior of the dynamic processes operating in the channel, including sedimentary, fluvial,

[11] In this second phase of work, the team formed a series of sub-teams that focused on discrete components of larger proposal, such as mobilizing sediment trapped behind upland dams, connecting the creek to the adjacent diked baylands, and the strategic placement of sediment near the mouth of the creek. The authors were primarily involved in the channel design team, which worked on the stretch of Alameda Creek from head of tide to Niles Canyon, and our account here focuses on that work.

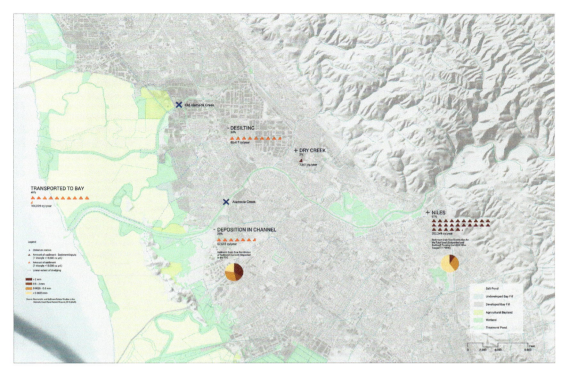

Figure 10.3 Channel sediment study.

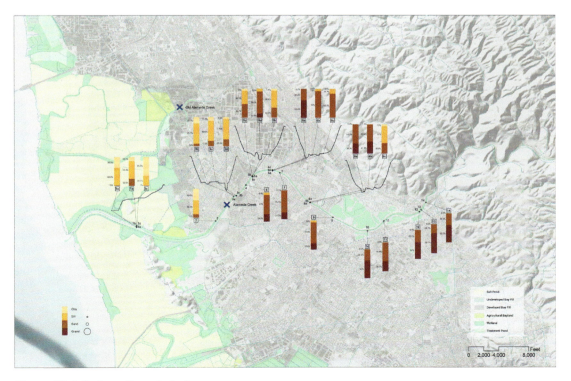

Figure 10.4 Bulk sediment study.

Figure 10.5 Channel dredging study.

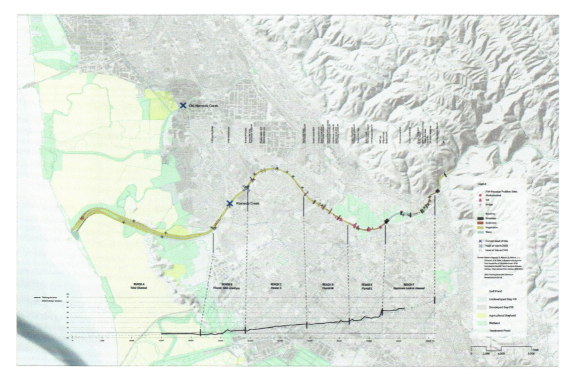

Figure 10.6 Channel profile, morphology, and barriers study.

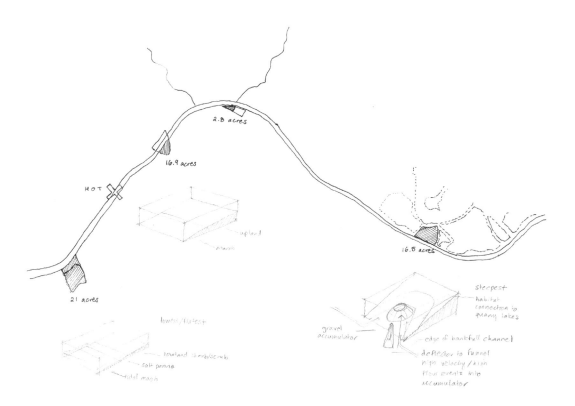

Figure 10.7 Initial ecological gradient and adjacent storage sketch.

tidal, geomorphological, and vegetative processes. As we focused in on the Creek, which had been channelized for flood control purposes in the 1970s, we were entering an ongoing conversation between scientists, engineers, and environmental planners about how to design the creek's channel and the relationships it has with adjacent landscapes.[12] We, as a project team, needed to understand their thinking. Making these drawings both helped those directly involved in making them to do that and helped us to share our findings with the full project team. As with the regional mappings, this often involved synthesizing information from existing sources, such as a 2012 technical report entitled "Geomorphic and Sediment-Related Studies in the Alameda Creek Flood Control Channel", and spatializing it. It also involved original measurement, annotation, and description: a channel morphology study (Figure 10.6), for instance, was based primarily on observations made from satellite photography in Google Earth, overlaid with some information drawn from scientific and technical reports.

Sketches

Where mappings were digitally assembled in Adobe Illustrator from GIS data, satellite aerial imagery, and the content of technical reports, many other drawings in the second phase were sketches

[12] The conversation we entered in the Bay generally and Alameda Creek specifically is a particularly sophisticated conversation. There is no other estuary in the United States whose sediments have been studied so carefully. The lack of such study in other places presents a major barrier to applying Public Sediment-like work in other contexts.

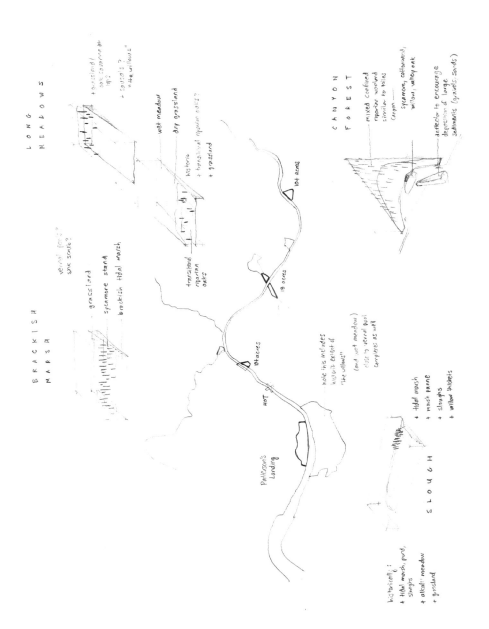

Figure 10.8 Ecological gradient and adjacent storage sketch.

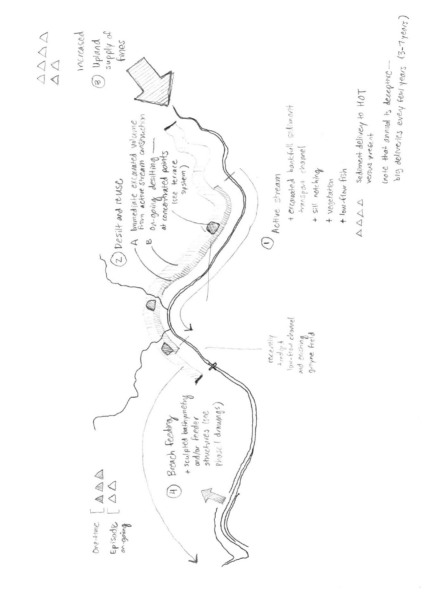

Figure 10.9 Sediment management and transport design concept for full channel.

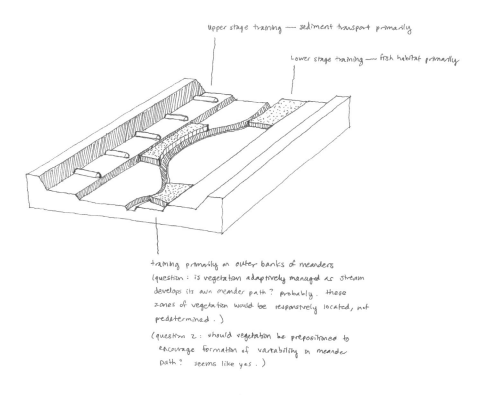

Figure 10.10 Initial low-flow and bankfull channel training design.

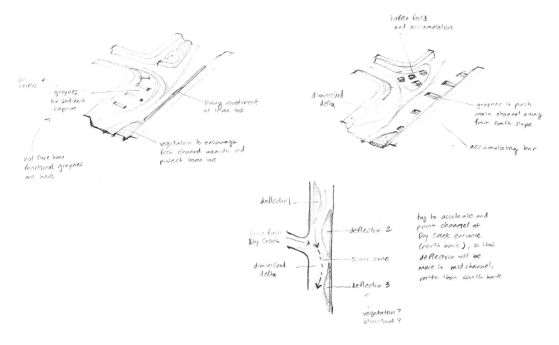

Figure 10.11 Initial concepts for Dry Creek confluence.

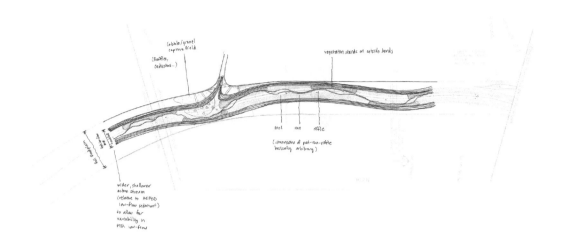

Figure 10.12 Design sketch for Dry Creek confluence channel design sketch.

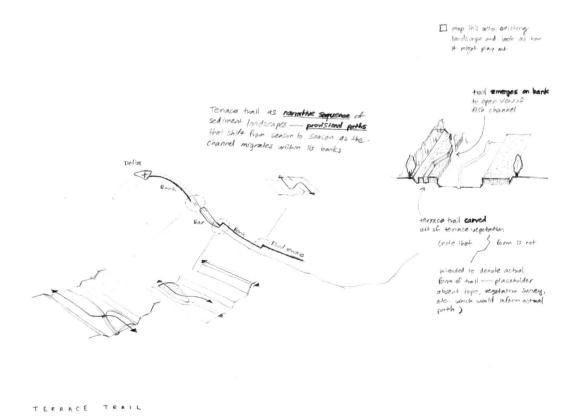

Figure 10.13 Initial concept sketches for pedestrian access in the channel.

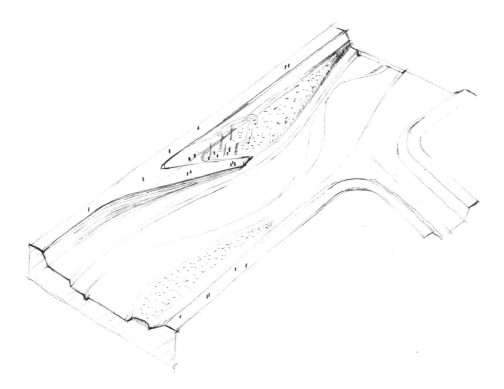

Figure 10.14 Design sketch for Dry Creek confluence with pedestrian access.

done in pen or pencil, typically on plain white paper (Figures 10.7–10.14). These sketches were produced for a variety of purposes, and with a variety of audiences—sometimes the sketcher, sometimes the channel design team, sometimes the whole project team.

Like the channel mappings, many of these, particularly those done earlier in the second phase, were efforts to synthesize and understand batches of scientific and engineering reports, covering topics like the use of channel vegetation to affect creek morphology, channel behavior at various stages of flow, and the placement of baffles, groynes, or other structures in the channel to modify sediment deposition rates. Relative to the channel mappings, though, these sketches were typically more abstract, attempting to spatialize general conditions, rather than describing conditions specifically for an entire reach or the full length of the channel.

As the work progressed, other sketches became more propositional. Some were efforts to collate ideas about what approaches to activating the channel were most promising in relationship to the goal of moving sediment more effectively downstream to the bay. Many were attempts to explore formal options for those promising approaches, such as potential baffle configurations and placements, or the patterning of vegetation blocks. Still others were primarily devices for internal team communication.

Toward the end of the competition, the sketches became more specific to particular locations in the channel, such the confluence with Dry Creek, a key site for both sediment transport and recreational use that became increasingly prominent in our thinking as the design progressed. (The bird's-eye section-perspective that is featured on the cover of the team's final report and at the top of the project website shows that confluence.) Some such sketches were still drawn freehand, while others were drawn on paper overlaid on maps or even directly on prints of Rhino model exports. As the SCAPE team developed digital design models and drawings, these sketches became raw material for generating some of those representations, and devices for communicating revisions to others.

In all these cases, though, sketches served to give spatial specificity to general intentions, such as training the channel course by placing groynes. This didn't always mean that they proposed precise forms—some of them are even annotated to explicitly note that this is not what they were doing—but they did always move in the direction of increasing spatial specificity, which is to say that they were form-giving even when they were not fully realized forms.

Models

To clarify our assumptions about channel morphology, members of the design team convened in Ithaca, New York, for a channel modeling workshop using a physical geomorphology table hosted by Brian Davis at Cornell University.[13] Such geomorphology tables function by continuously circulating a variable flow of water across sand-like plastic media to model hydrologic and sedimentary behaviors. Scientists (hydrologists and geomorphologists) and engineers have long used methods of both physical and digital computational modeling to study rivers. Physical modeling has been particularly important to knowing and designing within fluvial and coastal contexts because of the ability to seemingly reproduce complex and nonlinear phenomena at vastly different scales.[14]

The visual impact and ability for physical models to communicate these phenomena is quite important to the work of the modeler, in both interpreting the model and communicating its results or effects. Some modelers in this realm have recognized how the *scalelessness* of physical hydraulic models provide insights into autogenic processes.[15] While we had no ability to calibrate or scale our model to mimic real-world conditions, we recognize the value in working iteratively and intuitively with dynamic materials to provide insight into possible effects over time of specific design strategies through observable patterns and relationships of morphological change.

The format of the workshop was designed around a series of three scales and related questions that prompted a series of *approximations*—different table set-ups that calibrated the table to appear similar to the conditions of interest with interventions that reflect our design strategies. The three scales supported different

[13] Davis and his colleague Sean Burkholder had recently purchased an EM4 Little River geomorphology for a grant project, Healthy Port Futures. These relatively small EM River geomorphology tables have been used by Alexander Robinson, Bradley Cantrell, and Justine Holzman to advance landscape architecture research and design methods. Discussed in Alexander Robinson, *The Spoils of Dust: Reinventing the Lake that Made Los Angeles* (Novato, CA: Applied Research + Design Publishing, 2018) and Justine Holzman, "Hydraulic Modeling as Craft," ACSA Conference Proceedings, Shaping New Knowledges 2016.

[14] T. J. Coulthard and M. J. Van De Wiel, "Modelling River History and Evolution," *Philosophical Transactions Royal Society A*, 370 (2012): 2123–2142.

[15] Chris Paola, Kyle Straub, David Mohrig, and Liam Reinhardt, "The 'Unreasonable Effectiveness' of Stratigraphic and Geomorphic Experiments," *Earth Science Reviews* 97 (2009): 1–43.

aspects of the channel design. At the smallest scale, using the entire bed, we worked to understand modular devices for erosion control and planting individually and in aggregate. The mid-scale (Figures 10.15–10.19), reflecting an abstracted channel length, was where the majority of our modeling time was spent. Once a set-up was established that seemed to behave similar to what we know and have observed within the real channel, the set-up was modified using different spatial configurations of sediments as well as a range of materials from hard (engineered structures) to soft (vegetation strategies) to approximate design approaches that might achieve our broader goals for the Alameda Creek corridor. The largest scale (which we had the least confidence in because of its specificity to scale) used a simplified physical topo-bathy model of the Dry Creek and Alameda Creek confluence produced by SCAPE that was set within the geomorphology table.

Each approximation was documented and visually interpreted through meshes, photos, video, and point clouds to observe dynamics and characteristics (sediment transport and water currents) of a continuous low-flow channel meant to represent the flood controlled fluvial reach of Alameda Creek. The experience of working with the table and our extracted representations informed our final design proposal for the active channel. Importantly, the dynamic physical models provided the opportunity to capture video and stills that were later deployed at various public events

Figure 10.15 Public sediment team members working on the geomorphology table.

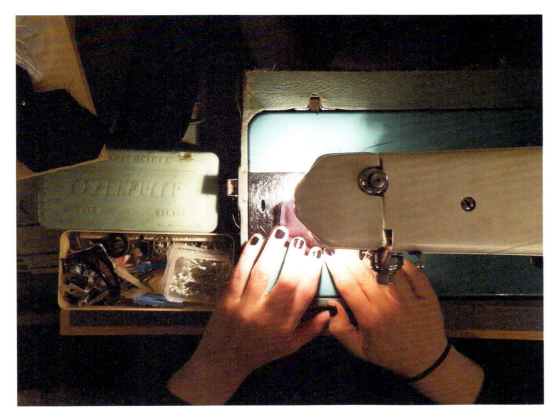

Figure 10.16 Sewing soft structures.

Figure 10.17 Setting up the geomorphology table bed.

Figure 10.18 Soft structures and setting up analogous behaviors.

Figure 10.19 Setting up analogues and photogrammetric scans of the geomorphology table bed.

and presentations to visually communicate the dynamic qualities of the creek, such as sediment transport, flood stages, meander, and bank erosion.

Interdisciplinarity, Institutions, and Form

What was unique about this work? What might its implications for landscape design processes more generally be?

One obvious starting point is that the interdisciplinarity of the project, the team, and the situation we were working with made distinct demands on the design process. Because scientists, engineers, and environmental planners have been studying, evaluating, and even making proposals for the Baylands generally and Alameda Creek specifically for decades now, our initial questions as we were conceptualizing the project often had to do with what those other fields (and, more specifically, other people) knew about the creek, the bay, and the prospects for sediment design, generally. Those questions quickly blurred into questions about how that knowledge might be deployed: given that we know that hundreds of thousands of cubic yards of sediment are trapped behind local dams, how might that sediment be mobilized? Given the constraints imposed on creek geomorphology by the banks of the flood control channel, how might the formation and continued presence of a low-flow channel that will facilitate fish passage be encouraged? Mappings and sketches were crucial to documenting, engaging, and answering such questions.

Moreover, the format and scope of the project was quite different from what is typically encountered in the average landscape design project in an average professional office. We were working to convince the public and decision-makers that Unlock Alameda Creek is worth investing in. We were trying to read and respond to the extensive scientific study of Bay sediment supply, cross-referenced with science on climate change, Bay communities, and the Baylands themselves. We were not trying complete a conceptual design that would then go through a design documentation and construction process. In some ways, this makes the value or success of drawings and models produced for the project more difficult to assess. We cannot ask whether the project has produced a rich and varied trail experience, immediately examine design details, or even evaluate its ecological contribution to the Baylands on anything less than a multi-decade timescale. Instead, Public Sediment must be evaluated in terms of institutional impact, the ways in which it is able to help many other people push the evolution of environmental policy, regulation, and planning in a direction that facilitates coping with the looming consequences of sea level rise, and whether it, over these decades, succeeds in contributing to the larger goal of building sediment publics. Early returns in the year after the competition finished have been promising, as components of the proposal have received funding from the National Fish and Wildlife Foundation, the National Oceanic and Atmospheric Administration, and in the 2019 California state budget, indicating continued support from local partners and momentum with funding agencies, but it is too soon to judge overall impact.

This is not to say that we were divorced from landscape architecture's traditional concern for form. The sketches and models make this particularly clear. The spatial specificity that they gave to more general intentions—both our intentions as a project team and the intentions of others, transmitted through conversations, engineering

Figure 10.20 Rendering of active channel design.

[16] Anita Berrizbeitia with Michel Desvigne, "On the Limits of Process: The Case for Precision in Landscape," filmed April 14, 2016 at Harvard Graduate School of Design, Cambridge, MA, video, 1:42:02, https://www.gsd.harvard.edu/event/anita-berrizbeitia-with-michel-desvigne-on-the-limits-of-process-the-case-for-precision-in-landscape/.
[17] This description of form as dynamic matter with consequential trajectories builds on Catherine Dee's description of "landscape forms as trajectories … acknowledg[ing] that landscape forms are dynamic to varying degrees" in her article "Form, Utility, and the Aesthetics of Thrift in Design Education," *Landscape Journal* 19, no. 1 (2010): 21–35.
[18] Rob Holmes, "Design with Change," in *Design with Nature Now*, ed. Frederick Steiner, Richard Weller, Karen M'Closkey, and Billy Fleming (Lincoln Institute of Land Policy, Cambridge, MA: Lincoln Institute of Land Policy, 2019).

documentation, and technical reports—was concretized in form. (This happened in the three approaches discussed in this essay, but also throughout other approaches within the project. SCAPE's GIS studies of bayland sediment needs, for instance, also projected from scientific generalities to spatially explicit maps, though at a much larger scale than the channel design.) This form given to the creek through drawings and models acted as a bridge between different concerns within the project: the migration needs of fish, the movement of flood water, access for people, and the transport of sediment (Figure 10.20). It was negotiated form. Crucially—and this is a second way, after institutional impact, that our proposal for Alameda Creek differs significantly from standard landscape design practices—this form is not a static form that can be opposed to dynamic landscape processes, or even thought of merely as a precise means for interacting with dynamic processes.[16] The proposed *active channel* is form understood as dynamic matter with consequential trajectories, both impacted by other forces (its uplands, tidal exchange with the Bay, rainfall linked to local and global climate) and affecting the trajectories of other landscapes around it (supplying sediment to subsided salt ponds, providing passage from bay to canyon and back for migrating salmonids, becoming accessible to adjacent neighborhoods).[17] Designing form in this fashion is crucial in the context of contemporary environmental challenges, including sea level rise and climate change.[18]

Working in this sort of expanded field of landscape agency will require more expansive, inclusive, and interdisciplinary design processes. The three approaches unpacked here begin to show how traditional conceptual design approaches like mapping, sketching, and modeling can be modified, redeployed, and recontextualized for such an expanded context. But they are only one small start; much work remains to be done.

Acknowledgments

Public Sediment for Alameda Creek is a collective work by the Public Sediment team and many partners. The proposal was created for the Resilient by Design Bay Area Challenge, a collaborative research and community-based design project to strengthen the region's resilience to sea level rise and climate change.

The Public Sediment team was led by SCAPE Landscape Architecture with the Dredge Research Collaborative, Arcadis, the UC Davis Departments of Human Ecology and Design, the Architectural Ecologies Lab, TS Studio, and Cy Keener. The team worked closely with many partners including the Alameda County Flood Control and Water Conservation District, the South Bay Salt Pond Restoration Project, East Bay Regional Park District, State Coastal Conservancy, the Alameda Creek Alliance, and the San Francisco Estuary Institute, as well as residents and students living and going to school in the Alameda Creek watershed.

Figures 10.1 and 10.20 were drawn by SCAPE Landscape Architecture. Photographs were taken by the Public Sediment team.

The mappings included here were drawn by Rob Holmes (DRC), Jingting Li (DRC), Yuanyuan Gao (Auburn University), and Yuzhou Jin (Auburn University).

The sketches were drawn by Rob Holmes (DRC).

Modeling happened during a workshop hosted by Brian Davis at Cornell University April 13–15, 2018. The workshop participants were Gena Wirth (SCAPE), Gena Morgis (SCAPE), Nick Shannon (SCAPE), Sophie Riedel (SCAPE), Justine Holzman (DRC), Rob Holmes (DRC), Brett Milligan (DRC), Sean Burkholder (DRC), Jingting Li (DRC), Brian Davis (Cornell/DRC), Zeynep Goksel (Cornell), Danielle Serigano (Cornell), Justin Leanza (Cornell), and Chris Devick (Arcadis).

Bibliography

Berrizbeitia, Anita with Michel Desvigne. "On the Limits of Process: The Case for Precision in Landscape." Filmed April 14, 2016 at Harvard Graduate School of Design, Cambridge, MA. Video, 1:42:02. https://www.gsd.harvard.edu/event/anita-berrizbeitia-with-michel-desvigne-on-the-limits-of-process-the-case-for-precision-in-landscape/.

Coulthard, T. J., and M. J. Van De Wiel. "Modelling River History and Evolution." *Philosophical Transactions Royal Society A*, 370 (2012): 2123–2142.

Dee, Catherine. "Form, Utility, and the Aesthetics of Thrift in Design Education." *Landscape Journal* 29, no. 1 (2010): 21–35.

Dee, Catherine. *Form and Fabric in Landscape Architecture: A Visual Introduction*. London: Taylor & Francis, 2004.

Dee, Catherine. *To Design Landscape: Art, Nature, and Utility*. New York: Routledge, 2012.

Descombes, Georges. "Shifting Sites: The Swiss Way, Geneva." In *Recovering Landscape: Essays in Contemporary Landscape Architecture*, 78–85. Edited by James Corner. New York: Princeton Architectural Press, 1999.

Desvigne, Michel, and Christine Dalnoky. *Desvigne & Dalnoky: The Return of the Landscape*. New York: Whitney Library of Design, 1997.

Dramstad, Wenche E., James D. Olson, and Richard T. T. Forman. *Landscape Ecology Principles in Landscape Architecture and Land-Use Planning*. Cambridge, MA: Harvard University Graduate School of Design, 1996.

Foxley, Alice and Günther Vogt. Distance and Engagement: Walking, Thinking, and Making Landscape. Zürich: Lars Müller, 2010.

Galí-Izard, Teresa. *The Same Landscapes: Ideas and Interpretations*. Barcelona: Gustavo Gili, 2005

Girot, Christophe, ed., et al. "Four Trace Concepts in Landscape Architecture." In *Recovering Landscape: Essays in Contemporary Landscape Architecture*, 58–67. Edited by James Corner. New York: Princeton Architectural Press, 1999.

Girot, Christophe. *Topology: Topical Thoughts on the Contemporary Landscape*. Landscript Vol. 3. Berlin: Jovis, 2013.

Holmes, Rob. "Design with Change." In Design with Nature Now, 258-265. Edited by Frederick Steiner, Richard Weller, Karen M'Closkey, and Billy Fleming. Cambridge, MA: Lincoln Institute of Land Policy, 2019.

Holzman, Justine. "Hydraulic Modeling as Craft." ACSA Conference Proceedings, Shaping New Knowledges 2016.

McHarg, Ian L. *Design with Nature*. Garden City, NY: Published for the American Museum of Natural History [by] the Natural History Press, 1969.

M'Closkey, Karen, and Keith Van Der Sys. *Dynamic Patterns: Visualizing Landscapes in a Digital Age*. London and New York: Routledge, 2017.

Meyer, Elizabeth. "Site Citations: The Grounds of Modern Landscape Architecture." In *Site Matters: Design Concepts, Histories, and Strategies*, 93–130. Edited by Carol J. Burns and Andrea Kahn. New York: Routledge, 2005.

Milligan, B., Holmes, R., Wirth, G., Maly, T., Burkholder, S., and Holzman, J. Dredge Research Collaborative. *DredgeFest California: Key Findings and Recommendations*, 2016. http://dredgeresearchcollaborative. org/works/dredgefest-californiawhite-paper/.

Paola, Chris, Kyle Straub, David Mohrig, and Liam Reinhardt. "The 'Unreasonable Effectiveness' of Stratigraphic and Geomorphic Experiments." *Earth Science Reviews* 97 (2009): 1–43.

Prominski, Martin, Antje Stokman, Daniel Stimberg, Hinnerk Voermanek, Susanne Zeller, and Katarina Bajc. *River.Space.Design: Planning Strategies, Methods and Projects for Urban Rivers*, 2nd ed. Basel and Boston: Birkhäuser, 2017.

Public Sediment Team. Public Sediment Volume I: Sediment is the Building Block of Resilience in San Francisco Bay. Research Report for the Resilient by Design Bay Area Challenge.

Public Sediment Team. Public Sediment Volume II: Public Sediment for Alameda Creek. Research Report for the Resilient by Design Bay Area Challenge.

Robinson, Alexander. *The Spoils of Dust: Reinventing the Lake that Made Los Angeles*. Novato, CA: Applied Research + Design Publishing, 2018.

11

GROUNDING THE SITE

Uncovering Concepts in the Landscape Architecture Design Process

Mary Pat McGuire

The fundamental activity of representing the world and the place of humans within it, the inventive relationships that underlie creative making, and the inventive opportunities that derive from making the best of what is found, are remarkably entangled. The common ground here is just that—the ground out of which all these relationships emerge.

—Robin Dripps[1]

Whether a landscape bears significance depends on what is ingrained in the terrain.

—Christophe Girot[2]

Landscape architects create landscapes both as concepts and constructions; that is, we imagine them and we build them. Understanding the relationship between concepts and constructions is essential, since landscapes in their constructed form—their physical and experiential manifestations—are both rooted in, and generative of, cultural, artistic, and productive ideas about humanity's relationship with land. The fundamental relationship between society and land and its resulting artifacts—"nature […] reshaped by human culture throughout history"—has been foundational to the work of the field and has evolved over time in response to changing social, cultural, and ecological agendas, desires, and contexts.[3] In recent decades, rapid urbanization, planetary disturbance, loss of a sense of place (and site) in everyday life, diminished ecological diversity, and social inequality have constituted intense areas of focus by landscape architecture.[4]

These alarming patterns of development, disturbance, and diminishment of land and society have restored attention on the practice of *grounding* in two senses: first, through reexamining and reengaging the material, earthly ground of landscape as physical home for the acts of settling and dwelling upon and within its surface; and second, in the epistemological sense, which concerns how a designer

[1] Robin Dripps. "Groundwork," in *Site Matters: Design Concepts, Histories, and Strategies*. Carol J. Burns and Andrea Kahn, Eds. (New York: Routledge, 2005), 77.

[2] Christophe Girot. *The Course of Landscape Architecture*. (New York: Thames & Hudson, 2016), 305.

[3] Ibid.

[4] See Pierre Belanger. "A Landscape Manifesto," in Landscape as Infrastructure. (Abingdon: Routledge, 2017); Christophe Girot and Dora Imhof. *Thinking the Contemporary Landscape*. (New York: Princeton Architectural Press, 2017); Susan Herrington. *Landscape Theory in Design*. (Abingdon: Routledge, 2017); and Charles Waldheim, Ed. *The Landscape Urbanism Reader*. (New York: Princeton Architectural Press, 2006).

[5] Isabelle Doucet. "Planning in Search of Ground: Committed Muddling through or a Critical View from Above?" in The Territorial Future of the City (Urban and Landscape Perspectives), vol. 3. Giovanni Maciocco, Ed. (Berlin: Springer Science+Business Media, 2008).

DOI: 10.4324/9781003053255-13

comes to know—to build knowledge—of a place/site/ground in order to act upon and restore it.[5] In the book *Groundswell*, curator Peter Reed describes landscape architecture design as combining "designer's aesthetic and theoretical ideas about landscape—an art of horizontal surfaces and systems, impermanence and change—but also the way a design[er] responds to the site, the most fundamental phenomenon underlying constructed landscapes."[6]

In both the conceiving and constructing of landscape, the physical ground and the creative design approach toward that ground are interlocked. In landscape architecture education, this dual grounding process can inform and address a vast array of contemporary concerns for the field—to design discreet project sites as well as to define new areas for contemporary research and creative work.

Of course, the ground has always been fundamental for our field. Landscapes are situated, defined, cultivated, and lived through the ground. As a core physical medium and canvas, the ground is a thick surface through which designers create site phenomena, programs, and experiences through materials and their organization.[7] In the beginning stages of design, we explore, analyze, interpret the existing physical and cultural aspects of the ground, and through the production of drawings, models, and other representations of the ground, we can communicate an understanding of the land and landscape as the foundation for design. As written by Carlo Lanfranco,

> [i]n the end, a defined site is not something given, but is instead something invented [...] site analysis creates not only the definition for the land within which a design is integrated, it creates the method of investigation that will influence the rest of the design process.[8]

Thinking and drawing are intertwined in design which creates an expression of place and of culture.

Over the course of one's landscape architectural education, students are exposed and trained to practice the full process of design from concept to construction. Early in the site design process, students often pose questions such as how does a designer create landscape concepts that are connected to the site? What are the tools and processes that achieve this? How do we know we are working through this process in a creative, productive way? While discovering and developing a concept may occasionally be a matter of luck or grace, most often design concepts emerge through a dedicated, diligent process. Exploring and studying the ground itself is a direct and productive way of both knowing and designing sites, with specific attitudes and techniques that aid in this process. The ground is a repository of history with ideas for each designer to uncover and with which to design. Insights are made simultaneous with drawings, models, and writing, the artifacts of which are physical, visible, sensorial, and/or textual. From the fragments of a sketch to iterative modeling, these artifacts can be shared with and experienced by others.

[6] See Peter Reed. *Groundswell: Constructing the Contemporary Landscape*. New York: Museum of Modern Art: 2005), 15. The Groundswell exhibition at MOMA (February 25–May 16, 2005) profiled exemplary works of contemporary public space design remade primarily from industrial, abandoned, and/or degraded urban sites.

[7] McGuire, Mary Pat. "Is Landscape Surface?," *Journal of Landscape Architecture*, Volume: 15, Issue: 1, 2020, 32–45.

[8] Carlo Lanfranco. *Site Divine: An Alternative Method of Site Analysis*. (New York: Montag Press, 2009), 17.

[9] Christophe Girot. "Four Trace Concepts in Landscape Architecture," in *Recovering Landscape: Essays in Contemporary Landscape Architecture*. James Corner, Ed. (New York: Princeton Architectural Press, 1999).

To explore this thread, I first revisit the concept of *grounding* put forth by Christophe Girot.[9] I then propose three themes for ground that I consider useful for students of landscape architecture today. The images that accompany the essay were created by my landscape architecture students who have engaged the grounding process; they represent a range of drawings and models of the ground that were generated in their beginning stages of site design.[10]

Grounding in the Design Process

In 1999, Christophe Girot's "Four Trace Concepts in Landscape Architecture" was published in the seminal collection *Recovering Landscape*, edited by James Corner.[11] Girot outlines four sequential traces (stages or phases) in the landscape architecture design process— *landing, grounding, finding*, and *founding*. The first trace is *Landing,* whereby a designer first encounters a site without pretense or judgment and takes in preliminary experiences and insights from the place. In *Landing*, a designer's initial sketches, photographs, or other first-person observations serve as tools to record site phenomena and patterns. Their observations may concentrate on a range of site subjects and phenomena, from the unusual and striking to the ordinary and every day. Their impressions may be fleeting (of little long-term consequence) or lasting (impactful to the longer-term design process).

Following the initial trace of *Landing*, the designer begins the *Grounding* process. *Grounding* is a process of discovering more about the place through a series of intentional studies that engage with both primary and secondary sources. As written by Girot,

> Grounding has to do with orientation and rootedness, both in the literal and figurative sense of the word […] Grounding is a process implying successive layers, both visible and invisible … those forces and events that undergird the evolution of a place.[12]

Through g*rounding*, the designer moves back and forth between their observations, perhaps entailing repeated site visits, and what they can learn about the site from other sources. Existing documents are explored, such as maps, surveys, and photographs, that literally and metaphorically peek through successive layers of ground to understand the historical, ecological, and cultural depth of a site. *Grounding* is an important and iterative exploration which allows for the third trace *finding* in which the designer identifies the core essential aspect(s) of the site for design. Finally, the fourth trace, *founding*, brings the first three traces together to initiate a construction or other design action for the site.

I consider the *grounding* process the most productive, revealing, and generative stage of Girot's process framework. *Grounding* extends the initial *landing* into a process of discovery that is the basis for and even overlaps with *finding.* In short, *finding* comes out of the *grounding*. In *grounding*, multiple kinds of information and insights converge, interact, and compete, through which the designer uses their interpretive skills, collecting information and

[10] The images and models were created by the author's undergraduate and graduate landscape architecture students at the University of Illinois - Urbana Champaign between 2015 and 2019.
[11] Girot, 1999.
[12] Ibid., 63.

[13] Nel Janssens. "Critical Design — The Implementation of "Designerly" Thinking to Explore the Futurity of Our Physical Environment," in *The Territorial Future of the City*. Giovanni Maciocco, Ed. (Berlin: Springer, 2010), 122.

[14] For a description of abduction or the "reflexive approach," see *Landscape Architecture Research: Inquiry, Strategy, Design*. M. Elen Deming and Simon Swaffield, Eds. (Hoboken: John Wiley & Sons, Inc., 2011), 7–9.

[15] James Corner. "Ecology and Landscape as Agents of Creativity," in *Ecological Design and Planning*. George F. Thompson and Frederick R. Steiner, Eds. (New York: John Wiley & Sons, 1997), 102.

[16] See Carol J. Burns and Andrea Kahn, Eds. *Site Matters: Design Concepts, Histories, and Strategies*. (New York: Routledge, 2005). In particular, see chapters: "Groundwork" by Robin Dripps, "Site Citations: The Grounds of Modern Landscape" by Elizabeth Meyer, "Shifting Sites" by Kristina Hill, and "Defining Urban Sites" by Andrea Kahn.

using designerly techniques to sort through site information. As described by Nel Janssens, designerly or 'critical' design gives "the capacity for prefiguration […] that makes prospective alternatives subject to discussion and anticipative reflection."[13] Largely non-hierarchical, the *grounding* process allows designers to reflexively sift through information to identify critical relationships and histories across and through the site.[14] These site relationships may be easily recognizable, such as evidence in plain view of a site disturbed by contamination and its sources, or they may be hidden, such as buried foundations or graves evident only through maps and archival records. Both visible and invisible patterns and traces may not be easy to resolve through design, but those discoveries may provide "the design of 'processes,' 'strategies,' 'agencies,' and 'scaffoldings," for new uses in an open, creative, interactive process.[15] The designer uses understanding and insight to find a design response that will alter the site for its next use.

In this process, associating the design project to the ground itself is paramount. Led by landscape scholars such as Elizabeth Meyer, Kristina Hill, Robin Dripps, Carol Burns, and Andrea Kahn, a renewed focus on terrain acknowledges a range of issues that revalue ground in the process of site knowledge and formation.[16] Concepts for thinking "with" the ground, as a material and deeply contextual medium, acknowledge the dynamic and shifting extent of sites that belie a singular definition. The ground itself carries multiple stories that are revealed through design. In the "Four Traces" framework, Girot suggests that *grounding* concerns the physical ground as well as the re/un-covering of landscape as a cultural imperative, such as reconnecting with cultural histories embedded in the ground—the earth's surface which records its histories. Thus landscape architects should understand and interpret the ground of a given project site to decide how to act upon it. The findings from the *grounding* process can be insightful, complex, and multi-directional in how we reconnect and further shape the terrain in response.

Three Key Themes of Ground

Building from this discourse, I outline three key themes of *ground* that I consider germane for landscape architecture students today: *Recovering ground*, which advocates a contemporary purpose for the field to address the issues outlined in the opening, *differentiating ground*, which suggests that the materiality of the ground plane guides performance and aesthetics, and *drawing ground*, which identifies techniques for creative exploration and communication of design concepts focused on the ground. Finally, at the end of this essay, I will briefly discuss *constructing ground*, which encompasses the translation of concepts into form.

Recovering ground returns our focus and design attention to the substance of the earth, positioning the ground surface as the most essential medium through which to intervene and impact at a territorial scale. In contrast with architecture or urban design for whom ground may be engaged or programmed but not necessarily designed or constructed, the ground is the primary design medium of landscape architecture. Across site scales, landscape architects have important opportunities to aggressively explore the role of the ground in the 21st-century imagination and to directly regenerate its ecological and social processes. As Andre Corboz writes,

> The land, so heavily charged with traces and with past readings, seems very similar to a palimpsest …. land is not a throw away wrapper or a consumer product which can be replaced. Every land is unique […] it is in fact evident that the foundation for planning can no longer be the city, but that territorial reserves to which it must be subordinated.[17]

Part of this importance lies in the loss of landscape histories and processes that have been erased, hidden, or buried by urbanization, agriculture, and industry. The ongoing project to locate these histories and develop material responses to them—metabolic, hydrologic, haptic, and cultural—forms a significant part of our work this century. For example, Robin Dripps cites the 1865 Viele map of Manhattan as an artifact of this purpose, when she writes that "being aware of the topographic past and its history of alteration provides a much broader temporal background to make effective imaginative decisions in the present."[18] Egbert L. Viele's depiction of the pre-urban waterways of the Manhattan peninsula once served as a visual tool for relating problems of disease to hydrology and is still used today to understand underground hydrologic characteristics for construction projects. Broadly speaking, the remaking of cities, infrastructure, coastlines, and other climate-adaptive design sites can be more effective when based on rethinking the performance of the ground itself and on re-establishing a human relationship with the earth. A significant role for landscape architects is to create better site knowledge, and to use the resources and tools of design to regenerate cyclical relationships through the ground at increasingly large scales.

Differentiating ground has to do with specifically recognizing the material qualities, textures, and substances of the earth's surface, which is especially important in urban and industrial contexts. Landscape architects continue to counter the misrepresentations of ground as an objective and featureless surface, for example as depicted through black and white figure-ground drawings presenting buildings as figures separate from surrounding ground shown as a blank nothingness. Worse yet, landscape architects also work against a legacy of engineering that has treated ground as urban "other"—a bulky mass to be smashed, scraped, compacted, or even excavated and discarded. Instead, landscape architects acknowledge and relish in the great topographic and textural variation of the ground as a rich prefiguring device for site occupation. Through a landscape perspective, the ground (even, urban ground) can be seen in a state of constant becoming, composed of a complex web of soil, air, roots, and living creatures, with a vast array of differentiated qualities, characteristics, densities, and vitality.

[17] Andre Corboz. "The Land as Palimsest," in *Diogenes*, Volume: 31 Issue: 121, published: March 1, 1983, 33.

[18] Dripps, *Groundwork*, 69–70. Note: the "Sanitary & Topographic Map of the City and Island of New York" is held in the collections of the New York Public Library. It can be viewed online through the David Rumsey Map Collection, http://www.david-rumsey.com/maps6128.html [accessed June 1, 2020.]

[19] Burns and Kahn, *Site Matters*, xv.
[20] Kenneth J. Helphand and Robert Z. Melnick. "Editor's Introduction" to *Eco-Revelatory Design: Nature Constructed/ Nature Revealed*, (Special issue of Landscape Journal, 1998), ix.

These qualities are not only aesthetic but representative of the rich ecological processes taking place through its thick surface.

Designing for metabolism (energetic and chemical processes in landscape), hydrology (flow and exchange of surface and ground waters), carbon sequestration (absorption of carbon through soil and plants), plant productivity (increasing planetary biomass and growing plants and edibles in urbanized areas), and soil stabilization (addressing vast issues associated soil erosion) helps to regenerate functional relationships with the earth. Equally vital is the design of human experiences of landscape, such as through visual perception, cultural meaning, and aesthetics. Re-engagement with the ground—combining all these aspects—signals a continued shift away from pictorial landscape production (image or scenery making) toward design of multi-sensorial, haptic, experiential, and performative grounds of a site. Human experience, re-connection with nature, and equitable healthy relationships with the world around us are urgently needed, and can be met through attention on grounding that is both ontological and directly rooted in the materiality of land.

Drawing ground has to do with understanding sites through representation, with a focus on the ground plane within landscapes. The essential acts of making maps, drawings, models, and other tangible tools for studying a site have the effect of creatively (re) imagining forms, flows, processes, structures, and textures of the site in both space and time. In *Site Matters*, architects Carol Burns and Andrea Kahn describe this as critical to the formation of site knowledge,

> modes of representation construe sites, and their formative role in the production of site knowledge should be revealed and expressed…Site and designer engage in a dialogic interaction […] [a] relational condition of the site derives from uninterrupted exchange between the real and the representational, the extrinsic and the intrinsic, and the world and the world-as-known.[19]

Further, as written by landscape architects Kenneth I. Helphand and Robert Z. Melnick for *Eco-Revelatory Design*,

> Design has the capacity to make the invisible visible […] it is our [landscape architecture's] task to comprehend patterns, divine meaning, and communicate understanding. The actions of drawing, mapping, modeling, marking, and making are methods and modes of visualizing and externalizing those understandings.[20]

We might then ask how the representation process allows for interpretations and insights to emerge such that a direction for design is created. This is where two- and three-dimensional techniques play a significant role. In order to study ground, students must be exposed to and use techniques where the material and spatial aspects of a site can be explored in ways that directly provide insights to that place.

Students might employ techniques such as those offered in James Corner's "Agency of Mapping," in which he advocates for instruments of spatial mapping that creatively imagine sites and our relationships with them.[21] Since Corner argues that the interrelationships across sites are often related to things, events, and processes, and less so fixed compositions, many of the techniques attempt to track relationships not normally found through other static references. Corner describes four techniques: *drift* (a recording of time-based movement through space that records moments and events of the everyday); *layering* (a process of multiple juxtapositions of site layers with varying scales to destabilize fixed readings of a site); *game-board* (mappings that anticipate or 'play out' scenarios of various agents and systems in relation with each other), and *rhizome* (drawings that emphasize the networks and evolutions of sites as systems, rather than as a fixed body). Across these techniques, the slippage of spatial and temporal scales is a recurring strategy through which a designer can explore, test, and interrogate relationships and events over time and space. Moving back and forth across temporal and spatial scales can generate critical insights into the relationship of a site within its larger region or historical setting. An event in time (frozen in an historical map, for example) may be better understood in a larger context of processes that generated that documented moment. By juxtaposing representations of the rational and analytic (e.g. data-driven modeling) and the intuitive process (e.g. aesthetic making),[22] stronger concepts emerge by loosening one's grip on fact, and instead seeing new formal, material relationships in the site.

When applied to the ground condition of a site, such techniques and their effects are essential. They help to avoid positivistic approaches to designing (such as to simply solve problems of drainage) and instead to invent new engagements with that ground that exceed functionality and allow for a renewed sense of intrinsic beauty and awareness such as that inherent to wetness and moisture. Techniques that employ materiality, pattern, and texture that occur across spatial difference are critical to achieving deeper insights into the nature of an area of ground. They lead to decisions for harnessing and enhancing those qualities in the design itself.

Constructing Ground

The themes of recovering ground, differentiating ground, and drawing ground provide a purposeful framework for site discovery. The *grounding* assignments that I give to my students in the early part of a semester are typically framed by a parallel set of considerations.

[21] James Corner. "Agency of Mapping," in *Mappings*. Denis Cosgrove, Ed. (London: Reaktion Books, 1999), 213–253.
[22] Corner, 1997, 89–90.

I introduce a site issue for students to interrogate, I emphasize materiality of the ground surface, and I suggest techniques to guide the discovery process. Techniques include multi-scalar layering, juxtaposition, abstraction, model-making, collage, and diagramming. I favor analog exercises in foundation studios working with materials such as paper and cardboard along with photography, while allowing for the integration of data, mapping tools, and digital surface modeling for advanced students. Both analog and digital techniques lead to creative insights, although my observation has been that working with one's hands through crafting leads to finding deeper relationships. Directly engaging with physical drawing and modeling materials translates into detailed thinking about the ground as a complex material substance. Design students also bring unique, subjective perspectives to site issues and their contexts. Learning to listen to the site and its occupants creates another lens through which to filter the grounding process. Sites contain multiple voices and bringing expression to their multiplicity is critical to the process.

Drawings generated in the grounding process can be so effective, strong, and evocative as to naturally lead to the concept itself— the *finding*. Many of the images presented here, that while speculating new understanding of a site through manipulating and experimenting with the ground, become strong form generators as well. Grounding creative speculations in the material of the site *as* the embodiment of its context and community readily reveals physical concepts which can be developed into constructible form.

As landscape architects move from concept to construction, they bring increased precision to material, formal, and spatial ideas. The height, width, and length of a site wall, for example, can be deeply meaningful to a design, along with the material and technique chosen for its construction. How people occupy that wall and how it engages the ground through topographic relationships can be profoundly connected to a series of concerns encompassing the ecological, the historical, and the social. Specific design decisions for soils, planting, pavements, structures, hydrology, and so forth shape a series of systems, elements, and processes for the site that can be envisioned as semi-fixed and/or open to rapid change and adaptation. Design attitudes and details within these visions and plans are rooted in the fundamentals of site discovery guided by the level of inclusiveness of what and who occupies sites. Good constructions are the result of well-developed concepts that are unearthed from a variety of sources and deeply grounded in the site. *Constructing ground* is an act of deep care for land and of realizing our conceptual imagination into new realities (Figures 11.1–11.12).

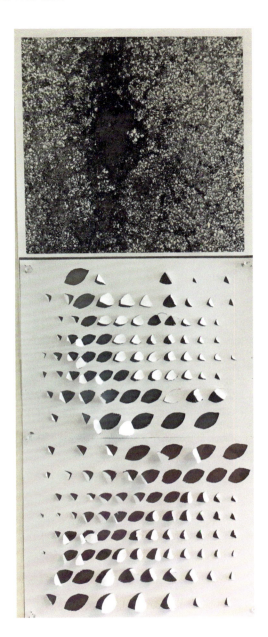

Figure 11.1 Surface puncture.
Surface puncture studies patterns of punctures in the surface of a
parking lot. The assignment asked students to observe the existing
processes of erosion, weathering, and material breakdown of asphalt,
and to explore small-scale interventions that continue to catalyze those
existing processes. The image presents a series of holes in varying
dimensions to mimic cracks and patterns in the surface. The openings
in the paper suggest that these are small portals for rain to enter the
surface and to slip beneath the surface. (Image by Yajing Zhao.)

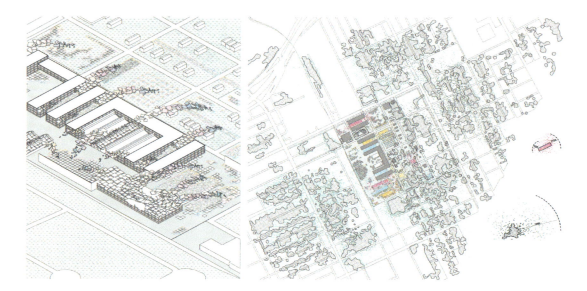

Figure 11.2 Material drift.

Material drift responds to found materials scattered across the ground in an abandoned, urban post-industrial landscape. The drawings explore how such sites might be catalysts for urban ecological processes through surface conditions afforded by vacancy, and specifically, how the ground might be both a launch site and a receiving site for seed dispersal for a larger seeding project to take hold. Wind patterns are studied across the surface of the site, and distances are studied for various species distribution. A subsequent design proposal entailed shaping the ground surface through excavation and mounding to capture seeds as a new landscape for the surrounding low-density neighborhood. (Image by Dawei Huang, in collaboration with Sydney Romero and Max Stuber.)

Figure 11.3 Soil patterning.

Soil patterning explores how soils can be engaged more creatively through a multi-scaled overlay of various patterns, qualities, and textures available from documented soil classifications to actual particles of those soils discovered on site. The patterns were later overlaid with the ground surface to imagine how to interpret soil patterns in the design of the landscape. (Image by Yuanyu Li.)

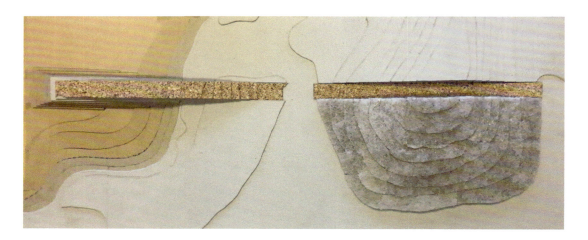

Figure 11.4 Cut/fill exposure.

Cut/fill exposure explores the artificiality of a graded park site. Originally the pond (left) was used to build the landform (right). The assignment asks the students to consider the spatial and temporal shifts in the site. This model provokes a reawakened relationship between cut and fill by slicing into the mound and displacing this soil back to the water as a bridge device. (Model by Wanhui Zuo.)

Figure 11.5 Landform study—perception and sequence.

Landform study—perception and sequence uses chipboard, cork, balsa wood, and dowels to abstract the three dimensionality of the ground surface. The study amplified small variations in the existing ground and varied the surface aspects so as to study different lighting effects, spatial sequencing, and potential microclimates. (Model by Yang Xia.)

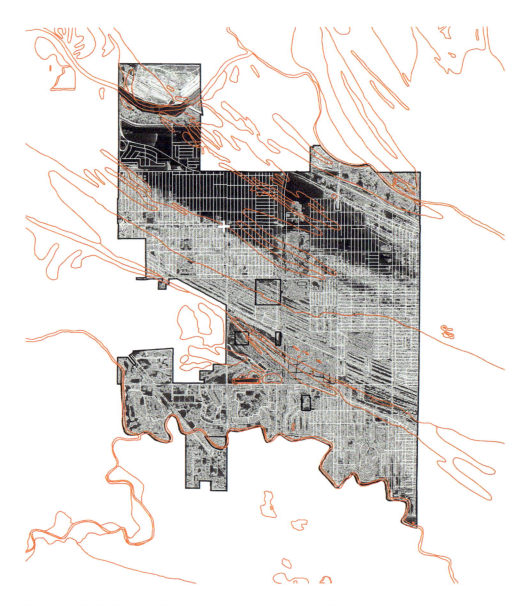

Figure 11.6 Geologic pattern, same-scale superimposition.

Geologic pattern, same-scale superimposition helped to develop a site concept using the geological soils and historic hydrologic patterns of a site. While the pattern of these soil and water systems were hidden and paved by urbanization, the team superimposed the former patterns across the site, and used this spatial-temporal study to reveal the underlying soils. The resulting design project won a 2019 ASLA Student Award. (Image by Xi Wang.)

Figure 11.7 Regional land surface study.

Regional land surface study invoked possible landscape templates for the ecological transformation of vacant land and an abandoned elevated train track. Regional patterns of vegetation and wetlands, in the form of printed photographs, were 'draped' across site models to provoke contrasts against the existing conditions of the site and to assess scale and texture for intervention. (Models by Garret Rock.)

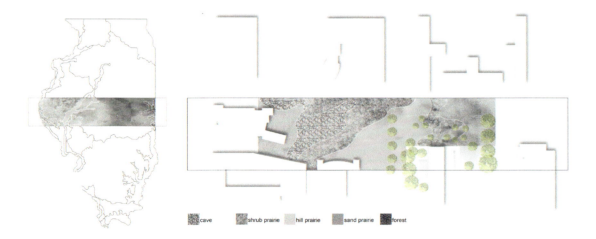

Figure 11.8 Geographic transect.

Geographic transect is a study of an ecological landscape sequence. With a desire to transform a monoculture of turf grass on the site, Illinois native landscape typologies were abstracted as a series of micro-scale landforms and associated dry and wet plant systems, based on high and low points in the site. The subsequent design provided subtle elevation changes to correspond to the low-lying topography of the Illinois prairie. Caves and underground experiences were carved into the park. (Model by Xinyuan Liu.)

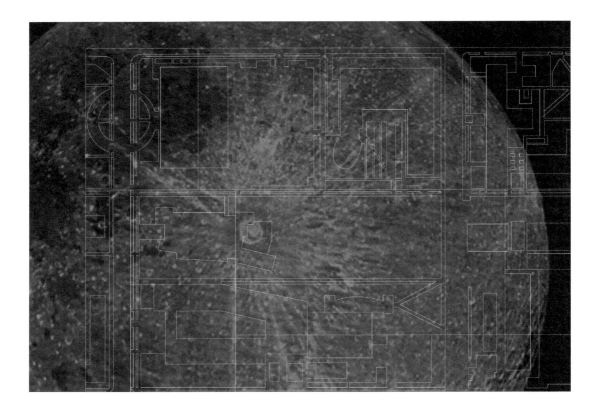

Figure 11.9 Tycho displacement.

Tycho displacement represents the concept of land displacement from a new building construction. Tycho is the term used to describe the craters that result from debris hitting the moon. The student envisioned the soil displacement from the building construction forming the landscape as a tycho with an explosion of debris dispersing through to the edges of the site—like a crater. The student subsequently (later in the formal design process) designed these displaced materials as long landform trails interspersed with pathways radiating outward from the new building site. (Image by Yizhu Liu.)

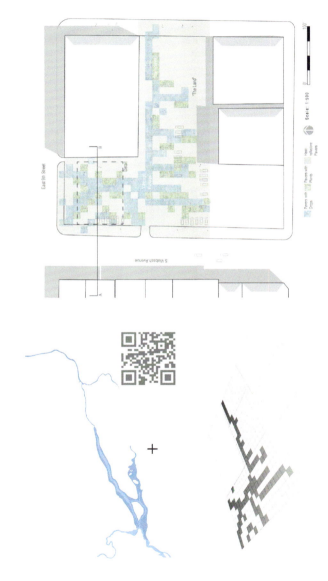

Figure 11.10 Flooding code.

Flooding code is a site study that takes its *inspiration* from the pattern of the historic Chicago Portage—a pre-urban, prairie wetland system that was located to the southeast of downtown Chicago. With a desire to embrace intermittent flooding in a parking lot, the students studied and then recalled the Portage as an abstracted figure for stormwater collection in the site. The pattern of the Portage serves as a "flooding code," a subtly lower portion of the site that slowly fills up in rain events, recalling the historic Portage seasonal flooding pattern. Later in the design process, the students designed a paver gradient pattern of "land" (highly porous pavers), "islands" (semi-porous pavers), and "portage" (water holding pavers). (Images by Zheng Cong and Henrik Lizell.)

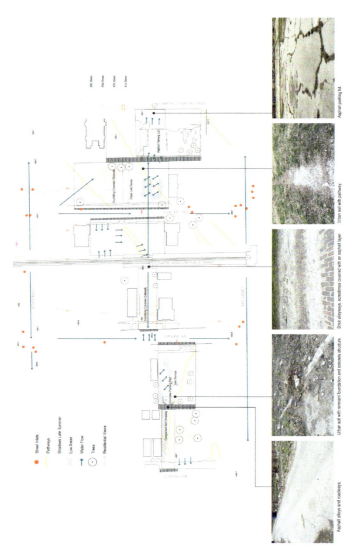

Figure 11.11 Interface.

Interface studies how to disrupt imperviousness and compacted soil in South Side Chicago. This drawing creatively inventoried the traces and surface conditions of the site, using an original series of graphic notations to locate patterns of lines and fields of textures. By drawing in this way, the designer established an attitude about design as a process of editing—using subtraction and additive material strategies—to transition the surface toward increased ecological and social performance. (Image by Liz Vogel, in collaboration with Thea Yang, Jie Bao, Yajing Zhao, and Yexuan Gu.)

Figure 11.12 Campus-walk.

Campus walk is an example of a drift mapping exercise, where students explored the ground surfaces of their university campus. They documented an interconnected series of asphalt, concrete, gravel, soil, and turf materials surfaces, and located infrastructure networks including drainage networks, electric service, and ventilation equipment. They invented their own signs, lines, and rules of navigation as well as using creatures encountered such as birds to guide the walk. The walk is time-stamped. The organization of the drift led to selective interventions to replace asphalt and fallow ground with new uses more pertinent to the students's desires for their campus. (Image by Litong Zeng, Zeyun Zheng, and Jinyu Shen.)

12

FROM IDEAS TO DESIGN ACTIONS

Yun Hye Hwang

Landscape architecture is increasingly synthesizing knowledge inputs from a range of disciplines (Arts et al. 2017) to address multifaceted concerns of the Anthropocene. As a pervasive profession (Kullmann 2016), one of its key roles of this field is to embrace relevant socioecological issues on specific sites and suggest wide-ranging holistic solutions to improve the environment and quality of life on those sites (ASLA 2019). No matter which approach a landscape architect uses to generate design concepts, the ultimate deliverables of design outputs in the field should be concrete and practical figures and grounds that are implementable in the real world. Even though an idea might be initiated by intuition and inspiration, the concept should be developed through systemic transformation processes. In this way, an idea evolves into convincing and impactful design actions. In fact, successful projects don't rely on impulse; they require effortful reflection. As Nassauer and Opdam see it, design is a science-driven, knowledge-based action towards landscape changes (Nassauer and Opdam 2008). By the same token, Steinitz advocates organizing objective and systematic investigations based on logical thinking processes into an iterative design development process (Steinitz 1995). The complexities inherent to such processes obviously call for a strong link between research and design (Van den Brink et al. 2016).

Understanding a site through research is key to establishing the credibility of a project. Therefore, site research should precede any design action. Design studios in the Master of Landscape Architecture Programme in the National University of Singapore (NUS MLA) examine various grounded social, ecological, and environmental demands within a site-specific context (i.e., an Asian high-rise, high-density built urban environment) with an emphasis on site research as a fundamental step to determine design direction (Hwang 2018). The studios rest on the assumption that powerful concepts devolve from the initial analytical efforts to apprehend the site – without critical investigation, in other words, there will be no convincing design actions.

The selected projects described in this chapter introduce the earliest stage of conceptualization processes led by the site research.

DOI: 10.4324/9781003053255-14

They show how designers read, represent, and transform site-related information into concepts that shape design actions towards sustainable, resilient, and liveable landscapes. The concept generation processes combine multiple research activities, including graphical interpretation of facts based on collected data, theoretical underpinnings, and field mapping through site observation, field sketches, measurement, and interviews.

Project A began with a theoretical investigation of different lifespans, looking at both rapidly changing housing estates with static urban greenery and steadily maturing tropical forests. It questioned conventional urban development that is entirely rebuilt from ground zero every few decades and argued that calibrating/redefining timescales of nature and the built environment represents an opportunity to design. It proposed evolving backyard gardens, starting from native tree nurseries in a semi-private strip park and ending with the development of a young primary forest over 100 years (Figure 12.1).

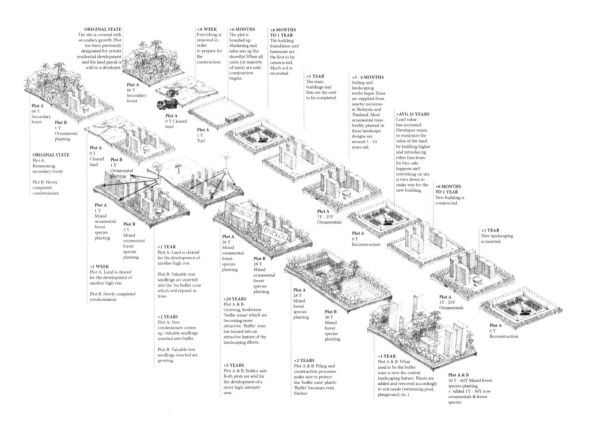

Figure 12.1 Diagram of *Project A*. The diagram visualizes the rapid transformation from a secondary forest into a low-rise housing estate and then into denser and higher new condominiums. The visualization triggered a proposal for evolutionary and heterogeneous landscape by promoting continuous growth of vegetation even as the built environment repeats its cycle of demolition and reconstruction (Yuanqiu Feng, NUS MLA 2016').

A key task of *Project B* was to transfer car-oriented outdoor spaces of a high-rise public housing estate into pedestrianized every-day landscapes promoting active interactions between humans and nature. The project concept came from a sketch of human flows that featured far more than dedicated footpaths; the sketch inspired a redesign of spatial configuration and usage towards an elastic, flexible, seamless network woven into cohesive and positive human and nature connections (Figure 12.2).

Figure 12.2 Human flow map for *Project B*. The map traces the movement of hundreds of residents in a high-dense public housing estate. The map shows that many portions of building in-outs, including void decks and immediate open spaces, are disconnected and underutilized. It verifies that highly tuned and programmed spaces seem less robust, as the flow patterns involve redundancy, overlap, and unpredictability (Yuqian Wang and Yu Liu, NUS MLA 2017').

Situated in an ecologically strategic location where the residential district immediately meets an ecologically rich forested area, *Project C* aimed to reduce physical barriers preventing wildlife movements. Spatial data based on field records and surveys with wildlife experts shed useful light on the dynamic relationship between fauna movements and required habitats. The data shaped the project concept through the following systemic design steps: identify wildlife gaps, find potential areas where design intervention is needed, aggregate available open spaces, connect isolated patches, and insert local habitats that could remove/alleviate barriers at the nested scale (Figure 12.3).

The objective of field research for *Project D* was to identify socioecologically valuable patches and determine the core forested areas to be conserved while allowing high-dense urban development in the less valuable areas. By doing this, the research supported alternative forms of protecting nature against loss of secondary forests and suggested a way for the built environment to accommodate a growing population (Figure 12.4).

As a landscape renewal project for an obsolete brownfield area, *Project E* prioritized scientific assessment of biophysical condition, including quality of soil and water. Spatial analysis of the biophysical site condition revealed the relevance of improving the quality of contaminated natural resources and pointed to the value of recyclable resources as landscape materials for new development. The project led to a comprehensive land use plan suggesting

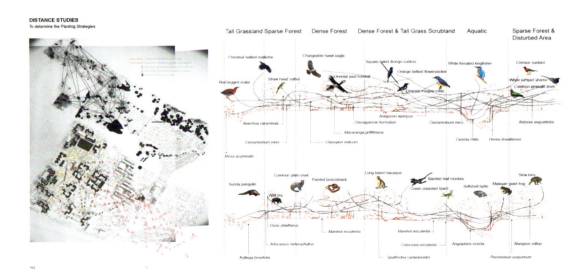

Figure 12.3 Animal movement map for *Project C*. The map identifies targeted fauna groups and their habitats based on collaborative field surveys with a nature society group and scholars in biology. It also identifies strategic areas to insert landscape elements as local habitats (Xiao Jun Kow NUS MLA 2016' (Left) and Zhuhui Bai, NUS MLA 2018' (Right)).

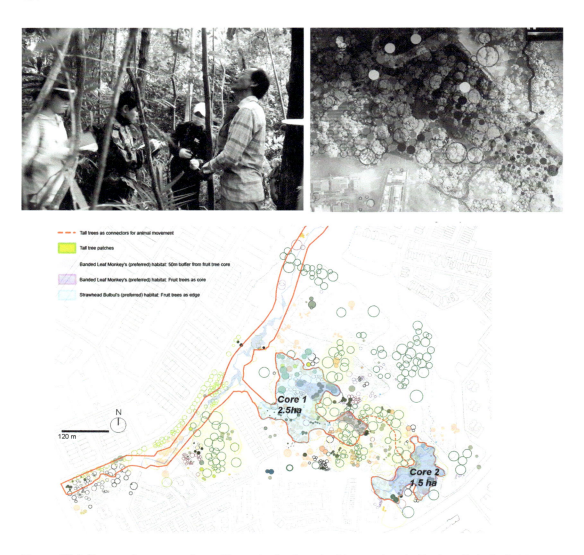

Figure 12.4 Research process to verify ecologically valuable patches in *Project D*. Left: field research to identify forest species in key transects of the forests. Center: mapping process to superimpose field data on a satellite map. Right: synthesis map highlighting areas to be preserved based on multiple layers of maps containing a higher biodiversity, large canopy trees, healthy soils, fauna-attractive plant species, types of habitat, and natural heritage (Hao Jen Sun, NUS MLA 2018').

Figure 12.5 Biophysical site information from field research injected evidence-based thinking into the design of a regional scale land use plan in *Project E*. Left: field research process to collect water and soil samples from a former industrial zone. Right: map differentiating pollution levels in soil and water (Junwei Dai, NUS MLA 2018').

different intensities of development and remediation plans in phases (Figure 12.5).

Situated on a strategic route connecting the city core of Jakarta and a tourist destination in Cimaja beach, site research for *Project F* verified the untapped tourist potential of the site and the alternative livelihood opportunities for those working on oil palm plantations. The fine-grained physical modeling of the terrain through examination of dynamic land forms and viewpoint analysis resulted in a viable plan for a scenic drive with ecotourism opportunities (Figure 12.6).

Sites in most landscape projects are complex enough to explore immense design possibilities, and ways of designing can be determined by site specificity. The projects displayed here seized the opportunity to elevate site information and incorporate scientific significance into creative conceptual landscapes. The examples show how physical material entities and site discovery processes can motivate initial thoughts and inspirations, which can then be cultivated in design actions. In sum, grounded and informative site research is imperative to develop convincing concepts and to trigger the instinctive part of designing. The ensuing transformation

Figure 12.6 *Project F*'s comprehensive understanding of existing oil palm farmlands and surrounding forests through topographic modelling, GIS maps, and perspective analysis influenced programmatic choices harnessing existing landscape resources to connect aesthetic landscapes and create a scenic and pleasant journey, ultimately contributing to the local economy (Wenjun Pu, Qingqing Zhang, and Wei Chen, NUS MLA 2017').

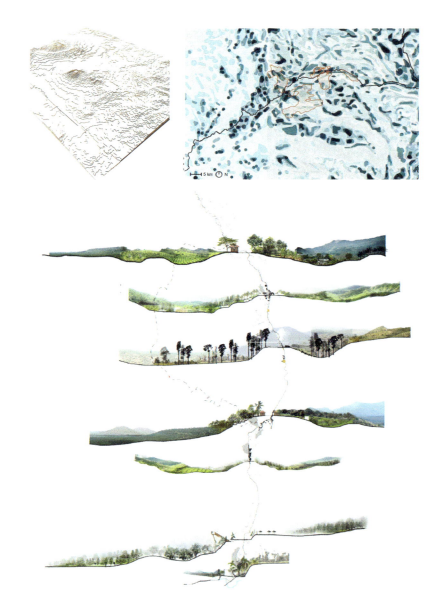

process captures the uniqueness of sites and leads to conceptually remarkable projects.

References

Arts, Bas, Marleen Buizer, Lumina Horlings, Verina Ingram, Cora Van Oosten, and Paul Opdam. 2017. "Landscape approaches: a state-of-the-art review." *Annual Review of Environment and Resources* 42: 439–463.

ASLA. 2019. "What is landscape architecture?" Accessed 1/8/2019. https://www.asla.org/aboutlandscapearchitecture.aspx.

Hwang, Yun Hye. 2018. "Site research in landscape design studios." *Asian Journal of the Scholarship of Teaching and Learning* 8 (1): 133–145.

Kullmann, Karl. 2016. "Disciplinary convergence: landscape architecture and the spatial design disciplines." *Journal of Landscape Architecture* 11 (1): 30–41.

Nassauer, Joan Iverson, and Paul Opdam. 2008. "Design in science: extending the landscape ecology paradigm." *Landscape ecology* 23 (6):633–644.

Steinitz, Carl. 1995. "Design is a verb; design is a noun." *Landscape Journal* 14 (2):188–200.

Van den Brink, Adri, Diedrich Bruns, Hilde Tobi, and Simon Bell. 2016. *Research in landscape architecture: methods and methodology*. London: Routledge.

13

TRANSLATIONS BETWEEN PATENT INNOVATION AND ENVIRONMENTAL DESIGN PEDAGOGY

Richard L. Hindle

Translations in Design Pedagogy

Translating patent innovation studies into environmental design pedagogy expands student knowledge and provides essential skills for future work. Readily accessible patent search tools and an evolving dossier of historical precedents that link the physical environment to patent innovation provided a valuable context through which to rethink research methods and outputs in design studio, workshops, and seminars. Recent publications in the field of architecture and technology have clearly identified the manifold ways in which intellectual property interacts with building systems, ranging from architectural components and systems to copyright.[1][2] An evolving body of literature also exists linking specific geographies and landscapes to the process of technological innovation using patent documents as a primary source.[3][4] These references clearly identify the role of patents in environmental design across scales but do not indicate how design educators might use this knowledge.

Integration of patent innovation studies into design processes is a powerful research and generative design tool that operates across a range of project types, from building systems to territorial infrastructure and issues related to the Anthropocene. Translation of patent innovation studies into design pedagogy requires methods that integrate the traditions of design process with establish methods for innovation studies. This hybrid yields distinct results and project types that can be replicated and further translated by others. Design studios and seminars are uniquely suited these processes as source material and research materials in seminars and studios are open to interpretation based on the desired pedagogical objectives. In courses where technology is integral, patent innovation might be considered a generative research topic. In technology classes, patent research may generate a broad understanding of particular systems that relate to the built environment. In studio

[1] Decker, Martina, "Novelty and Ownership: Intellectual Property in Architecture and Design," *Technology|Architecture + Design* 1, no. 1 (n.d.): 41–47.
[2] Wendy W. Fok and Antoine Picon, *Digital Property Open-Source Architecture* (Oxford: John Wiley & Sons, 2016).
[3] Richard Hindle, "Prototyping the Mississippi Delta: Patents, Alternative Futures, and the Design of Complex Environmental Systems," *Journal of Landscape Architecture* 12, no. 2 (n.d.): 32–47, https://doi.org/10.1080/18626033.2017.1361084.
[4] Richard L. Hindle, "Patent Scenarios for the Mississippi River," *Journal of Architectural Education* 71, no. 2 (2017): 280–285.

DOI: 10.4324/9781003053255-15

and design seminar, patent research may play a primary role in framing topics and analysis of particular landscape conditions.

Patent Search Tools and Methods

Translations of patent research into environmental design projects require working knowledge of patent search methods. A wealth of peer-reviewed literature exists for tracking innovation through patents, ranging from papers that link the rate of scientific publications to patent innovation, asses university research outputs through patent metrics, and use patents as a primary source to understand innovation in specific sectors of technology. [5,6,7] A review of this literature is valuable for advanced study in a specific sector of technology, yet in the field of environmental design few sources exist that explicitly address the subject of urbanization, infrastructure, or regional landscapes. This means that innovation studies must be conducted on a project by project basis, using the established methods of citation networks, keyword searches, classification searches, and the more advanced process of patent mapping. Many of these core search and analysis processes can be accomplished through easily accessible web searches such as Google Patents (www.patents.google.com), the United States Patent office (www.uspto.gov), and the European Patent Office (https://worldwide.espacenet.com/).

Citation networks essentially link prior art, and future inventions, through the use of citations. Just as in scientific literature, patents include citations of prior art and nonpatent citations to ensure the claims made by the patent are novel and constitute a substantively new contribution. Citation networks provide an important window into specific sectors of technology. Citation searches are among the simplest to conduct as bibliographic data is associated with each patent for citations and future reference to each patent. Accessing this information is simple through free online searches, and the data acquired in this manner can also be used to construct more robust network mappings or serve as the basis for advanced research in a specific sector. For example, recent publications on the subject of building sector innovation use patent citations as the primary method, concluding advances in computer, communication technology in the industry, and recommend incentives for energy technology.[8] Google patents, the USPTO, and European Patent office can all be used to construct citations networks that situate individual patents within a context or prior art and evaluate their relationship to future inventions. They can expand the notion of a singular invention and suggest areas for further research. Importantly, they provide context for design interpretation through recognition of prior-art.

Keyword Searches provide another robust search tool within patent search databases. When coupled with customized date ranges, and issuing patent office criteria, assignee, and other meta-data keyword searches can provide a window into the innovation

[5] Angela Hullmann and Martin Meyer, "Publications and Patents in Nanotechnology," *Scientometrics* 58, no. 3 (2003): 507–527.

[6] Lee Branstetter and Yoshiaki Ogura, "Is Academic Science Driving a Surge in Industrial Innovation? Evidence from Patent Citations" (National Bureau of Economic Research, 2005).

[7] Eibert C, Engelsman and Anthony F. J. van Raan, "A Patent-Based Cartography of Technology," *Research Policy* 23, no. 1 (1994): 1–26.

[8] Joy E. Altwies and Gregory F. Nemet, "Innovation in the US Building Sector: An Assessment of Patent Citations in Building Energy Control Technology," *Energy Policy* 52 (2013): 819–831.

landscape associated with particular types of technology. In simple terms, keyword searches function like other web searches allowing searchers to find specific documents, asses the relative frequency occurrence of a particular term, or gain knowledge about its relative scarcity within the assigned search criteria. This intuitive type of patent search is invaluable as a starting point for research but also can be generative for more complex innovation studies. For example, researchers use keyword search networks to map sectors of technology and evaluate amount of patent innovation occurring in specific sectors. Importantly, this approach can also be used to identify areas in which patent innovation is lacking, therefore suggesting areas of technology where new investment, research, and development may be warranted.[9] The mining of patent text also yields interesting insights about technology, with new tools available for analysis of massive textual data sets.[10]

Patent classification searches may also provide insights about technological trends. Patent classification systems have evolved over time to group and organize patented inventions by sector. For example, the Cooperative Patent Classification (E) refers to "Fixed Constructions" and the subclass (E01) refers to "construction of roads, railways, and bridges" further subdividing the class based on specific criteria. Patent classification is a system of sorting inventions and their documents into technical fields covering all areas of technology, including areas of new technology that are not yet classified. By organizing patent by classification, each document can be found based on sector as well as through keywords, and so on, facilitating searches and insights about technological concepts and their relationships.[11] Benefits of patent classification Patent classification systems make it easier to file and retrieve patent documents, and also to look back in time to find antecedents of technology. There are two main international classification systems, and many more national systems. The International Patent Classification system (IPC) was introduced in 1968, and the IPC is used by all patent offices worldwide. The Cooperative Patent Classification system (CPC) is an extension of the IPC and is used by the European Patent Office, the United States Patent and Trademark Office other national offices. The CPC subgroups are added to the IPC symbol. While the IPC has 70,000 entries, the CPC has more than 250,000, making it much more precise. Classification searches can help designers situate their research and design inquiries into known categories of invention.

Visualization and mapping of patents is robust area of research. Each patent document archived by global patent office has associated metadata and these data sets, in combination with the requisite textual and graphic description of the particular invention, are a treasure trove of information for technologists and information scientists. Analysis of patent documents is used to assess the efficacy of university research, link scientific discoveries to industry applications, identify emerging technology sectors,[12] and generate high-level analysis of technology trends over time and by

[9] Sungjoo Lee, Byungun Yoon, and Yongtae Park, "An Approach to Discovering New Technology Opportunities: Keyword-Based Patent Map Approach," *Technovation* 29, nos. 6–7 (2009): 481–497.
[10] YunYun Yang et al., "Text Mining and Visualization Tools–Impressions of Emerging Capabilities," *World Patent Information* 30, no. 4 (2008): 280–293.
[11] Tiziano Montecchi, Davide Russo, and Ying Liu, "Searching in Cooperative Patent Classification: Comparison between Keyword and Concept-Based Search," *Advanced Engineering Informatics* 27, no. 3 (2013): 335–345.
[12] Young Gil Kim, Jong Hwan Suh, and Sang Chan Park, "Visualization of Patent Analysis for Emerging Technology," *Expert Systems with Applications* 34, no. 3 (2008): 1804–1812.

location.[13] Visualization and mapping has evolved into a distinct area of research, as well as an area of innovation and business opportunity within itself. Numerous commercial software platforms now offer patent mapping and data mining to industry and academic clients. The relational diagrams that define this type of research reveal interconnectivity between patents and can be powerful sources to asses technology sectors. Free online tools such as (lens.org)[14] are also readily accessible to researchers and can offer students of environmental design easy tools to start exploring patent innovation for sectors of the built environment.

[13] "PatentsView," accessed May 28, 2019, http://www.patentsview.org/web/#viz/locations.
[14] "The Lens - Free & Open Patent and Scholarly Search," The Lens - Free & Open Patent and Scholarly Search, accessed May 28, 2019, https://www.lens.org/lens.

Case Studies: Translating Patent Innovation Studies into Design Pedagogy

The availability of patent search tools, and new case studies in environmental innovation, now facilitates the creation of experimental pedagogies that integrate patent innovation into site, building, and territorial design processes. Translating patent research into design pedagogy can take many forms from a detailed investigation of a single invention to high-level analysis of technological trends or abstraction of imagery and text. The following examples discuss, and reflect, on observations in process for experimental pedagogy and professional projects that situate patent innovation studies a source research material and/or outcome of a design process in landscape architecture and environmental design. Within each project, patent innovation is integrated either in the initial project framing, as part of the research process, through iterative design exercises, or as a final outcome and deliverable. The exercises use source material from keyword searches, citation networks, mapping exercise, and classification analysis, as part of the design process. This source material ranges from images associated with

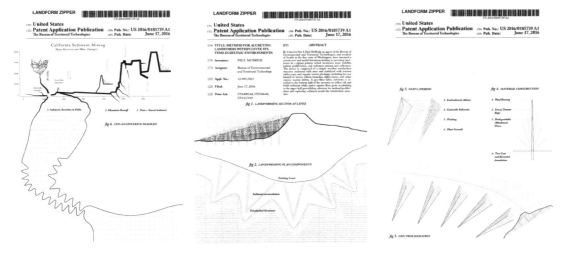

Figure 13.1 Patent documents often include textual and graphic descriptions of an invention, including plan, section, elevation, and diagrams. This faux patent document for a "Landscape Zipper" was created by Paul McBride as part of workshop during Dredgefest California (2016). It describes a speculative method, invented during the workshop, of sediment capture and management integrated across scales from the site detail to the larger region.

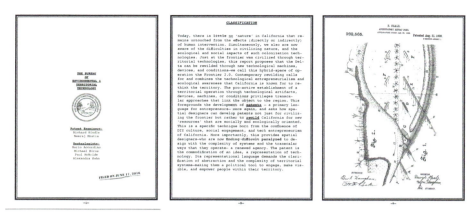

Figure 13.2 The Bureau of Environmental and Territorial Technology was conceived of during Dredgefest California (2016) by Neeraj Bhatia and Richard Hindle as a hypothetical branch of the patent office founded to manage sequential innovation in the emerging sector of ecological technology. It builds upon the forgotten history of the patent office as part of the United States Department of Interior from 1849–1925.

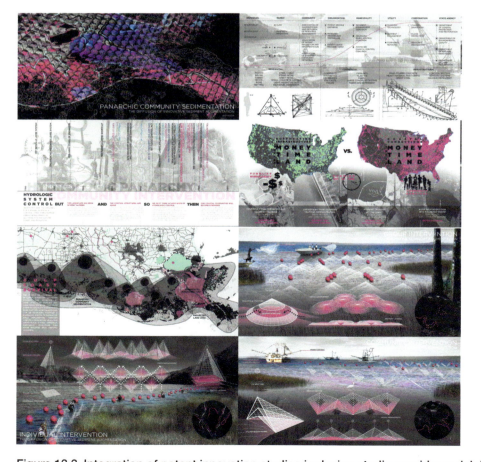

Figure 13.3 Integration of patent innovation studies in design studio provides a rich heuristic for design studios. Sean Passler's project "Panarchic Community Sedimentation" project was developed at Louisiana State University (2014) as a community based sediment capturing process in which the technologies of coastal adaptation where designed and scaled for local participation

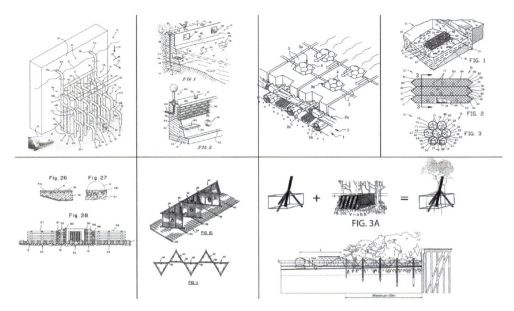

Figure 13.4 Patent searches and research provides detailed information about innovation within each sector or technology. The image shows a sample of patents related to the construction and design habitats integrated with coastal infrastructure.

Figure 13.5 Translation between patent research and design pedagogy can take many forms by helping shape research processes and project rational. The course "Hard Habitats" at UC Berkeley integrates patent innovation studies into the course syllabus, helping to guide individual design project. Noah Pitts' (pictured here) project from 2018 used fabric forming processes to develop ecological seawall prototypes for the San Francisco Embarcadero.

Figure 13.6 Patent source images can be hybridized with other modes of landscape representation to envision new potentials and highlight technical aspects of design thinking.

patent documents to textual descriptions of a particular invention that revel technical specifications of how a technology works.

Three pedagogical approaches are discussed and analyzed in this essay. The first results from the LAEP Innovation Seminar taught at UC Berkeley (2016–2019) focusing on the fabrication of hard habitats for coastal armoring. The second focuses on a workshop for Dredgefest California (2016) in which scenarios were tested at the scale of the Sacramento – San Joaquin Delta using discrete technologies. The third results from the "Inventing Rivers and Coasts" studio taught at Louisiana State University (2014) focusing on the reciprocal relationship between technological innovation and large-scale hydrologic systems and questions related to design agency in the Anthropocene. In each, integration of patent innovation studies served as a heuristic for problem solving, a research method for skill building, and generative part of the design process through interpretation and abstraction (Figures 13.1–13.6).

Part 3

Forming Futures

14

DESIGNING PARKS – THE ART OF CREATING LIVELY PLACES

Leonard Grosch

Location – A Need for History

Carefully analyzing the characteristics of a location and evaluating and interpreting them remains the basis for every landscape architecture design. The qualities of a location are unique. They already exist. At a time of increasing global alignment, it is important to design distinct locations through intensifying their specific qualities. At the same time, it is necessary to conserve resources and to derive the basic spatial and functional framework from the location. Building history further in such a way increases many people's acceptance: Such open spaces are taken as a matter of course. Through appreciating the legacy of past times, a prudent and reflected examination of a location develops. It is about the desire to find meaning in locations. Arbitrariness is rejected. Last but not least, it is also simpler for landscape architects: Why devise something that is not intrinsic to the location when careful observation of the location is able to provide the spatial and thematic concept? (Figures 14.1–14.3).

What, therefore, does location mean? In my understanding, a location is made up of spatial qualities, of the concrete, of the structural legacies left behind by people of past eras, of an atmosphere that provides information about what a location needs, what would be suitable and what would be detrimental there, of technical constraints, and all this: at a particular point in time.

Framework – Stability and Orientation

A strong framework ensures the superordinate spatial qualities and the functional and staging connections of a park in the long run – even if the contents of individual spaces change over the course of time. It makes it possible to hold together different atmospheres and aesthetics – subareas designed by planners as well as by citizens – spatially, functionally, and in terms of design. In the future, the codetermination and joint designing of parks by civil society and its diverse desires and demands will only gain more in importance. This makes robust park structures that much more

DOI: 10.4324/9781003053255-17

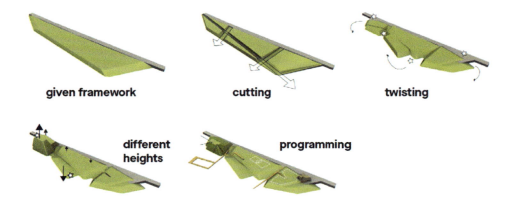

Figure 14.1 Baakenpark framework.

Baakenpark Hamburg – Baakenpark has a remarkable topography with several plateaus of different heights. The highest peak at the eastern end of the peninsula is the 15 m high *Himmelsberg*, a panoramic point visible from afar. When exploring the park, visitors are offered surprising shifts in perspective and varied insights and views. As a green area, the park offers recreation with a variety of sports, play and recreation possibilities and is an optical-aesthetic point of reference in the middle of the harbor basin.

Figure 14.2 Baakenpark scale.

Baakenpark Hamburg – The Baakenpark is the green center of the eastern HafenCity. The 1.6 hectare peninsula, artificially created with sand from the river Elbe, is located in the middle of the former harbor basin of Baakenhafen. With its wild shoreline, the green embankments right up to the water and its characteristic topography, the park forms an atmospheric counterpoint to its surroundings. A park that invites visitors to explore and only unfolds when walking through it. A park with a variety of offers for all visitors, with lively meeting points, wide meadows and playgrounds, but also with quieter, isolated places.

Figure 14.3 Baakenpark atmosphere.
Baakenpark Hamburg – Due to the special flood protection requirements, the playgrounds and lawns of the park were laid out on three plateaus. The three plateaus are clearly different in their uses and atmospheres: in the western part, a sport and play area dominates; the middle level offers a play and sunbathing area with the gallery of banks; in the east, the *Himmelsberg* rises away from the hustle and bustle as the highlight.

important. A strong framework corresponds to many people's need for a balance of secure orientation and consistent spatial and functional interconnections, on the one hand, with variety and the possibility to transform the contents, on the other hand.

So what does framework mean? A park framework is comparable to the structural statics of a building: It is composed of the spatial framework, the network of paths, the structuring of the areas that thus arises, and the most important structuring – and generally also staging – installations. The components of this framework determine one another. When designing, it is possible to verify the framework by successively leaving out structure-giving components: At what point does the spatial and functional cohesion disintegrate?

Program – Activity and Community

People should experience things in the park. A park expands their living space into the open air – particularly in a densely built-up city. For this, it requires a program with the most varied and attractive offerings. This program should reflect the social diversity and, if possible, speak to all age, population, and interest groups. Cleverly concentrating offerings at hotspots makes it possible for intensity and, thus, urbanity to arise in the park. What is crucial for acceptance is imaginatively formulating the program by means of landscape architecture. This is simultaneously also one of the bases for developing different atmospheres in the park.

Multilayered Coding – Everyday Usability and Self-Realization

It should not only be possible to use the elements of a park in an outstanding way; in an ideal case, they should also inspire creative use and unforeseen activities. For this reason, for me, a park should also include elements whose use is not clearly recognizable and that offer so much sophistication that they animate people to appropriate or use them in unexpected ways. Free objects and installations and areas with specific purposes should be so stimulating in form and material that people want to touch them, climb on them, or desire to use them in some way. In other words: They should make people want to appropriate them. The hope, so to say, is that animation will be able to speak to a majority. It is specifically indeterminateness with respect to use that entices.

Multilayered coding coincides with the idea of so-called *soft edges* and can easily be transferred quite well to park planning. While studying in Copenhagen, I was impressed by a presentation by the urban planner Jan Gehl. He repeated the term *soft edges* like a mantra. What he means with this are first and foremost lively ground floor zones. They are extremely important for a varied, livable city because this is the area where the building and its residents come into contact with the rest of the city population. The animating effect can result from shops; from a projection from a wall on which it is possible to sit, such as the former loading ramps in SoHo in New York; from attractive front gardens, which, on the one hand, produce a social distance to passersby but, on the other hand, also please them with arrangements of flowers; or from garden cafés, as are found in Amsterdam or Berlin. The building, therefore, becomes a hybrid. It no longer only serves the use ascribed to it, but with its contact areas, it contributes additionally to the liveliness of the city. This is exactly what occurs in connection with elements in the park that can be used in other ways than actually intended.

What plays a big role is intuitively designing and positioning such objects and locations outside the context of the program. As planners, we anticipate that particular uses will take place at particular locations and facilitate this in the design without being able to specify the whole spectrum of actions in advance. The more unforeseen uses and activities take place, the more pleased I am. For me, a range of uses at one spot is proof of their ability to animate. In my understanding, it is then practical to classify them as autonomous objects or elements with specific purposes:

Stage and Stands – Great Cinema

A park should bring people together. It should give rise to a feeling of social closeness and a shared identity. Creating a relaxed atmosphere can contribute to mitigating social tensions or even prevent them from arising in the first place. To achieve this, it is first necessary to encourage communication in a targeted manner and, second, to produce a feeling of togetherness. How can this be realized using the means of landscape architecture?

The stages-and-stands principle orchestrates the coming together of people who would, otherwise, never take note of each other. People should do things and want to do things in the park: to enjoy life and show off, to let others share in their abilities and hobbies. For this, there needs to be someone who does something and someone who watches, and perhaps even marvels. This results in interaction and communication.

Scale – Security and Freedom

Parks should satisfy people's needs in terms of the size and proportions of spaces in them. Spaces that are oriented toward the human scale should alternate with scenic expanse. Depending on the mood, atmospheric conditions, and frequency, park visitors are, therefore, able to choose between protected and open spaces. The scale of the spaces to be designed is based on the tailoring and size of the site, what is found there, the concentration and location of the necessary framework of paths, the program, and the atmospheres envisaged. The scale of individual objects is, in turn, oriented toward the scale of the space.

Types of Nature – Wildness and Design

Wildness is important in a city and should be a basic component of its parks. And not only that. Different forms of vegetation should – just like the program – reflect the variety of city dwellers' needs and desires for nature. These needs can be of a purely contemplative or atmospheric sort or be expressed as a desire to participate, for instance, through gardening together. The contrast between wild and designed forms of vegetation makes both seem more valuable.

Detail – Precision and Sensuousness

It is through being used that what can be understood by everyone develops its effect. The details of an element should, therefore, be as simple as possible and as complex as necessary so that its ability to animate people is intensified. Simple elements explain themselves and are intelligible in themselves. This ensures acceptance. Design that is simple, robust, and appropriate to the particular material also leads directly to durability and easier maintenance. The longevity of the site that results from this further increases acceptance and brings greater appreciation in society with it.

Atmospheres – In the Middle of Things and Truly Outdoors

The atmosphere of a space determines whether I feel comfortable or uncomfortable there. When designing a park, the focus should, therefore, be on creating atmospheres in which as many people as possible feel good. Feeling good is used here in its more neutral interpretation as being without perceived interference. Seen positively, it might stand for a wide range of sentiments that we associate with well-being: lively, protected, free, inspired, vital, happy. Only a wealth of different atmospheres is able to give people, with their individual perceptions and needs, a sense of well-being or even delight them with the design of locations. Favorite spaces, niches, and locations for personal fulfillment are possible where different atmospheres are planned and different aesthetics are permitted. From this stance, we promised ourselves that many population groups will feel integrated (and included). To construct atmospheres in a park, all of the strategies presented here have to work together. It is, however, not possible to plan a specific atmosphere since each person perceives it differently. Nevertheless, the philosopher Gernot Böhme states that there is almost something objective inherent in atmospheres because people experience them in a shared way and, despite the subjectivity of feeling, are able to agree on their character.[1]

A design, therefore, involves targeting atmospheres – and hoping that they then end up speaking to a majority in how they are received. I am naturally aware of the fact that, in spite of this intersubjectivity, other factors such as the weather, time of day and season of the year, one's personal state of mind, or other people can have a substantial influence on how the atmosphere of a location is perceived. My focus, however, is on constructing atmospheres. How is it possible to design parks that radiate a distinct atmosphere as a whole? How is it possible to create multilayered and multifaceted locations in a park structure that are also easy to read? And how can this readability of atmospheres be achieved? (Figures 14.4–14.10)

A short time ago, I visited a garden that Lawrence Johnston had created in the heart of England starting in 1907. There, Johnston had the individual garden spaces separated from one another by hedges taller than a man and correlated them by means of an elaborate structure of visual axes. In his garden, I would equate the individual spaces with atmospheres since there it is only possible to experience what is located within one hedged room. In a contemporary park, however, all the spaces cannot and should not be completely separated from one another. They should flow into each other. The atmosphere moreover changes through moving within the space. This flowing-into-one-another of spaces, for various reasons, makes it more difficult to create incisive locations since a changing and, therefore, hardly foreseeable range of stimuli influence the viewer.

framework   communication   ecology

Figure 14.4 Campbell barracks framework.
Campbell Barracks Heidelberg – A framework of different, identity-strong surfaces, characteristic vegetation and furniture that creates communication provides a framework for the user to take part in a variety of activities. In the negotiation of concrete content, participation in a participation process is desirable. The drafts are, thus, concertized cooperatively, directly at the site of the event and with the neighbors and users. There are flexible areas where appropriation is possible at any time. These areas are freely playable. The challenge is to create a balance between animation and appropriation. Therefore, it is more about curating functions – guiding and encouraging in order to anchor the design in the broad city public.

Figure 14.5 Campbell barracks detail.
Campbell Barracks Heidelberg – The preservation of historical monuments requires the *Paradeplatz* to be kept open. The small-scale setting achieves a balance between the requirements of monument conservation and everyday usability.

Figure 14.6 Campbell barrack stage and stands.
Campbell Barracks Heidelberg – People are to be brought together in the park. A feeling of social closeness and togetherness is to be created. To achieve this, it is necessary to promote communication in a targeted way and to create a feeling of togetherness. That is why large parts of the park are based on the stage-stand principle. This is how interaction and communication arise.

Figure 14.7 Campbell barracks location.
Campbell Barracks Heidelberg – The relics of military use will be integrated and, where possible, reinterpreted. For example, the former checkpoints will become meeting points in the park or a one-man-museum.

Figure 14.8 Campbell barracks program.
Campbell Barracks Heidelberg – Arranging offerings compactly within a hotspot is an expedient way to encourage interpersonal interaction and communication to develop. All the intensively programmed areas are also designed as stage and stands locations in order to intensify (visual) communication between visitors, the intensity of shared experiences, people putting themselves on show or observing, and the feeling of security.

Figure 14.9 Campbell barracks multilayered coding.
Campbell Barracks Heidelberg – Through clever positioning on-site this has the side effect of attracting people of different ages or particular uses that would otherwise not be found there. We have observed, for instance, that senior citizens are also drawn by the spectacular tricks of the skaters or the loud soccer and basketball matches and sit down in order to be part of things.

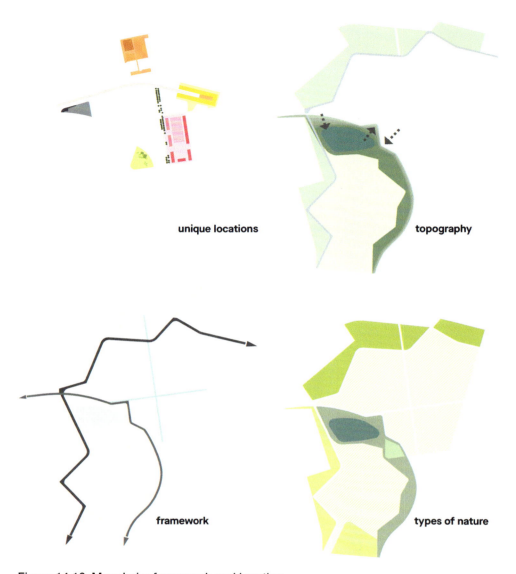

unique locations

topography

framework

types of nature

Figure 14.10 Mannheim framework and location.
Green Belt Mannheim – With the closure of the barracks on the periphery of Mannheim, an enormous area was opened up which is to be developed into a green belt. Programs and localities will be created out of the relics and embedded in a framework of paths. Topography and various forms of nature support this spatial structure.

At this point, I would, therefore, like to introduce the German term *Gestaltungseinheit* (design unit). I understand this to mean that a location is designed with recognizably connected and consistent means. These mean clearly differ from the design units adjacent to them. Through structuring the atmospheres in the park into design units – effectively sub-atmospheres – the unit in which one finds oneself becomes the immediate atmosphere and the surrounding, clearly distinguishable units become an atmospheric backdrop.

Such structuring helps above all in getting a grip on large parks in terms of atmosphere. The atmospheric conciseness of a location as a whole is achieved through distinguishability and, thus, the readability of its individual design units. It should provide a clear design response to a location, its program, and the atmospheres envisaged. Moreover, the allocation of means within a design unit should be as simple as possible and as varied as necessary.

Figure 14.11 Mannheim program.
Green Belt Mannheim – Richness and openness characterize the landscape park. The individual hotspots ensure that the programs are concentrated. The facets of the park range from extensive biotopes to artificially sculpted spots.

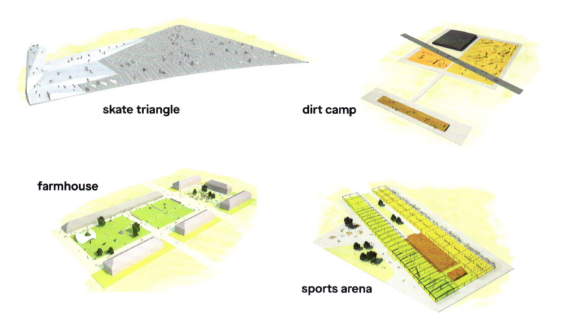

skate triangle

dirt camp

farmhouse

sports arena

Figure 14.12 Mannheim program.
Green Belt Mannheim – Strategically locating and arranging the offerings is essential to the success of a park. To create truly lively locations, it is necessary to concentrate offerings in hotspots. This concentration of offerings has two positive effects: It intensifies the active locations and relieves the calm ones. Park visitors, therefore, have a choice to communicate or remain on their own.

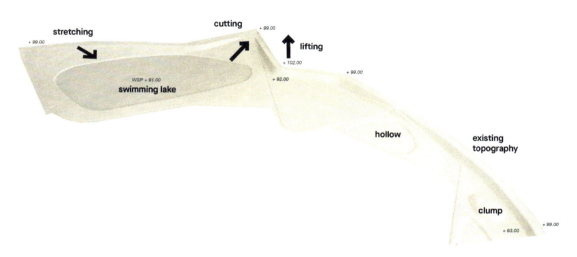

Figure 14.13 Mannheim scale.
Green Belt Mannheim – Using sand models, we simulate the topography and try out variations with our own hands. It is a very intuitive tool for designing complex situations.

Figure 14.14 Mannheim atmosphere.
Green Belt Mannheim – The large sand model can be further developed for simple perspectives. For the competition in Mannheim we built the topography with sand and rendered the object. This way of visualization allows a greater imagination. The image or design is still in a process.

Through limiting oneself to just a few, precise means, a location can develop a great vitality and simultaneously the presence required to awaken the desired acceptance, enthusiasm, and appropriation. Atmospheric intensity and acceptance ultimately encourage inter-personal communication (Figures 14.11–14.14).

Reference

[1] Böhme, Gernot (2006), *Architektur und Atmosphäre*, Munich. Page 26.

15

DISRUPTED DIGITAL FUTURES

The Rise of Speculative Digital Landscape Simulation in Conceptual Design

Aidan Ackerman

Conceptual design is an iterative process, repeatedly asking the fundamental question: *How should I evolve my design concept?* Yet, an equally important question is: *How will my design continue to evolve even after it is built?* This second question embraces change and uncertainty in landscape design, asking the designer to play with future possibilities and examine them over space and time. This is not a novel development – landscape architects have always incorporated impermanence into their conceptual design work. Any design which incorporates living systems must, by its very nature, be dynamic and flexible. By repositioning the landscape design process as "design with nature", Ian McHarg acknowledged the fundamental truth that landscape architects work not with the materiality of nature alone, but with its processes.[1] In *Plotting Time in Landscape Architecture*, Sonja Duempelmann and Susan Herrington argue that landscapes are themselves the "markers and makers of time".[2] This signifies a need to rethink the paradigm of iterative design; we must consider a landscape not merely as a singular space whose existence begins upon completion of construction, but rather as a complex collection of processes which evolve over time. Within this paradigm of *landscape as time*, I argue that we can embrace this complexity through incorporating digital simulation at the earliest possible point in the conceptual design process.

Digital simulations at the earliest stages of the design process can take the form of animations, fabricated models, virtual reality simulations, and other visualization techniques which allow the designer to visualize alternative environmental scenarios and their outcomes across space and time.[3] Contrary to the notion that the design process might become inhibited by data overload and complex calculations, computational tools have enabled experimentation

[1] McHarg, 1969. McHarg's seminal text introduced a method of layering complex spatial data and its processes to determine a site's suitability.

[2] Duempelmann and Herrington, 2014. Here the fundamental link between time and the landscape is framed through numerous lenses, suggesting that if the landscape is itself allows us to experience and trace time.

[3] Cureton, 2017. This primer on digital landscape design theory and technique offers a thorough overview of the many ways landscape architects use visual media for communication and iteration.

DOI: 10.4324/9781003053255-18

Figure 15.1 Reforestation composite.
Renderings of stages of landscape reforestation were created in Lumion using the built-in tree library coupled with custom ground textures. The three images were overlaid in Photoshop with transparency and offset alignment in order to communicate the passage of time within one image.

and freedom in the design process. The firm Nervous System creates data-derived tangible products such as wearable jewelry and home furnishings inspired by ecology. Landscape firms such as Peg Office use software simulation of complex ecological systems to produce a range of future scenarios, resulting in sophisticated visualization of landscape potential. The visual output of digital landscape simulation tends to exist as multiples, rather as discrete representations of states at moments in time, or as one model or image that compresses multiple moments into a singular visualization. In this work, the primacy of the fixed image representing a single state is replaced by multiform, variegated, composite image making (Figure 15.1).

The inherent complexity of this image making requires a particular partnership between the designer and the computer, recognizing the strengths of each. As analog beings, humans are exceptionally good at contextualizing information. We possess social systems, cultural knowledge, value systems, and the ability to understand how small differences signify large changes, as well as the ways in which these all impact how individuals and groups process visual information.[4] However, humans are not adept at manipulating and recombining large amounts of data. Landscape simulation is a cyclical process that requires millions of calculations of potential steps forward in space and time, exploring possibilities too vast to be captured by analog effort alone. This is where computation steps in, as it can expedite the creation of variations showing the range of possibilities contained in a natural system's observed behavior in an infinitesimal fraction of the time it would take even

[4] Mcwhinnie et al., 1970. This text investigates how people in different cultures around the world do not interpret geometric illusions identically, because of how inference habits are learned differently across societies.

Figure 15.2 Reforestation early.
A rendering of the earliest stage of reforestation was created in Lumion, using the built-in tree library and custom textures for the tire-marked ground surface. 3D models of the stumps were taken from photogrammetry of actual tree stumps. The composition of the image was created based on actual forestry monitoring data and photographs.

[5] Ervin, 2018. Three different modes of computational interaction used by landscape architects are explored: landscapes designed with computation, without computation, and aided by computation.
[6] Gigerenzer, 1987. Cognitive processes and their origin in statistics are discussed, particularly intuition and intelligence.

the most well-trained human brain. The role of the designer then becomes distant from the data-processing endeavor: we decide the data inputs, and we evaluate the outputs. Eventually, we arrive at a design solution that is inherently human yet aided by, as Stephen Ervin writes in *Codify*, the "heavy math" of computational fluid dynamics calculations or the generation of multiple formal solutions for evaluation.[5] At this point, we are no longer designing just landscapes, but rather designing systems of evaluation and prediction that will allow us to design landscapes with more contextual information, to go beyond given information to infer conceptual meaning (Figures 15.2–15.4).[6]

I call this process *speculative digital landscape simulation*. As a conceptual design approach, speculative digital landscape simulation requires a fascination with identifying the underlying algorithmic logic of a landscape – the code of some particular natural landscape formation – and then developing a workflow to enact that code upon a digitized physical space. The workflow to generate a digital simulation of a natural system is then set loose to play itself out over a length of time and expanse of space. This is an open-ended, organic process that can yield surprises with every iteration, standing in contrast to the relative predictability of architectural performance simulation. This predictability stems from the

Figure 15.3 Reforestation mid.
A rendering of a midpoint phase of reforestation was created in Lumion, using the built-in tree and plant library. 3D grass textures were applied to the ground to mimic the sparse grass beginning to fill in the cleared area. The composition of the image was created based on actual forestry monitoring data and photographs.

Figure 15.4 Reforestation advanced.
A rendering of a midpoint phase of reforestation was created in Lumion, using the built-in tree and plant library. The use of atmospheric illumination shows the limited light filtering through the forest canopy, indicating an advanced stage of forest canopy regeneration. The composition of the image was created based on actual forestry monitoring data and photographs.

idea that designers are generally able to accurately forecast the service life prediction of manufactured materials and their applications.[7] We do not possess this same command over natural systems. Our knowledge of the natural world is derivative; it emerges not from invention but from study and observation. This limit to our "knowability" of natural elements means that our ability to design with them comes from direct experience. If we wish to design intuitively with natural elements in all their complexity, we need digital tools that predictively model landscape futures. The designer must then decide if they are comfortable with the leap of faith necessary to design based on simulation. Can we reliably channel data to behave in ways that elucidate ecological patterns? Can we take individual data points and make them converge to indicate the forces and interactions which create ecological processes?[8]

The answer might be simpler than we think. We can consider our visual perception of natural systems to rely on a shorthand, or heuristic, which for the most part can correctly identify patterns in nature. Knowing this, we might give ourselves permission to trust our instincts about whether our natural systems simulations "look right", with the assurance that the instinct's underlying rationale will reliably point us in the right direction most of the time. Humans rely on visual heuristics to navigate much of their surroundings, often in ways that appear to be based on intuition rather than reason. The human eye and brain are remarkably adept at processing and evaluating visual information from our environments. Take, for example, the *gaze heuristic*, in which humans interact with moving objects, such as catching a ball, based on nothing more than adjusting their position to keep their eye uniformly trained on a moving object.[9] This heuristic does not require that the ball catcher calculate the velocity, distance, and angle of the ball but instead employs guiding principles inherited by humans over thousands of years of evolution. Many other examples exist, such as the ways that humans are remarkably skilled at visually identifying materials and their properties (whether they are real or rendered), immediately distinguishing similar-looking materials such as soap and pate.[10] A phenomenon called the Uncanny Valley allows humans to excel at identifying when a simulation of a human being is incorrect, and the smaller the aberration – such as a slightly delayed movement of the mouth when speaking – the more something appears strange to the observer.[11] As in assessing the physical world and simulated humans, these cognitive phenomena indicate that we can trust our instincts when evaluating simulations and renderings of natural environments. Additionally, the more realistic the visuals appear, the greater the chances the designer has of forming instinctual reactions based on cognitive heuristics. Lastly, our ability to visually assess simulations of natural systems, refining them until they look as though they behave correctly, is strong enough that we can comfortably incorporate speculative simulation in conceptual design (Figures 15.5–15.7).

[7] Masters and Brandt, 1989. This paper proposes a systematic method for evaluating the period of time after building materials are used where they perform their intended function.

[8] MCloskey and VanDerSys, 2017. An exploration of innovations in how landscape architects engaging with patterns using digital media.

[9] Gigerenzer, 2008. An exploration of intuition as an evolved, neurologically based behavior that enables rapid response in humans when faced with a problem.

[10] Fleming, 2014. A study of how the human brain uses generative models to visually infer actual physical parameters from images.

[11] Mori, 1970. Mori first hypothesized that the uncanny valley is an emotional response to an object's resemblance to a human. The viewer's feelings of revulsion or strangeness is directly related to the degree to which a humanoid resembles an actual human being. The imperfections of simulated humanoids become increasingly apparent with movement, meaning that animation and robotics are especially likely to cause viewers to experience the uncanny valley.

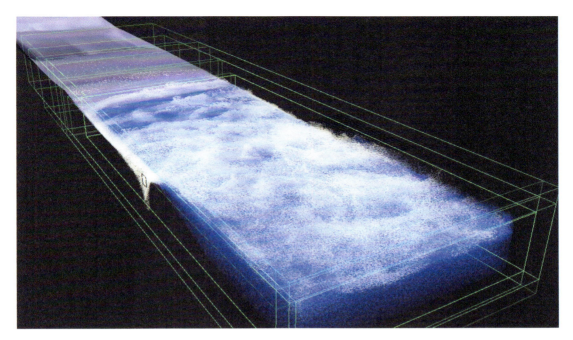

Figure 15.5 Wave overlays.
Using Bifröst, the Autodesk Maya fluid simulation engine, waves were animated to crash on a shoreline section of Misquamicut Beach, Rhode Island. These waves accurately mimic the direction, height, and force of a Category 1 Hurricane based on historic data from NOAA. Frames from the animation were captured and transparently overlaid in Photoshop, drawing out the patterns that can be found in the waves' continual movement towards and away from shore.

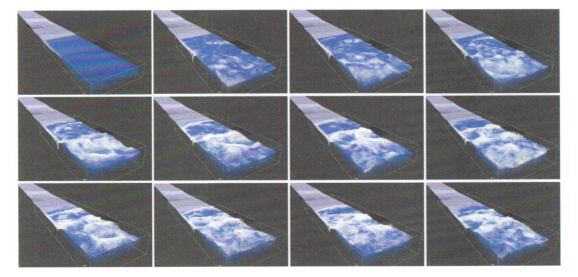

Figure 15.6 Frames from wave animation.
Using Bifröst, the Autodesk Maya fluid simulation engine, waves were animated to crash on a shoreline section of Misquamicut Beach, Rhode Island. These waves accurately mimic the direction, height, and force of a Category 1 Hurricane based on historic data from NOAA. Frames from the animation were captured and laid out in a grid to illustrate the progression of the waves' movement towards and away from shore.

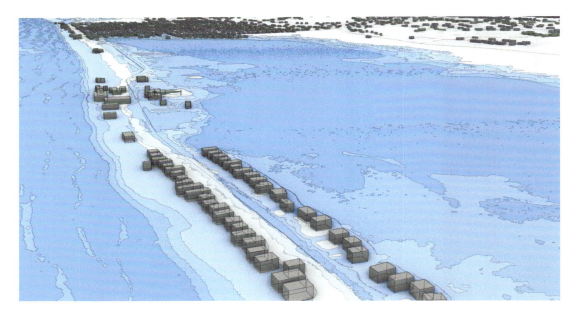

Figure 15.7 Erosion and sea level rise.
A Digital Elevation Model (DEM) of Misquamicut Beach, Rhode Island was imported into Photoshop using the geographic Imager plugin, which enables geospatial image editing in Photoshop. The DEM was then edited four times with brush tools to gradually erase the shoreline to simulate erosion, using Geographic Imager's measurement tools to ensure accurate erasure. Each DEM was then exported to Rhino and rendered as a three-dimensional view. Each view was then overlaid with transparency in Photoshop, allowing a single image to communicate the dramatic decrease in the shoreline and its impact on existing buildings.

Speculative digital landscape simulations can be seductive, and we might find ourselves failing to question the validity of the simulations we create. However, we must also acknowledge that even the most powerful of algorithms will be unlikely to perfectly predict the future of a landscape's ecological development. The chances that we will happen to model an exact future scenario are incalculably small. Humbly accepting this is a challenge. Humans have never had so much information at our disposal, so many open-source options such as Grasshopper or Processing to input complex variables and receive hundreds of possible outcomes in visual format. We can produce digital patterns based on ecological data which can be used as computational design fabric, with which we can assemble form and process as animated growth, movement, change, and regeneration. We might be able to convincingly model a plant bending in the wind, a series of waves on a shoreline, a leaf uncurling as a branch extends; and to simulate natural relationships: to generate a Perlin noise terrain, to make a bunch of polygons flock using attractors. These real-looking, growing, swaying, flowing, complex natural landscapes created from algorithms provide us with a shorthand for the underlying behavioral complexity of natural systems, which are infinitely too complex to categorize and replicate.

We are far better off with speculative digital simulation of landscape design than we are without it, for it offers the designer *more*. When we depict something, we are forced to confront and investigate it. The more we can visualize, the more we can interrogate what we have visualized for its accuracy, potential, and viability. The very act of simulating the landscape demands that we have access to more: that we import the most data, as frequently as possible, form this data into the most complex geometry possible without crashing the computer, populate the largest possible surface area of the landscape, show the landscape changing over

Figure 15.8 Orbes fantasia ice world.
An invented landscape of frozen ice floes, visualized as a barren planet and an intimate physical landscape. The planet and the landscape were modeled in 3ds Max, textured in Photoshop, and animated in Lumion.

as long a time period as possible, and include as many alternative scenarios as we possibly can. In pursuing this future, we must keep in mind that more information does not necessarily lead to more predictable design outcomes; rather, it allows us to pursue design avenues that otherwise would be unavailable. More information can, if unchecked, paralyze the creative senses, but it can also open the door to freedom from entrenched design processes which lead to uninspiring projects. Design with data and applied with heuristics can allow us to connect factual information with our deepest design instincts, fostering a true marriage of the analytical and the intuitive. The rise of speculative digital landscape

Figure 15.9 Orbes fantasia tree world.
An invented landscape of oversize trees and futuristic buildings, visualized as a lush planet and an intimate physical landscape. The planet and the landscape were modeled in 3ds Max, textured in Photoshop, and animated in Lumion.

simulation in conceptual design promises to wake us up from a stupor of predictability, injecting fresh information and thoroughly disrupting our collective sense of how to move through a design project. The projects produced with these tools will be phenomenally creative and ingenious. The design world eagerly awaits (Figures 15.8 and 15.9).

References

Cureton, Paul. *Strategies for Landscape Representation: Digital and Analogue Techniques*. London: Routledge, 2017.

Duempelmann, Sonja, and Susan Herrington. "Plotting Time in Landscape Architecture." *Studies in the History of Gardens & Designed Landscapes* 34, no. 1 (2014): 1–14.

Ervin, Stephen. "Turing Landscapes." In *Codify: Parametric and Computational Design in Landscape Architecture*, by Bradley Cantrell and Adam Mekies, London: Routledge, 2018, pp. 89–115.

Fleming, Roland W. "Visual Perception of Materials and Their Properties." *Vision Research* 94 (2014): 62–75.

Gigerenzer, Gerd. *Cognition as Intuitive Statistics*. Hillsdale, NJ: L. Erlbaum Associates, 1987.

Gigerenzer, Gerd. *Gut Feelings: Short Cuts to Better Decision Making*. London: Penguin Books, 2008.

Masters, Larry W., and Erik Brandt. "Systematic Methodology for Service Life Prediction of Building Materials and Components." *Materials and Structures* 22, no. 5 (1989): 385–392.

MCloskey, Karen, and Keith VanDerSys. *Dynamic Patterns: Visualizing Landscapes in a Digital Age*. London: Routledge, Taylor & Francis Group, 2017.

McHarg, Ian. *Design with Nature*. Garden City, NY: Natural History Press, 1969.

Mcwhinnie, Harold J., Marshall Segall, Donald Campbell, and Merville Herskovits. "The Influence of Culture on Visual Perception." *Art Education* 23, no. 6 (1970): 30.

Mori, M. The Uncanny Valley. *Energy* 7 (1970): 33–35.

16

LANDSCAPE

"For Illustration Purposes Only"

Fadi Masoud

In small fine print, a cautionary text typically accompanies the rendering of a proposed housing development, public square, or waterfront park. They alert the observer that the images that they are examining are *"illustrations for artistic purposes only"* or that *"impressions in these representations are artist's interpretation only"*. It goes without saying that rendered images are the quintessential means for designers and their clients to communicate change in the environment to mass audiences; a critical tool for engaging reaction. "This may seem innocuous enough, but it does imply something peculiar about it, as though our reaction to the image is exchangeable with our perceptions of the world in a way it is not with other kinds of pictures" (Zerner, 1989). As if the insertion of that simple cautionary text averts the binding legality of these impending reactions. As if it allows for the disassociation with expectations of what is, what it portrays, and what is to be. These cautions simply and subliminally remind us that all images are artist's interpretations and all acts of looking are subject to embedded reactions engrained in our social, political, and intellectual conscience.

Like most design disciplines, landscape architecture is inherently tied to the processes, methods, and outcomes of its representation. The way we measure, perceive, design, and ultimately construct landscapes is intertwined with its various modes of representation and communication. Originating with the pictorial gaze that once dominated the image and perception of landscape through painting, the effects of technological advancement on landscape architecture are profound.

The conception of landscape as a form of visual representation, illustration, or image making is not far from a string of evolutionary associations with our perceptions of the visual experience, and their direct links with what exists, what is perceived, and what is proposed. Clear lineages have been drawn between the evolution of the profession of landscape architecture and the genre

DOI: 10.4324/9781003053255-19

Figure 16.1 Rendering by Paisajes Emergentes/LCLA "Parque del lago" Quito Airport Competition Proposal (2008).

of landscape painting that emerged in highly urbanized parts of Europe. With a surplus of labor and income in an urbanizing continent, a loss of direct relation with the idea of perceived "nature" began taking hold with the "urban elites" and artists. Painters, and later photographers, chose to represent a cultural construct of what they perceived the landscape "out there" to be. The invention of mediating devices for vision such as the Claude glass and the stereoscope dating from the 18th and 19th centuries was intended to manipulate vision, creating both a frame and an atmosphere for a particular landscape in order to generate a specific experience for the viewer (Harris and Ruggles, 2007). Making it clear the intention of the distortion of accuracy and reality for the sake of artistic representation and illustration (Figure 16.1).

Many generations later, and through technological advancements, these types of images continue to surface in the photography of people like Ansel Adams and the Sierra Club Calendars. With a notable absence of human presence, "out there" the landscape is shown as a primeval place of enchantment and contemplation rather than a place of habitation. Zerner (1989) reiterates Ruskin's 1859 review

> … for the first time in history, we have, by help of art the power of visiting a place, reasoning about it, and knowing it, just as if we were there - except only that we cannot stir from out place, nor look behind us.

These images articulated positions in space and the perception of space by a human viewer. They presented an important opportunity to reconsider landscape as neither an object nor a contextual field but as always simultaneously both (Harris and Ruggles, 2007).

While the earlier associations with painting led to the ideas of the Picturesque in landscape design, "the Picturesque becomes a mode of composition that stands next to nature, but does not imagine it is natural. By choosing to represent nature in three-dimensions, to make an artefact that employs natural elements or the appearance of natural forces, it does not convey nature directly" (Robinson, 1991). This is where the distinction between the predisposition of representations of Landscape as an "image" or "illustration" stand in contrast to the ideas of the future of landscape as a field of design and intervention. In paintings, the landscape's elements (water, geology, light, vegetation) have always existed in absence of all forms of human management and design. Even when human habitation or occupation is evident in those paintings, they seemed subservient and passive, and rarely propositional (Harris and Ruggles, 2007). Today's pictorial renderings stand in sharp contrast to primarily show human agency, while the preexisting context evolves to both inform it and then to absorb it (Figures 16.2–16.4).

It is in the moment of intervention that image-making, painting, photomontage, and photography become a tool for an artist's interpretative illustration of human's transformation – rather than an artist's interpretation of what simply "exists". In his essay titled Flatness (2007), Adriaan Geueze points to remarkable parallels between paintings of the Dutch landscape and the polders that make the nation habitable; where one and the other are hard to distinguish. Making no clear distinctions between artificially manipulated landscapes and the natural context it sits in. These were representations of landscape that were motivated from the outset by intellectual, cultural, or political investments made harder to divorce from the viewer's own subjectivity.

By the end of the 20th century computer generated renderings, that in their own way evolved from painting, collage, and photography, become the predominate way to show and emphasize proposed alteration of a site. Critical to the photorealism generated, is that it no longer ingrained in society's psyche the notion that landscape is preexisting and primordial – but a precursor to a new altered and projective reality that is yet to come. Now more than ever, the adoption and application of these new digital technologies in

Figure 16.2 Humphry Repton (1792) Humphry Repton, Mosely (sic) Hall near Birmingham, a seat of John Taylor. Album with ink and watercolor, 22.2 × 29.2 × 1.3 cm.

Figures 16.3, and 16.4 John Nolen: Menton, la Promenade du midi – Nice, France (1908). John Nolen Papers, #2903. Division of Rare and Manuscript Collections, Cornell University Library.

Figure 16.5 Lake/City/Horizon, Töölönlahti Park, Helsinki, 1997. Photomontage, 35.6 × 55.9 cm. Photo credit: James Corner.

landscape representation has become too standardized and simplified. Interfacing with technological platforms requires little mathematical knowledge and the software is highly accessible and customizable. New technologies are applied regularly to modify and enhance the experience of landscapes as well as to increase understanding analysis. Beyond merely digitizing a formerly analogue design process, technology is now an essential tool used in the creative process, helping landscape architects navigate complex sites and multifaceted design requirements.[1] A criticism of the advent of digital representation is the transformation of the role of representation from one that is exploratory and experimental to one that is either technical or illustrative. "With the rise of technology, drawing as a significant architectural act withered away. From the mid-'90s onward … the act of drawing became increasingly anachronistic" (Walliss and Rahmann, 2016).

Technology enabled the creation of drawings that are infinitely more precise, but also more standardized. The vast processing powers of render software enabled landscape architects to generate images at speeds that subsumed the "drawing as design and design through the drawing process" as Walliss and Rahmann (2016) described it. This also created a generic-ness in the form of photorealistic photomontaged images. Resulting in a type

[1] By the end of 2022, Text to Image deep learning algorithms, through general artificial intelligence, have begun to profoundly change the conversation around digital representation and image creation - its full impact on landscape architecture is yet to unfold.

of "authored anonymousness in the representation of landscape works by flatting contexts, sites, and ultimately designs. Speed in production rather than ingenuity in the creative process became the name of the game" (Masoud et al, 2023).

A return to the architectural drawing style began to appear in the works of many design offices and creative practices as photorealism fatigue became evident, toward the end of 2010.

The post-digital drawing renders space and experience with similar format and conceptualization to paintings from Hockney to Sheeler, and the method of landscape photocollage evident in work as early as from Repton (1792) to John Nolan's 1908 European travels. This was masterfully documented by Waldheim and Hansen in Composite Landscapes Photomontage and Landscape Architecture book and exhibition (2015). Where we see clear parallels between photomontage and the "post-digital's" embryotic influences in the contemporary work of landscape architects. Drawings by James Corner (1990's), MVVA (1997), Cormier (2015) lacked "precision", but played a fundamental role in using drawing as design "device". Freed from the illusion of impending realism and exact implementation also made them timeless (Figure 16.5).

> Instead of striving for pseudo-photo-realism, this new cult of drawing explores and exploits its artificiality, making us as viewers aware that we are looking at space as a fictional form of representation. This is in strict opposition to the digital rendering's desire to make the fiction seem 'real'.
>
> (Walliss and Rahmann, 2016)

Even though the return of drawing in the digital age is a "reinvigoration of the tradition of drawing", its techniques, tools, and media make it fundamentally new. Drawing in infinite space, in multiple dimensions on a screen with pixels is technically and conceptually different from drawing on paper (Jacob, 2017). Drawing digitally has also meant that landscape architects have access to an infinite web-repository of images and precedents, in addition to real-time data, metrics, and feedback responses (Masoud et al, 2023). Jacob (2017) states that through the screen, the designer is "vibrantly connected to the world". In that context, individuality and originality in representation is a sign of creative identity and attainment. Ghosh (2018) critiques this phenomenon as "merely substituting one base form of representation with another, one set of smooth algorithmic processes for another". (Figures 16.6–16.7).

Maybe then the cautionary texts below design renderings serve to remind us that the representation of what exists and what is proposed could not be regarded as a fixed and neutral; but a complex relationship among the artist, their modes and methods of representation, its audience, and the work itself. Each playing a role

Figure 16.6 Fionn Byrne (Sulfer Pyramid).

Figure 16.7 Claude Cormier, Garrison Point with Toronto Skyline over
David Hockney's 'Paper Pool 25,' 2013.

Figures 16.8 and 16.9 Michel Desvigne Paysagiste Parco Centrale in Prato, Italy (2016).

Figure 16.10 Bonnie Tung, Likun Lu, Alexandre DosSantons - SuParkbia (2020).

Figure 16.11 Ambika Pharma and Hillary DeWildt - SuParkbia (2020).

Figure 16.12 Monica Hutton – The Everglades (2017) – MIT Seeking Resilience in South Florida Studio – Instructors: Fadi Masoud, Miho Mazereeuw.

and a position, all aspects of which are unstable, interdependent, and as Harris and Ruggles (2007) assert "continuously articulating some kind of power" (Figures 16.8–16.12).

References

Ghosh, Swarnbh. "Can't Be Bothered: The Chic Indifference of Post-Digital Drawing." *Metropolis*, August 1, 2018. https://www.metropolismag.com/architecture/postdigital-drawing-aesthetic/.

Geuze, Adriaan, "Flatness." *Mosaics*, ed. West8 (Basel: Birkhäuser, 2007).

Harris, Dianne and D. Fairchild Ruggles, "Landscape and Vision," *Sites Unseen: Landscape and Vision*, ed. Dianne Harris and D. Fairchild Ruggles (Pittsburgh: University of Pittsburgh Press, 2007), 5–29.

Jacob, Sam. "Architecture Enters the Age of Post-Digital Drawing." *Metropolis Magazine*, March 21, 2017. http://www.metropolismag.com/architecture/architecture-enters-age-post-digital-drawing/.

Masoud, Fadi, Matthew Spremulli, Shadi Ramos. "Technology Driven Shift in the Digital Representation of Landscape Architecture" in *Innate Terrain*: ed. Alissa North. (Toronto: University of Toronto Press, 2023), 253–275.

Robinson, Sidney K. "Artifice," *Inquiry into the Picturesque* (Chicago: University of Chicago Press, 1991), 93–116.

Waldheim, Charles, Andrea Hansen, *Composite Landscapes: Photomontage and Landscape Architecture* (Boston: Isabella Stewart Gardner Museum, 2014).

Walliss, Jillian and Heike Rahmann, *Landscape Architecture and Digital Technologies: Re-conceptualising Design and Making* (New York: Routledge, 2016).

Zerner, Henri. "On Landscape," *Rudolf L. Baumfeld Collection of Landscape Drawings and Prints* (Los Angeles: The Grunwald Center for the Graphic Arts, 1989), 29–32.

17

CONCEPTUALIZING THE DESIGN OF FLUID GEOGRAPHIES

Kees Lokman

This short essay is structured in two parts. The first part outlines my perspective on the role of the conceptual design process in generating design interventions (futures). Part two describes modes of representation and design approaches that challenge the dichotomy between land and water—generating new understandings and imaginations of water as a framework for design. Taken together, this contribution repositions water from *a matter of fact* to *a matter of concern*—a basis for conceptualizing hybrid and dynamic environments.[1]

Conceptual Design

"Design is a reflective practice in which critical assessment, comparability and evaluation takes place through ... the continual weaving between problem and solution in an iterative movement between inquiry and proposal."[2]—Roggema (2017). Design is a fluid and iterative process. It is both an object of study and a process to implement this study.[3] Research is a critical component of the design process, involving inquiries into the cultural, social–ecological, spatial, aesthetic, and ethical issues of places as well as the testing and development of design methods, protocols, and approaches. Drawings and models are arguably the most important tools for designers. They not only communicate how we understand the world but also provide a platform for the generation and representation of ideas and solutions. Collectively, these tools and techniques enable unique "designerly ways of knowing."[4]

The conceptual design phase engages modes and methods that orient towards the future by simultaneously providing descriptions of what exists and what is envisioned. Throughout this process, designers are asked to position themselves in relation to the site, and to other humans, nonhumans, and things. Here, drawing and modelmaking—both analogue and digital—enable the manifestation of new insights into relationships between the seen and unseen, myth and materiality, the past and present, all the while indicating potentials for future interventions.

[1] Latour, Bruno. 2004. "Why Has Critique Run Out of Steam? From Matters of Fact to Matters of Concern." Critical Inquiry 30 (2): 225–248.

[2] Roggema, R. *Research by Design: Proposition for a Methodological Approach.* Urban Sci. 2017, 1, 2. https://doi.org/10.3390/urbansci1010002

[3] Glanville, Ranulph. 1999. "Researching Design and Designing Research." *Design Issues* 15 (2): 80–91. doi:10.2307/1511844.

[4] Cross, Nigel, ed. 1984. *Developments in Design Methodology*. Chichester: John Wiley & Sons.

DOI: 10.4324/9781003053255-20

These *projective moments* of the design process, as Martin Prominski calls them, are key in framing certain assumptions and premises—pointing to potential design directions and actions.[5] In my teaching, I emphasize the importance of moving (quickly) between sketches and concept models to digitized drawings, animations, and scaled models, in order to uncover and reformulate physical and symbolic layers of hybrid water/land environments. Understood as working documents—constantly updated, clarified, and refined over the course of the design process—drawings and models have the ability to transform, juxtapose, and choreograph multiple subjects and sources of information into new figures, scales, and coordinates. It is through this continual process of investigation, discovery, and re-representation that landscapes derive meaning and new knowledge of the built environment is produced (Figures 17.1–17.3).[6]

[5] Prominski, Martin. 2019. "Design Research as a Non-Linear Interplay." In Prominski, Martin and Hille von Seggern (eds.), *Design Research for Urban Landscapes: Theories and Methods*. New York; Abingdon; Oxon: Routledge, pp. 33–49.
[6] Corner, James. 1999. "The Agency of Mapping: Speculation, Critique and Invention." In Denis Cosgrove (ed.), *Mappings*. London: Reaktion Books, pp. 213–252.

Figure 17.1 Map model.
This interactive model has three components. The three stacked plexiglass layers up top reflect changing shoreline (at mean sea level) conditions in 1900, 1940, and 1980. Then there are three plexiglass squares (one each for 1900, 1940, and 1980) that show a section of the shoreline in more detail by highlighting land uses, transportation, buildings, and so on. The bottom part shows a prototypical photograph taken at the site, again referencing 1900 (bottom left), 1940 (middle), and 1980 (bottom right). Taken together, the model allows users to play around with the plexiglass squares, either placing them in relation to the changing shoreline conditions, or atop of the photographs. Different time periods can be stacked, thereby collapsing time as well as prompting questions as to how the site might, or could, evolve in the future. (Model by Sam Luo, Shavonne Yu, Yang Lee).

Figure 17.2 Before/after flood.
Similar to how Humphry Repton drew the existing scenery on folded flaps, which could be lifted to reveal the proposed design interventions underneath, this model uses simple frames with inserts to reveal how sea level rise may affect the study area in the future. The eye-level perspective allows for an exploration of different aspects of the site, while the inserts make it clear which buildings and landscape elements will potentially be lost. The model set the stage for an urban proposal that embraced the dynamics of flooding. (Model by Sam Luo, Shavonne Yu, Yang Lee).

Photography, perspective composites, video work, (section) models, diagrams, or map overlays all enable different ways to represent and explore how space is connected to, and inhabited by, social and ecological processes that register across multiple spatial and temporal scales. Where the open-ended format of mapping allows for interpretative readings of spatial patterns, logics and social–ecological processes, physical models, on the other hand, enable a different way of knowledge creation and sharing. As Paul Cureton explains, "the feedback from touch and working of materials and the responses it provides has a particular agency and heuristic; a way of learning through making."[7]

[7] Cureton, Paul. 2016. *Strategies for Landscape Representation: Digital and Analogue Techniques*. London: Routledge.

By moving between spatial and temporal scales as well as between concrete and abstract representations of the site, new insights, spatial knowledge, and potential interventions come to the fore. This spatial knowledge ranges from specific site strategies to those

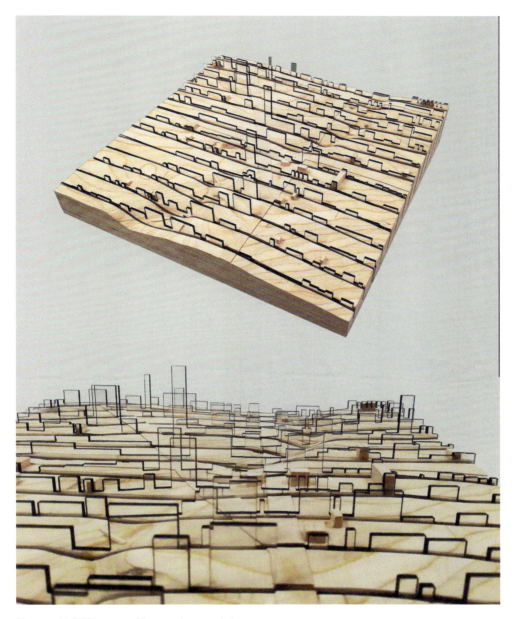

Figure 17.3 Topographic overlay model.
This base (wood) of this CNC milled model shows the topography which features a prominent creek, as well as a road system and number of buildings that were present at this area in Vancouver in the late 1800s. The acrylic section insets illustrate the existing conditions of the site; the creek is filled in and regraded, while the area has developed in a high-density neighborhood. The model not only reveals how much the landscape has changed, it also questions what future relationships—both tangible and intangible—can be developed between the buried creek and the urban fabric. (Model by Sarah Baxendale, Jordan Haylor, Veronica Troughton).

[8] Deming, M. Elen and Simon R. Swaffield. 2011. *Landscape Architecture Research: Inquiry, Strategy, Design*. 1st ed. Hoboken, NJ: Wiley.

[9] Wood, Denis and John Fels. 2008. *The Natures of Maps: Cartographic Constructions of the Natural World*. Chicago: University of Chicago Press.

[10] Kwan, Mei-Po, 2015. "Critical Visualization in Landscape and Urban Planning: Making the Invisible Visible." *Landscape and Urban Planning* 142: 243–244.

[11] Lahiri-Dutt, Kuntala. 2014. "Beyond the Water-Land Binary in Geography: Water/lands of Bengal Re-Visioning Hybridity." *ACME: An International E-Journal for Critical Geographies* 13 (3): 505–529.

[12] Mathur, Anuradha, Dilip da Cunha. 2014. *Design in the Terrain of Water*. Applied Research + Design Publishing with the University of Pennsylvania School of Design.

[13] Karr, J. R., and I. J. Schlosser (1978). "Water Resources and the Land-Water Interface." *Science* 201 (4352): 229–234.

that can be scaled up and/or replicated elsewhere. As suggested by Deming and Swaffield, "there is a clear difference between finding a specific design solution to a situated problem and identifying a general principle that may reliably and clearly inform others in [the] future."[8]

Finally, drawings and models are never neutral: they represent particular ways of seeing—framing specific arguments and perspectives.[9] For designers, it is critical to recognize *who, what,* and *why* certain perspectives (human and/or nonhuman) and values are foregrounded and prioritized. At the same time, this opens up possibilities for activism and public engagement. As suggested by Kwan, critical modes of representation "not only enables us to see how social injustices were obfuscated; it also seeks to challenge and transform the prevalent dynamics of social power with the hope of bringing forth progressive change."[10] As such, (conceptual) design is much more than the creation of visual products but instead a process of engaging the cognitive, social, cultural, and political realms of spatial practice (Figures 17.4–17.6).

Fluid Geographies

"… apparent hard edges are the historical product of a determined effort to imagine lines where none exist and then to make them survive in the face of an aqueous terrain which constantly defeats their materiality"[11]—Lahiri-Dutt, Kuntala (2014). The work in this section explores the histories, materiality, fluidity, and temporality of water. In a sense, it fundamentally confronts the definition of term *land*scape architecture, which inherently suggests prioritizing *terra firma* over the spatial, temporal, and social–ecological complexities of fluid geographies—including oceans, rivers, estuaries, swamps, and rain. The work is informed by literature and conceptual frameworks that seek to oppose the binaries of land/water, wet/dry, permanent/temporary, and so on. The emphasis shifts from describing clear boundaries between where the water 'stops' and the land 'starts,' to imagining and visualizing *gradients* and *hybrid relationships* as a means the interrogate the dynamic and ever-changing conditions of land–water interfaces (Figures 17.7 and 17.8).

Mathur and Da Cuna, among others, have long explored the notion of "water as a ground in design."[12] This involves investigating the ubiquitous, transient, and cultural presence of water—from the inherent connections between rain and rivers, or the ever-changing hydromorphological conditions of deltas. These spatial conditions are a result of the complex interplay of biological, geological, chemical, physical, and social phenomena in both terrestrial and aquatic environments.[13] Consequently, the work in this section asks: How can we visualize, celebrate, materialize, and politicize the presence of water in all its forms and functions? How can water become the basis of a new imagination of spatial environments?

Figure 17.4 Temporal renderings.
Landscapes are ever-changing and always in flux. Photomontage provides a relatively quick and effective way of showing how landscapes change over both short and long periods of time—due to maintenance, seasonal variations, or as a result of floods or other extreme events. This series of collages explores how periodic flooding can affect/enable different landscape functions. The series of drawings on the right, for example, shows how a single site can accommodate a range of programs, including recreation, agricultural use, and temporary flood storage. The perspective 3d wireframe is created in Rhino; textures and entourage are added in Photoshop. (Drawings by Emily Chen).

Water is also at the center of many contemporary challenges and conflicts, including flooding, water scarcity, water pollution, aquifer depletion, and water rights, to name just a few. In order to create insight and solutions to these issues requires examining relationships that bring together the large and small, the near and far, and the weak and strong.[14] Moving from the watershed planning to the redesign of a street section, it is essential to explore "ways in which

[14] Lahoud, Adrian. 2016. "Scale as Problem, Architecture as Trap." In *Climates: Architecture and the Planetary Imaginary*. New York: Columbia Books on Architecture and the City, p. 85.

Figure 17.5 Managed retreat.
Rather than drawing a series of phasing diagrams, it is also possible to tell a story within one drawing. This section perspective tells a story of what managed retreat in a specific section along a river may look like. The drawing shows removal of armored edges in favor of habitat restoration. Moreover, houses in the floodplain are demolished and rebuild on higher ground. This section perspective combines elements drawn in Rhino with textures and entourage arranged in Photoshop. (Drawing by Sam McFaul).

Figure 17.6 Mining futures.
Sometimes, it is necessary to boil down an idea to its pure essence. These physical concept models do just that. One illustrates the planting of grids of willow trees in mine tailings ponds to remove heavy metals and hydrocarbons from the soil. The other speaks to an idea of redesigning haul roads of abandoned surface mines to swales in order to manage water runoff and contamination. Models are accompanied by "New Yorker-style" illustrations. Neither lose-reality nor hyper realistic, these drawings enable loose narratives that still leave room for imagination. They combine clean lines, subtle color fields while hinting at spatial and aesthetic qualities. The physical models were created with plexiglass, wood, and Styrofoam. The drawings were created in Illustrator. (Models and drawings by Lee Patola and Shaheed Karim).

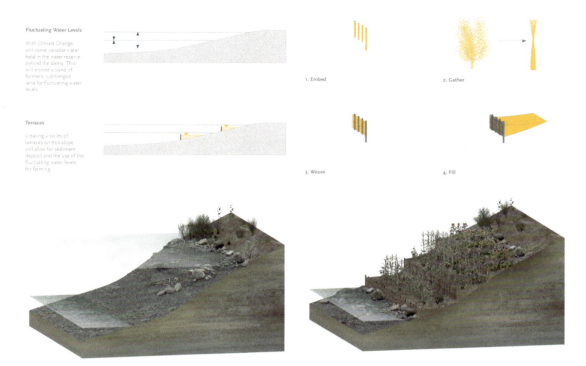

Figure 17.7 Reservoir edge terraces.
Climate change will have profound effects on the land–water interfaces along coastal conditions, rivers, lakes, and reservoirs. This provides necessities and opportunities for new design explorations. This series of drawings supposes that water levels of reservoirs in the Missouri River will drop, thereby exposing a new strip of land. Simple techniques, such as willow wattle fences, could be used to catch and retain sediment—over time creating a terrace system that can be used for agricultural practices. Line work drawings are created in Illustrator. The illustrative sections perspectives are created in Photoshop. (Drawing by Sam McFaul).

history shaped and intertwined human lives, lands, and waters at different geographical scales."[15] Sea level rise and coastal habitat squeeze is impacting migratory pathways of birds and fish species. Upstream dams hold back sediments critical for coastal wetlands and other intertidal ecosystems. Agricultural runoff (including nitrogen and phosphorus) causes nutrient pollution and hypoxic (low-oxygen zones) at the mouth of rivers. Combined sewer overflows impact water quality, beaches, and public health. Suffice to say: water is the common denominator and we need to develop a transdisciplinary and multiscalar approach to envision alternative land–water interfaces.

The discipline of landscape architecture is uniquely positioned to contribute to ongoing experimentation, conceptualization, and creation of methods, frameworks, and approaches that explore the perception and material conditions of water/lands. The fact that landscape architects are generalists with the ability to frame positions from multiple perspectives allows for a deeper, more

[15] Lahiri-Dutt, Kuntala. 2014. "Beyond the Water-Land Binary in Geography: Water/lands of Bengal Re-Visioning Hybridity." *ACME: An International E-Journal for Critical Geographies*, 13 (3): 505–529.

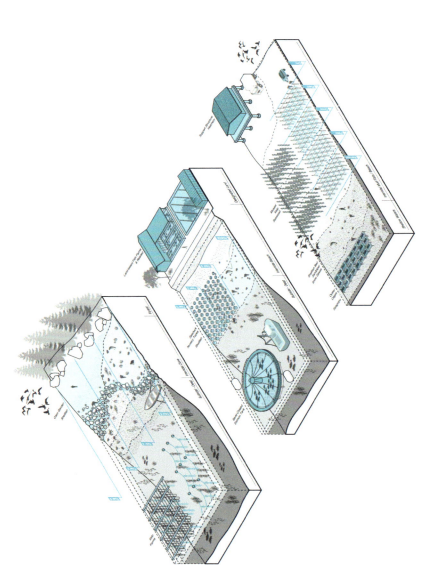

Figure 17.8 Mariculture.
There are a number of ways to apply spatial knowledge learned from case studies in the design process. In this case, Jessica researched the different spatial and temporal scales as well as programmatic conditions associated with mariculture practices around the globe. These findings were then abstracted and represented in a sequence of axonometric drawings showing a range of plausible coastal landscape conditions. Particular attention was paid to showing how different mariculture practices are situated along the gradient of the subtidal–intertidal–beach zone, as well as changes in low/high water levels, phasing, and development over time. Base linework for the drawing was setup in Rhino and further developed in Illustrator. (Drawing by Jessica Hoang).

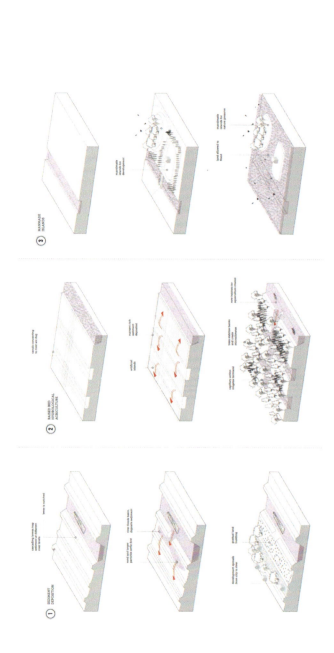

Figure 17.9 Staging interventions.

All designed landscapes are constructed. Particularly for projects that operate on large scales, it is often necessary to illustrate how operations are phased to generate specific landscape conditions and processes. These diagrams show the staging of different interventions that allow the river to reengage—periodically or permanently—with existing and proposed floodplain conditions. The generic nature of these axonometric allows for exploration and experimentation without having to address too many issues at once. The drawings were created in Illustrator. (Drawings by Emily Chen).

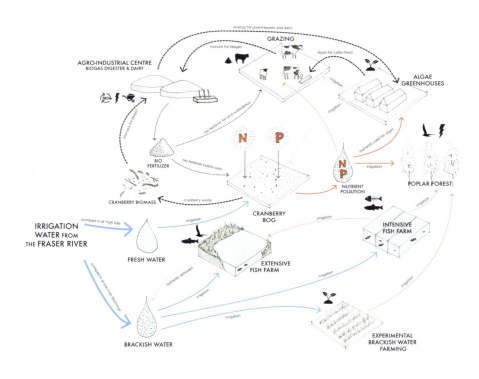

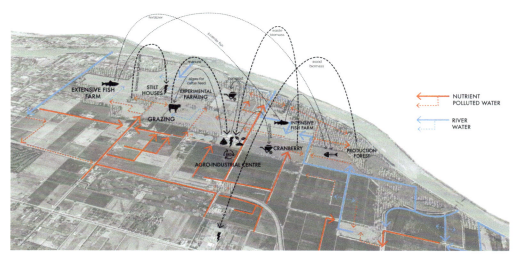

Figure 17.10 Reconfiguring metabolic flows
System diagrams are often a great way to begin to map how to create feedback systems and closed loop systems between various resource flows (of water, waste, energy, and food). This concept diagram explores how agricultural practices in the floodplain can be recalibrated to accommodate temporary flooding while providing multiple benefits, including carbon sequestration, climate regulation, and nutrient cycling. By spatializing this information (bottom diagram), one can begin to project how manure from floodplain grazers and the organic waste from cranberry farming and surrounding municipalities can be used to produce renewable energy. Similarly, a network of aquaculture and hydroponics produces food while recycling and purifying nutrient rich water. The aerial map (Photoshop cut out) is taken from Google Earth; the icons and arrows are drawn in Illustrator and connect a series of simple hand drawings axos. (Drawing by Miyo Takeda).

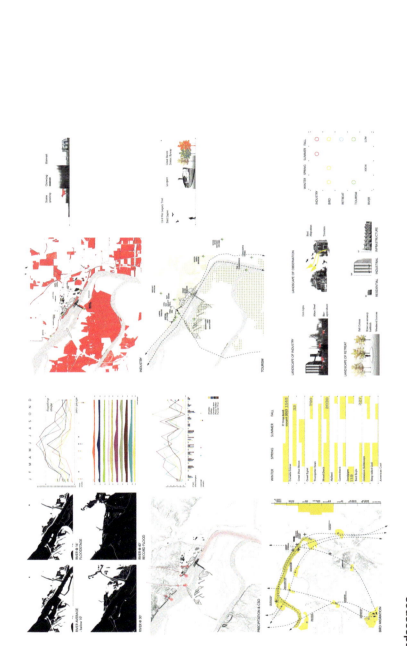

Figure 17.11 Cyclical landscapes

All landscapes, but especially hydrological landscapes, are dynamic. Mapping and diagramming these spatial and temporal dynamics are often a first entry point into developing design interventions. This sequence of drawings shows the dynamics associated with a range of different systems (river pulse, rainfall, stormwater outflows, bird migration, agricultural cycles, and tourism) operating in Alton, MO, located at the confluence of the Missouri and Mississippi River. This series of drawings evolved into a proposal focusing on alternative floodplain management strategies to link the seasonal dynamics of the river to flexible land uses and programs. A range of different software programs were used to create the diagrams. All map-based drawings rely on geospatial data from GIS, which was edited in Illustrator. The graphs are generated in Excel and edited in Illustrator. Finally, there are a number of collages which were created in Photoshops with vector overlays in Illustrator. (Drawings by Emily Chen).

Figure 17.12 Metabolic flow animation.
This is a sequence of stills from an animation which shows the risks and vulnerabilities of drinking water and waste water infrastructure in the Metro Vancouver Area as it relates to potential floods and earthquakes. The animation concludes by proposing a number of initial strategies that approach water management not as a linear but circular metabolism. Animations have a major advantage over singular drawings in that information can be introduced successively, allowing for a specific narrative to be illustrated and spatialized. The animation was created using a number of software programs. Geospatial data was analyzed and processed in GIS, exported, and subsequently imported in Illustrator for refinement of line work, colors, and labels. Finally, this vector data was edited in Adobe After Effects as a movie with animated actions, transitions, and voiceovers. (Animation by Celia Winters and Jessica Hoang).

informed debate surrounding water as a ground for design. As such, the work in this section shows a few examples of how different modes of representation can be used to analyze, visualize, and imagine fluid geographies across multiple spatial and temporal scales (Figures 17.9–17.12).

18

UX FOR LANDSCAPE ARCHITECTS

A New Paradigm for Conceptual Design

Andrea Hansen-Phillips

Introduction: Conceptual Drawing in the Digital Age

It is the undeniable truth that we are living in a digital age. For landscape architecture, this has profound implications, one of which is the transformation of the conceptual design process. While landscape architects of previous generations favored pen and pencil, sketchbook and study model, as a professor, I am noticing more and more students produce many (if not most) of their conceptual drawings digitally. This perhaps comes as no surprise when considering the average age of the landscape architecture graduate— 24 for undergraduate (BLA) students and 30 for graduate (MLA) students.[1]

At the time of writing, this means the average landscape architecture student was born sometime between 1989 and 1999— hence, most of these students have never known a world without computers.[2]

Nevertheless, digital drawing has some distinct disadvantages when compared to analog drawing, especially in the early stages of a design project. The architect Michael Graves articulates the advantages of hand drawing as follows: (1) hand drawings "express the interaction of our minds, eyes and hands" by creating a direct physical connection between the hand and the drawing that is cannot be replicated between mouse and screen; (2) drawing something by hand makes a visceral imprint on one's memory, whereas drawing by computer feels more like a trance state; (3) drawing by hand allows for an iterative, nonlinear process, such as when Graves uses trace paper to "layer one drawing on top of another," building on what [he has] drawn before; and (4) the act of drawing by hand leaves "intonations, traces of intentions and speculation," the marks of an individual artist that are obscured by digital drawing software.[3]

[1] American Society of Landscape Architects. "2014 Survey of Graduating Landscape Architecture Students," "Ideation Method: Mash-Up," IDEO U, accessed September 4, 2019, https://www.ideou.com/pages/ideation-method-mash-up.

[2] For context, the IBM PC was introduced in 1981, AOL was launched in 1991, the iMac was introduced in 1998, and Google made its debut in 1998.

[3] Michael Graves, "Opinion | Architecture and the Lost Art of Drawing," *The New York Times*, September 1, 2012, sec. Opinion, https://www.nytimes.com/2012/09/02/opinion/sunday/architecture-and-the-lost-art-of-drawing.html.

DOI: 10.4324/9781003053255-21

4 Seymour Simmons, "Drawing in the Digital Age: Observations and Implications for Education," *Arts* 8, no. 1 (March 2019): 33. https://doi.org/10.3390/arts8010033.

The artist Seymour Simmons, in his essay "Drawing in the Digital Age: Observations and Implications for Education," offers the additional advantage that hand drawn concept sketches have rapid generative potential, explaining that "sketches are rough, typically done by hand with pen or pencil on paper including on the proverbial napkin or envelope. As such, the process remains fluid, facilitating experimentation, correction, and communication among colleagues or with clients. Equally important, for the trained eye and hand, even mistakes may suggest unforeseen possibilities."[4] And according to John Maeda, *"skill in the digital age is confused with mastery of digital tools, masking the importance of understanding materials and mastering the elements of form."*

Thus, a dilemma emerges in which the mode of conceptual drawing creation preferred by more and more landscape architecture students for its familiarity and convenience—digital drawing—is inferior in many ways to analog drawing, especially when it comes to the critical early stages of design, when the drawing process must be (to summarize Graves and Simmons) interactive, memorable, iterative, individualistic, rapid, and generative. While the sketchbook will and should remain a key part of the landscape architect's arsenal, it is also unrealistic to attempt to stop the trajectory of digital drawing becoming the primary medium for conceptual design among the next generation of landscape architects. So then, we must adapt, and find ways of bringing digital conceptual drawings up to speed. This essay will outline how landscape architects can address the aforementioned inadequacies of digital conceptual drawing by borrowing techniques from User Experience Design, or UX.

Adapting UX to Landscape Architecture

In my own practice, Datum Digital Studio, digital design is at the heart of every project, as the firm's name implies. Datum specializes in web design and development, mapping, and data visualization for the built environment. Since 2010, I have worked with architects, landscape architects, local governments, universities, nonprofits, builders, and community organizations to build unique websites and data visualizations that emphasize sustainability, urbanism, community engagement, and smart growth while keeping usability and accessibility top-of-mind. Datum's recent projects have included an interactive landscape history website for the Landscape Studies Initiative at UVA; the Littoral Gradients Atlas (littoralgradients.daniels.utoronto.ca), which maps land reclamation projects around the world; Transforming Community Spaces (transformingcommunityspaces.org), an interactive toolkit which helps communities confront the spatial legacies of colonialism, slavery, and white supremacy; and MainStreet21 (mainstreet21.org), an outreach portal for an NSF grant-funded project investigating needs and best practices for the 21st century Main Street in Virginia.

Given the siteless and entirely digital nature of my work at Datum, I have had to find new conceptual design methods and strategies, and for this, I have looked to the field of User Experience Design, or UX. UX designers specialize in researching how user needs shape the development of many different kinds of products, ranging from consumer goods to web designs and applications. The field is broadly split into two groups, UX research and UX design (though there is a good amount of overlap between the two), with the former focusing on understanding users through interviews and workshops, and the latter focusing on the creation of sketches, mockups, and prototypes and testing them with various user groups. Though most landscape architects do not use the same terminology as UX practitioners, we are clearly concerned with user experience in our daily practice, and the best landscape projects succeed because they have done the hard work of trying to understand how the project can best meet the needs of both human and nonhuman agents. By studying the theory behind UX, and the tools commonly used by UX researchers and designers, landscape architects can make better decisions about incorporating user needs throughout the design process, but especially in the early conceptual stages.

The term "user experience" was coined by Don Norman, a designer and professor with a background in psychology, computer science, and cognitive science. Norman's insight about product design has helped to develop a general attitude about the importance of UX in tech, and today, UX is an indispensable group at nearly every tech company. Norman's words are highly applicable to landscape architecture as well. For instance, in the following quote, we could replace the word "product" with "landscape," and end up with a fundamental maxim one could use to explain what is needed to create a successful landscape project:

> No product is an island. A product is more than the product. It is a cohesive, integrated set of experiences. Think through all of the stages of a product or service – from initial intentions through final reflections, from first usage to help, service, and maintenance. Make them all work together seamlessly. That's systems thinking.[5]

No *landscape* is an island. A *landscape* is more than the *landscape*. It is a cohesive, integrated set of experiences. Think through all of the stages of a *landscape design*—from initial intentions through final reflections, from first usage to help, service, and maintenance. Make them all work together seamlessly. That's systems thinking.

If landscape architects are to look to UX for inspiration, it is important to understand UX not just as a set of principles, but as a process. Just as there is not a universal design process among landscape architects, there is no universally defined set of principles and tools among UX designers. However, just as most landscape architecture projects follow a defined roadmap through a

[5] Norman, Donald. "The Way I See It - Systems Thinking: A Product Is More than the Product," *Interactions* 16 (September 1, 2009): 52–54. https://doi.org/10.1145/1572626.1572637.

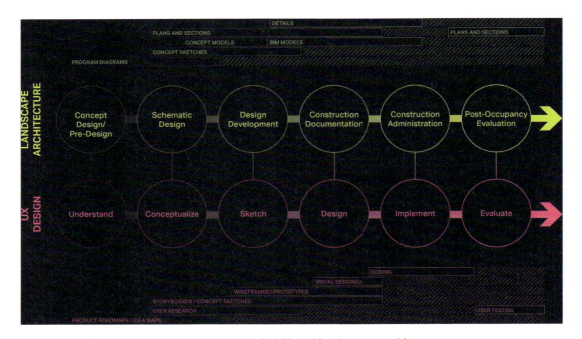

Figure 18.1 Comparing the design process in UX and landscape architecture.
This diagram shows the typical phases of a landscape architecture project (top) and a UX project (bottom), along with the different types of drawings and other deliverables commonly created in each stage, in order to compare the similarities between the design processes for each discipline. *Created by Andrea Hansen-Phillips.*

series of stages, with certain tools and deliverables common to each, there is also a general structure that UX tends to follow. We can divide the UX process into six phases (though not every UX practitioner will use the same names): Understand, Conceptualize, Sketch, Design, Implement, and Evaluate. These six stages have many similarities to the six main phases of a landscape architecture project: Concept Design/Pre-Design, Schematic Design, Design Development, Construction Documentation, Construction Administration, and Post-Occupancy Evaluation.

The diagram in Figure 18.1 compares the stages of the two disciplines to one another, while also showing the different types of deliverables that are commonly created during each stage. For instance, the Concept Design/Pre-Design phase (landscape architecture) and the Understand phase (UX) are both focused on understanding a project and user needs and documenting those needs through various types of diagrams. Meanwhile, later design phases such as Design Development (landscape architecture) and Sketch (UX) are focused on creating scaled design drawings with fixed dimensions and greater detail.

The remainder of this essay will focus on the types of rapid prototyping drawings created in the first three phases of UX: Understand (which parallels Concept Design in landscape architecture), Conceptualize (which parallels Schematic Design in landscape architecture), and Sketch (which parallels Design Development in landscape architecture).

UX Phase 1: Understand (Concept Design)

The first phase of any design project, regardless of discipline, involves understanding the design problem. In professional landscape architecture, early stage design work might involve reviewing an RFP and submitting a proposal, or reviewing a client brief to understand program, site, and context. Lists, site diagrams, massing models, and sketches, often developed during collaborative charettes, help to provide a holistic, spatial and visual understanding of the design problem, and the foundation for further site design. These internal exercises are often paired with interviews with various stakeholders, especially in public projects.

In UX, the process is similar, and the "Understand" phase involves collaborative planning, research, and early stage sketching and visualization. Some of the more common techniques include user research interviews, workshops with various stakeholders, roadmap diagrams which outline the project timeline, goals, and milestones, and idea maps, which are visual diagrams documenting a rapid brainstorming process.

There are as many different kinds of idea maps as there are designers. Like landscape architects, some designers prefer the use of pen and paper at this early stage, while others may use digital tools such as Illustrator. Three kinds of idea maps I have used in my teaching are Mind Maps, Decision Trees, and Ideation Mashups. Mind maps are essentially word diagrams, typically laid out as a web or network, in which different elements of a project are classified and interconnected. Decision trees use a hierarchical, tree-like structure to model decisions and their consequences. They often start with a question or questions, and then offer different alternatives based on a user's answer to that question, thereby making them highly useful for trying to understand user needs, whether for a website or a landscape site.

The final kind of idea map, an ideation mash-up, involves a brainstorming exercise devised by the global design firm Ideo. In this exercise, participants come up with lists in two categories—one relating to the project type (for instance, if the project is the redesign of a community park, Column A might include things typically found in a park), and one relating to a completely different industry or industries (Column B might include things typically found in hotels, shopping malls, etc.). Next, users will pick one item from Column A and one from Column B and create a mash-up, such as a park with a food court. This exercise encourages quantity over quality, and by bringing seemingly unrelated things together, allows for fresh, unexpected ideas to emerge. To document the mashup exercise, Ideo has provided a template that has space to expand upon individual mash-up ideas both in writing and visually (Figures 18.2–18.6).[6]

[6] "Ideation Method: Mash-Up," IDEO U, accessed September 4, 2019, https://www.ideou.com/pages/ideation-method-mash-up.

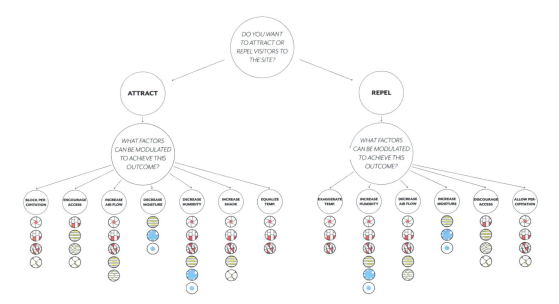

Figure 18.2 Decision Tree (Daniel Rose).
Decision Tree showing alternatives for attracting or repelling visitors. Different options for modulating the façade and hardscape patterning are listed at the bottom of the diagram, classified by the desired outcome. *University of Tennessee College of Architecture and Design, Graduate Landscape Architecture Studio, "Cause and Effect: Space, Form and Program in the Relational Landscape." Student: Daniel Rose. Instructor: Andrea Hansen-Phillips (Spring 2017).*

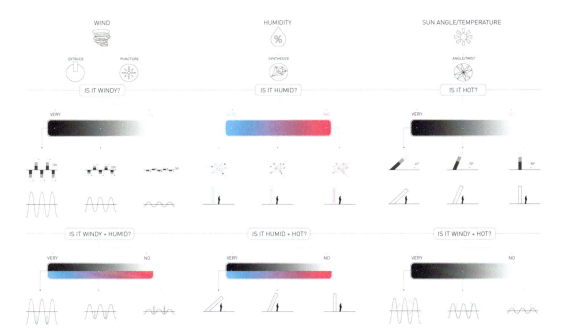

Figure 18.3 Decision Tree (Alexa Macri).
Decision Tree comparing different human comfort factors (wind, humidity, dry bulb temperature) and combinations thereof, to understand how landscape elements could be used to module climatic comfort. *University of Tennessee College of Architecture and Design, Graduate Landscape Architecture Studio, "Cause and Effect: Space, Form and Program in the Relational Landscape." Student: Alexa Macri. Instructor: Andrea Hansen-Phillips (Spring 2017).*

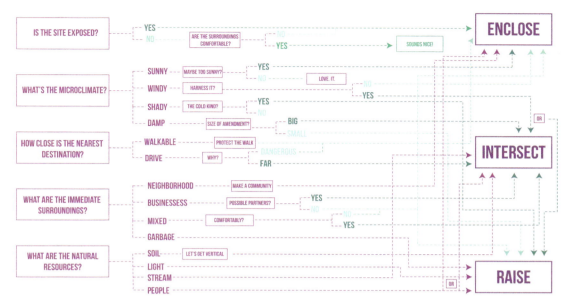

Figure 18.4 Decision Tree (Natalie McCarthy).
Decision Tree posing a number of different questions related to site context. This student was interested in flexible, temporary program elements and the possibility of multiple configurations on a single site, and this decision tree formed the basis for creating different types of landscape experiences at a granular level. *University of Tennessee College of Architecture and Design, Graduate Landscape Architecture Studio, "Cause and Effect: Space, Form and Program in the Relational Landscape." Student: Natalie McCarthy. Instructor: Andrea Hansen-Phillips (Spring 2017).*

UX Phase 2: Conceptualize (Schematic Design)

The second phase of a landscape architecture project, Schematic Design, involves preliminary design drawings that illustrate the basic design concept. These drawings are often quite rough at this stage, and may include hand-drawn sketches (plans, sections, views, etc.) as well as initial digital drawings and renderings. Rather than focusing on the details, these drawings outline the overall concept.

In UX, the second phase, Conceptualize, involves translating the initial research performed in Phase 1 (Understanding) into a preliminary design idea. Some of the tools used in Phase 1, such as mind maps, idea maps, and decision trees, continue to be refined and iterated upon in this phase, while other new formats are introduced as well. Two of these formats are Storyboards and Wireframes.

Storyboards, borrowed from the film industry, are highly useful for projects that have a narrative component, such as videos, games, or choreographed paths or trails. They are typically linear in nature, progressing from beginning to end without breaks or alternate paths. Wireframes can be seen as an interactive version of a storyboard, and are often used in the early stages of website or app design. The aim of a wireframe is to focus on the general structure,

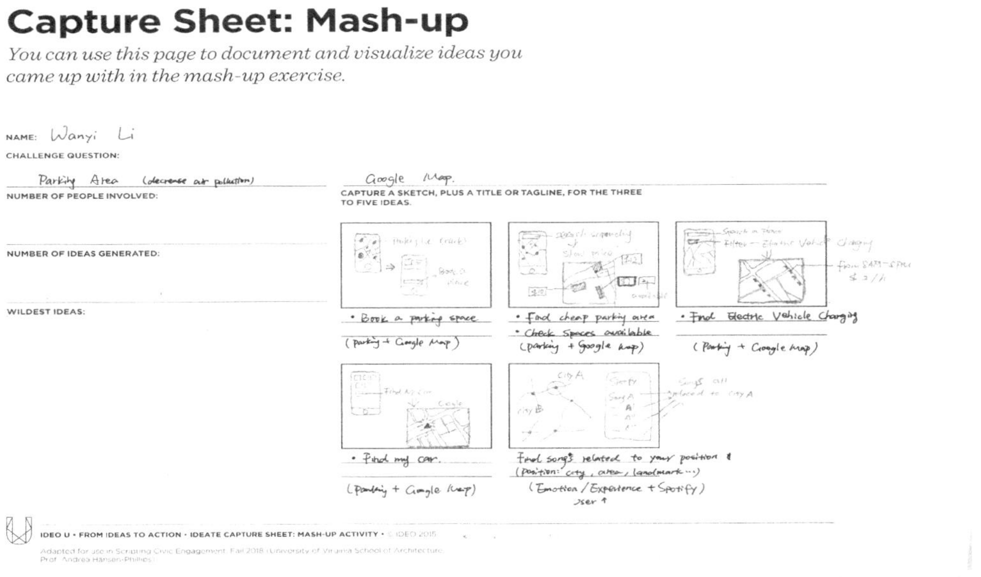

Figure 18.5 Ideation Mash-up (Wanyi Li).
In this exercise, students brainstormed a list of "big problems" that landscape architecture could help to solve, as well as a list of popular websites or apps, and then were asked to create several "mash-ups" of the two. This student came up with several interesting ideas, including "Google Maps for Parking" (nearby parking lots and their ratings/availability) and "Geo-tagged Spotify" (A playlist that would automatically find songs related to places close to your current map position). *University of Virginia School of Architecture, Scripting Civic Engagement Seminar. Student: Wanyi Li. Instructor: Andrea Hansen-Phillips (Fall 2018).*

layout, and usability an interface without focusing on its design (i.e., colors, fonts, and graphics). Wireframes are typically drawn in black and white or grayscale so as to focus attention away from color, but color is sometimes used for color-coding. Wireframes are also sometimes rendered in a sketchy or cartoon-like manner (most prominently by the wireframing tool Balsamiq Mockups), again this is to make it clear that the wireframe is focused on interface usability rather than design. Both storyboards and wireframes can be made in a variety of ways, either using pen and paper or using specialized software (Figures 18.7–18.9).

UX Phase 3: Sketch (Design Development)

The third phase of a landscape architecture project, Design Development, builds upon the basic design ideas laid out in the Schematic Design phase and begins to refine and increase the level of the granularity. During this phase, most designers will switch from creating drawings by hand or in Photoshop, Illustrator, or Rhino to using more precise software such as AutoCAD or Revit due to the need for more precise scale and measurements.

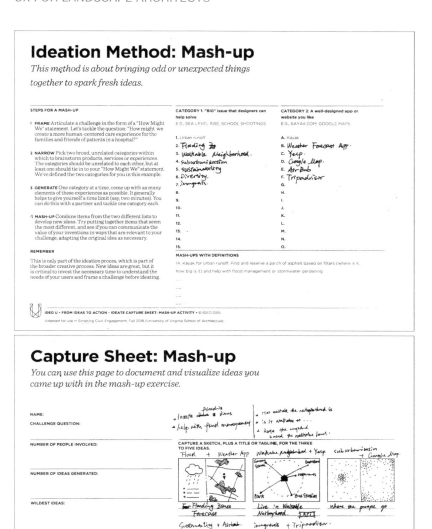

Figure 18.6 Ideation Mash-up (Ziqing Ye).
In this exercise, students brainstormed a list of "big problems" that landscape architecture could help to solve, as well as a list of popular websites or apps, and then were asked to create several "mash-ups" of the two. This student came up with several interesting ideas, including "Yelp for Walkable Neighborhoods" (neighbors could "rate" their neighborhood's walkability) and "TripAdvisor for Immigrants" (a listing of immigrant-friendly resources and activities in a community). *University of Virginia School of Architecture, Scripting Civic Engagement Seminar. Student: Ziqing Ye. Instructor: Andrea Hansen-Phillips (Fall 2018)*

Figure 18.7 Storyboard (Daniel Rose).
Storyboard for a video showing guiding principles, site strategy, and three-dimensional parti diagram for set of vacant lots in Knoxville, Tennessee. *University of Tennessee College of Architecture and Design, Graduate Landscape Architecture Studio, "Cause and Effect: Space, Form and Program in the Relational Landscape." Student: Daniel Rose. Instructor: Andrea Hansen-Phillips (Spring 2017).*

AERO-SPACE *aural windscapes*

Figure 18.8 Storyboard (Sarah Newton).
Storyboard showing a topographic landscape designed to shape and curate wind, and how that wind will produce desired plant textures and effects. *University of Tennessee College of Architecture and Design, Graduate Landscape Architecture Studio, "Cause and Effect: Space, Form and Program in the Relational Landscape." Student: Sarah Newton. Instructor: Andrea Hansen-Phillips (Spring 2017).*

Figure 18.9 Wireframe (Fangli Zhang).
Wireframe for Candy Crush, a mobile app geared at bridging the divide between social media and real life by encouraging users to collect "candies" by having face-to-face meetups with other nearby users. *University of Virginia School of Architecture, Scripting Civic Engagement Seminar. Student: Fangli Zhang. Instructor: Andrea Hansen-Phillips (Fall 2018).*

Similarly, in UX, the initial design ideas that were developed through idea maps, storyboards, and wireframes are refined and detailed in Phase 3 (Sketch).[7] While the previous stage (Conceptualize) was focused on usability rather than design, the Sketch phase starts to integrate visual design (also called UI, or User Interface Design) into the mix. The visual designs created by UI designers are often aesthetically stunning and highly stylized; however, UI designers are primarily focused on how the visual design of an interface appeals to a user's wants and needs rather than pure aesthetics. In other words, as in many landscape architecture projects, in UX and UI, form follows function.

Two tools are predominantly used in this phase: Mockups and Prototypes. A mockup is a pixel-perfect visual rendering of the user interface of a website, app, and so on. It uses the same color swatches, fonts, images, and graphics that will be used on the live site, and it is often shown projected onto the device it is intended to be used on (e.g., phone, tablet, or desktop), so as to simulate the actual user experience. A prototype, rather than being an entirely separate format, is an interactive mockup: it shows the interactivity and connections between different pages/screens (e.g., it has working buttons, dropdown menus, animations, etc.), and is typically shown either as an interactive interface (typically on the device it is intended to be used on) or as a set of individual screens laid out into a networked structure and connected by wires showing which elements are connected (linked) to one another (Figures 18.10–18.12).

Conclusion

The UX tools described above offer all six of the characteristics identified earlier as being important to digital concept drawings: they are interactive (whether by being generated collaboratively or by diagramming and expressing the interactivity of an interface or

[7] As the name implies, the Sketch phase in UX is somewhat looser than the Design Development in a landscape architecture project, primarily because it remains far easier to modify a wireframe or a mockup than a set of landscape architecture drawings.

Figure 18.10 Wireframe (Qiyao Li).
Wireframe for a mobile app designed to let users take care of a "pet tree" by watering it, fertilizing it, and making sure it has enough sunlight, and then watching it grow from seed to sapling to mature tree. *University of Virginia School of Architecture, Scripting Civic Engagement Seminar. Student: Qiyao Li. Instructor: Andrea Hansen-Phillips (Fall 2018).*

Figure 18.11 Wireframe (Landscape Studies Initiative).
Wireframe for the ISLAND (Interactive Studies in Landscape Architecture iNterface and Database) website showing various timeline alternatives. *Landscape Studies Initiative, University of Virginia School of Architecture. Wireframe created by Qiyao Li. Principal investigators: Elizabeth Meyer, Michael Lee, Worthy Martin. Project Manager: Allison James. Interface Design: Andrea Hansen-Phillips. Research Assistants: Qiyao Li, Heather Courtenay, Reid Farnsworth, Eva Lucy Alvarado. (Summer 2019).*

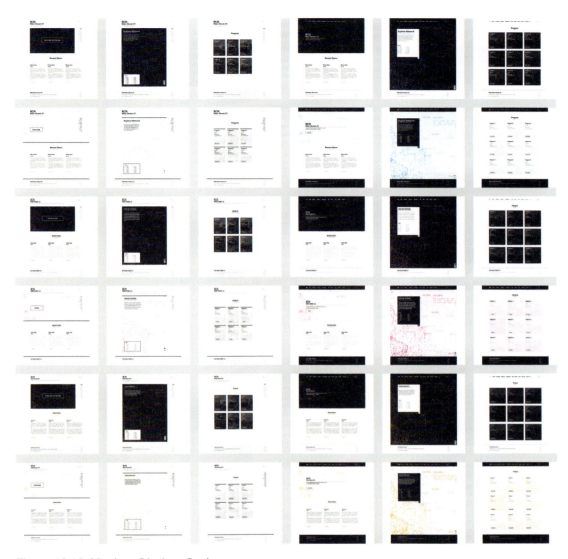

Figure 18.12 Mockup (Yuchen Sun).
Mockup for the Field Mix app, designed to let users survey a site and add landscape and hardscape features such as trees, plants, sidewalks, paving, and so on. *University of Virginia School of Architecture, Scripting Civic Engagement Seminar. Student: Yuchen Sun. Instructor: Andrea Hansen-Phillips (Fall 2018).*

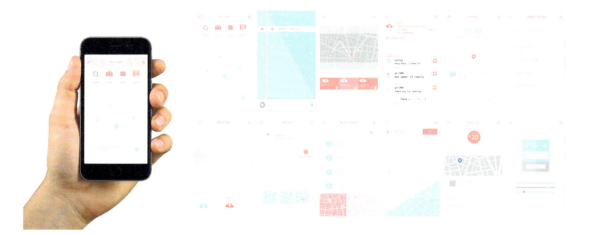

Figure 18.13 Mockup (Qiuheng Xu).
Mockup for the Wi-Fi Tracker app, an "Airbnb" for wifi hotspots designed to let users share their Wi-Fi hotspot with other users, or see hotspots in the area that can be checked out. *University of Virginia School of Architecture, Scripting Civic Engagement Seminar. Student: Qiuheng Xu. Instructor: Andrea Hansen-Phillips (Fall 2018).*

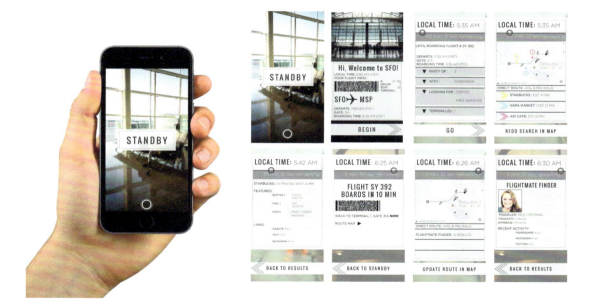

Figure 18.14 Mockup (Megan Freeman).
Mockup for the Standby app, designed to let guide users through the airport check-in and waiting process by keeping them informed about flight changes and providing information about nearby amenities. *California College of the Arts, The Data-Driven City Seminar. Student: Megan Freeman. Instructor: Andrea Hansen-Phillips (Fall 2014).*

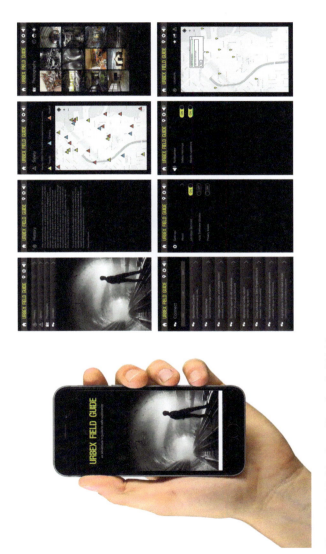

Figure 18.15 Mockup (Stephanie Tabb).
Mockup for the Urbex Field Guide app, an app for urban explorers providing information about interesting sights on vacant and abandoned properties, as well as safety tips and access information. *California College of the Arts, The Data-Driven City Seminar. Student: Stephanie Tabb. Instructor: Andrea Hansen-Phillips (Fall 2014).*

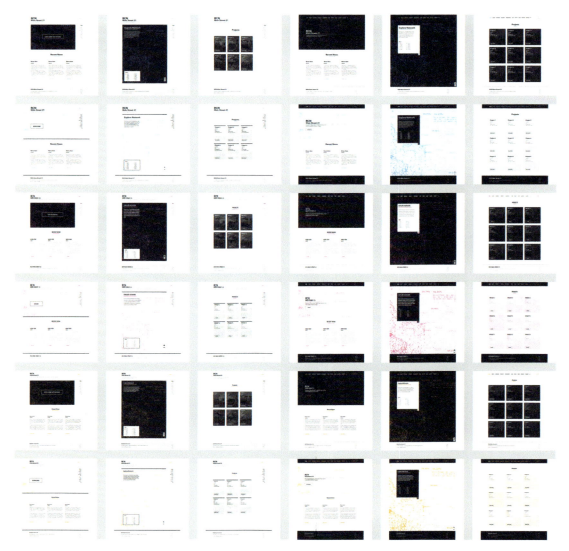

Figure 18.16 Mockup (Mainstreet21).
Mockup showing color and typography alternatives for the RCN Mainstreet21 website. RCN
Mainstreet21, University of Virginia School of Architecture. Mockup created by Andrea Hansen-
Phillips. Principal Investigator: Ila Berman. Collaborators: Mona El Khafif, Zihao Zhang. Research
Assistant: Taro Matsuno.

Figure 18.17 Mockup (Landscape Studies Initiative).
Mockup for the ISLAND (Interactive Studies in Landscape Architecture iNterface and Database) website showing different design alternatives. *Landscape Studies Initiative, University of Virginia School of Architecture. Mockups created by Andrea Hansen-Phillips. Principal Investigators: Elizabeth Meyer, Michael Lee, Worthy Martin. Project Manager: Allison James. Interface Design: Andrea Hansen-Phillips. Research Assistants: Qiyao Li, Heather Courtenay, Reid Farnsworth, Eva Lucy Alvarado. (Summer 2019).*

PROTOTYPE |CANDY

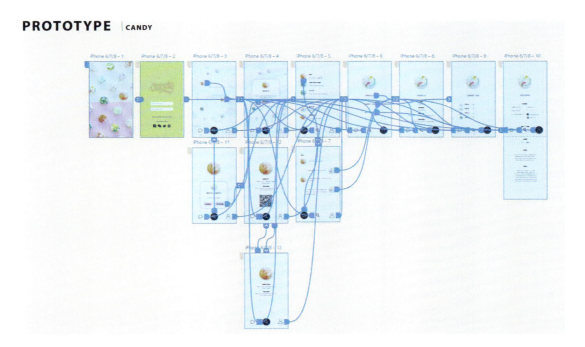

Figure 18.18 Prototype (Fangli Zhang).
Prototype showing the interactivity of the Candy Crush app, a mobile app geared at bridging the divide between social media and real life by encouraging users to collect "candies" by having face-to-face meetups with other nearby users. *University of Virginia School of Architecture, Scripting Civic Engagement Seminar. Student: Fangli Zhang. Instructor: Andrea Hansen-Phillips (Fall 2018).*

site design), they are memorable, they are highly iterative, they are individualized (and explicitly focused on user needs), they are rapid and easy to create, and they are full of generative potential. While these drawings are not intended to replace the digital drawings most commonly used by landscape architecture students today (e.g., plans, sections, renderings, maps, and diagrams), they offer a far less time-consuming alternative that can augment and supplement the conceptual drawing arsenal and address the inadequacies presented by the current process (Figures 18.13–18.18).

AFTERWORD

A Concept, in Five Parts

Simon M. Bussiere

I'm writing this as if speaking to myself as a first-year landscape architecture student, from two decades ahead, in the hopes, there is something of value in my experience for you. I don't know whether ideas miraculously pop out or not, but certain parts seem to when conditions are right. Concepts certainly don't emerge suddenly, or fully formed. But when I've done my homework, prepared, revised, and actually focused, a few odd fragments start to line up, a few errant data points relate, and the dots start to connect for me. It's said the harder you work, the luckier you get. Making concepts in my experience seems to require the ability to quickly test hypotheses, identify correlations or missing links, and find strategies and applications for new ways to put people, materials, and their uses, into beautiful, meaningful juxtaposition. My experience has validated my creative instincts and has crucially given me a very practical sense of how to harness my strengths and temper my weaknesses. I've bolstered those whenever possible through practice, and I've asked for help, leading to collaborations that leverage team strengths to make up for certain areas of knowledge. This essay is an effort to recollect some of the better lessons I've benefited from in landscape architecture. The recommendations I offer are that of both a teacher and a student and are intended to help you in forming meaningful design concepts, while also remaining alert to broader professional and creative ambitions.

Much of what I've learned about conceptual design has been born out of experimentation. Making things, and regarding the process of making itself somewhat carefully. I'm interested in the ways things come together, how they fit or don't, how time or other pressures change them, how they react to stimuli, how it all gets organized and communicated, and how it might all become persuasive. Always improvising when I can to figure out somewhat imprecisely where the limits are. I'm excited to do this kind of work, and to read the work of others, all considering better ways to make landscapes operate. Fortunately, conceptual thinking, in general, is a natural tendency for me. I also genuinely like to and need to learn, and don't we all? I'm grateful for an instinctively curious imagination and I enjoy anticipating those moments of discovery that I know are just ahead. As it happens though, for an oddly frantic yet

DOI: 10.4324/9781003053255-22

relaxed mind like mine, it's a constant challenge to record, to write it all down for later. Yet deliberate, radical reflection is an absolutely critical part of the process of conceptualization, and unlike some less rational parts of the creative trajectory, documentation, or the act of classifying and organizing evidence, requires linear precision.

Michael Graves once said, "my favorite project is the next one." To me, this statement makes a lot of sense. In my experience, you'll learn a lot with each new project. Your knowledge and skills will grow wider and deeper as you explore. Some early efforts will be one-offs, leading to little more than short-term economic gain. While others build cumulatively and help shape a career and an identity as a designer. You'll find that some projects build on one another, too, contributing meaningfully to a pattern of professional evolution. They'll be creatively fulfilling, and as they accrue, you'll gain insight into your core values as a person; your core principles as a designer. Each passing project will teach you how you learn, and how you design. You'll discover a palate of techniques, design principles, and workflows. And you'll inevitably evolve as you form new concepts, developing each project and shedding light on the things you value with each forged relationship, failure, or victory. It's important to have a trajectory in mind for yourself and your work, even if it's somewhat ambiguous at the outset.

A precise five-year plan is impossible, let alone a projection out a year or two. But as you get going, you need to gain momentum somehow, doing so while forecasting the near-term storms and aiming toward some end-goal. Saying yes can be a great way to get into good sorts of trouble, even if you're not completely confident you can achieve a high degree of success. I'm not proposing you take on more than you can handle. Instead, I'd ask you to recall the tools and methods of research, analysis, and design you've learned, and anticipate yourself rising to meet new challenges with a prospective and optimistic attitude. Be open to opportunities and entrepreneurial in the manner in which you conduct yourself. You have enormous privilege and opportunity if you've found yourself here; or at the nearly annual crossroads between taking an existing position somewhere or making a new one, forging ahead for yourself. Take stock of the case studies and lessons from lectures, field trips, and studio projects, the myriad outcomes of your prior coursework and life experience. Actively and deliberately build on the friendships you made in school, and capitalize on that network of smart and industrious people around you. As you develop a method of conceptualization and more broadly grow as a designer, you'll need help. So ask.

As my students graduate every year, I worry their passion for design might fade; they might wander for too long, or be absorbed into a corporate giant. But I'm encouraged by the creative erosion of outdated modalities in practice, some bad habits and attitudes seem to be waning. Design is becoming more democratized.

Offices, institutions, agencies, and associations have made great strides in the direction of diversity, equity, and inclusion. One only needs to look back a few decades to see that this is the very best time in human history to be alive for the greatest number of people. But there is so much to repair and correct, so many opportunities to improve ecosystems and people's lives. So much potential for landscape architecture to contribute to our planet and species. And as we're all constantly remaking ourselves, our organizations, and our communities, I'm assured by the bright, healthy, and productive former students who keep in touch. They tell me enough to know that the future is promising.

Concept Zero

My career in landscape architecture started not long after I finished my undergraduate degree. I didn't take an internship or work on the side through school. A job wasn't waiting for me after graduation. I also didn't know then what sort of work I'd be best suited for exactly, so planning ahead was difficult. Despite enjoying my evenings and weekends in college, very much, I took studio pretty seriously and thankfully spent most of my time in school trying to make projects that I could build a portfolio with. I'd seen the power of finishing something, the permanence of a line on the CV. Once I had a professional degree in hand, I looked everywhere around me for opportunities to make landscapes.

My first built project, a small garden, started as a conversation about a basement that was flooding periodically. Chris Meyerhoff, a BSLA classmate/design partner and I partnered up and I got to work evaluating the flooding problem, looking for a way to leverage a solution into a more meaningful and interesting concept. Water was sheeting across a gently sloping compacted suburban lawn into a perimeter planting along the sill of the house, seeping through the foundation wall during the heavy rains in the Spring. It was easy to diagnose the issue, and we were happy to offer ideas. Knowing just a little bit about green infrastructure, at least in theory, we proposed grading the yard to accommodate a vegetated swale that would wrap around the structure to draw that runoff into a water feature at a low point in the backyard. That was really it in the beginning. A simple tactical solution to an obvious problem; a swale to allow some of the stormwater to infiltrate, away from the house, and thus keep the basement dry. We did a quick cost-estimate. The client agreed to a budget. We rented a skid steer from the local hardware store, called 1–800-DIG-SAFE to locate underground utilities, and got on with excavating the swale, by eye, as if drawing three-dimensional contour lines with the blade of the Bobcat©. Chris knew how to safely operate heavy equipment, and he quickly gave me a crash course. From the first dip of the bucket into the ground, we started pulling up beautiful New England cobbles and boulders from the subsoil. Free materials! The swale was dug quickly and delineated with some of the more eccentric found stones. We cut the lawn wider than we needed to, adding a band of smaller cobbles on the uphill edge of the swale to reduce erosion and increase permeability.

The surplus cut soil was nutrient-rich and made for a planted berm which we used to define a small contemplative space near the edge of the property. We transplanted Lily of the Valley plugs from the nearby woods, and some even took. More free material for a well-defined landform enclosure! With the swale excavated, the first problem seemed solved, but now came the chance to try adding design value. We advised on a planting strategy that might help reduce peak runoff. Moisture-tolerant plants could absorb some of the stormwater, their roots could help stabilize soils. The client was also an amateur ornithologist, a lover of birds, and with that, a palate of plant materials came together. Pollinators and insects would be excellent bait for the local birds, so we massed together native flowering shrubs and trees. The plants were incorporated into the swale, which was starting to feel like a meandering pathway through a garden. We let the path continue down and around the yard. Some of the larger boulders were low and flat, making for good steps, others were rounded and large with flat tops, making for good seating. The cobbles were suitable edge materials. With an order of pea-gravel to comprise the walking surface, one load in a tri-axle 22-ton truck from the nearest quarry, we had all the hardscape elements required to realize the concept and finish the first phase of the job.

After solving the principle drainage issue at hand, the rest of the process was highly iterative and improvisational. The work unfurled yes-and, a bit like jazz, with just enough structure to keep time and rhythm, and yet not without the flexibility to adapt and respond to new information and subtle cues that made the work and process unique and site-dependent, a term I learned later from Julie Bargmann. Site dependence goes beyond site-specificity to require a deeper and perhaps truer sense of place, authenticity, and intention. Being site-dependent means that the work grows from the layered existing conditions, and emerges through a careful reconfiguration of and building onto a site's physical matter, registering existing patterns and embracing its inherent qualities through design. Each discovery, from the rocks below to the birds overhead, required open communication, thoughtful, collaborative analysis, and interpretation, as well as skillful implementation in order to achieve some degree of synthesis. The success of the project resulted both from the client's willingness to trust in our qualifications, knowledge, and intentions, and in our openness to embody her practical vision for the landscape as an extension of her home.

I tell this story of my first "real" project because there is a lesson in the way it came together. The formation of a concept occurred through the act of reading and making landscape. A string of small residential garden projects followed for the next two years. But even with great collaborators, it was a struggle to do good work while simultaneously marketing and winning new work. I knew enough to know I needed to know more. In the winter of 2006, I worked as hard as I'd ever worked on anything to produce an application to the Harvard Graduate School of Design. It doesn't make any sense, but I didn't apply anywhere else. I visited Gund Hall earlier that year and decided I'd try and get in. My mentors and friends from UMass helped me shape a letter and frame my interest in advanced pursuits more clearly. Then, once in graduate school, the projects became much larger and more complex, by orders of magnitude. The expanded nature of the work better illustrated the potential scope and capacity of landscape. More detailed ecological frameworks and more lucid representational theories sharpened my conceptual design focus and grew my understanding of how landscape media and processes work together. The travel associated with the projects in school played a pivotal role as well. It's difficult to overstate the importance of exposure and immersion through on-site, first-hand, in-person fieldwork in design education. Experiential learning, a term I didn't know at the time, has become a kind of beacon for me since.

With each failure or success, I gained experience and confidence in my ability to read a place, understand a client, their vision, and the nature of a problem. I learned, in other words, how to help others form a design concept. Perhaps most significantly over the years, I've grown a deeper appreciation for and understanding of landscape architecture's capacity to add real and tangible value to the world.

Now in this short essay and the five steps that follow, I have not intended to offer a prescription or formulae, but instead a summary of the critical elements I've found most useful in strategically composing the earliest stages of a design concept. Each is a time-tested and proven lens through which you can learn to simplify and understand the complexity of the challenge you face in forming a solid and suitable concept. Each comes with challenges, but as you focus on each discrete part, site, people, principles, framing, and forming, you should begin to realize that good decisions have the power to build cumulatively. I recommend that you build similarly on this outline, reshuffling the parts and their sequencing as needed.

Site

Place, Territory, Identity, Kuleana

Go and walk the site. Camp out for a full day or two if you can. Observe and learn from the variations that occur from day to day, season to season. Wake up to the sun rising there, feel the moist early air, and the warm middle part of the day, and watch for the inflections, pulses, and other abrupt signals that stand out against the surrounding patterns. Witness the rising and falling activity throughout and toward the evening. John Stilgoe urges us to abandon, even momentarily, the sleek modern technology that consumes so much time and money now, and seek out the resting place of a technology almost forgotten. Go outside and walk a bit, long enough to forget programming, long enough to take in and record new surroundings.

Sit and walk, drawing and thinking deeply about the site, on-site. Generate visual notes in your sketchbook with a list of questions to start conversations with stakeholders. Before you sit down with them, conduct an exhaustive inventory of everything you deem useful, along with everything hidden that rises above the noise or through the fog for you somehow.

I think it's optimal to start a project with an intimate personal familiarity with a site, but that's my bias. A site, while complex, guarantees a first-hand opportunity to probe, test, and understand a place from a physical, tangible, and arguably actual perspective. The timing and prioritization of landscape architectural services is highly variable. Regardless of when you enter the project timeline, my advice is to first explore the site as you would as a child, freely if possible before attempting to absorb too much history. There's likely one or more directions or a plans being discussed already, clients or stakeholder groups who have published their sets of ideas. I recommend you study them before your first visit. Let your skills come into focus on site as you identify problems in need of solutions. Wear your PPEs and perform a layered and critical analysis, looking for correlations of note. Highlight any imbalance; too much of something, too little. Is it too hot? It's getting hotter out there, particularly in the city. Could a healthy tree canopy help provide shade? How's the soil? Could a water feature help decrease the temperature? Too loud? A planted berm might screen a surrounding disturbance, lowering the decibel level, framing a gathering space, and anchoring a gateway. Might you also consider the work and its evolution as being grounded in a completely unique site? As you draw on the greatest extent of available historical information, selectively retrace important physical registrations in the landscape. Draw these out, mapping the patterns and hierarchies. You are a new arrival, but the site is a powerful and rich palimpsest to gain insight from. An inventory with good data will lead you to a conscientious analysis; analytical thought through action – writing, mapping, sketching, modeling – as connections begin to combine and calibrate.

The patterns and signals may not be obvious at first, so be patient and open, with all your facilities and sensors on high alert. Eyes, ears, nose, open and discerning, on full volume. As with the presence of unwanted water and the subsequent unraveling of material and formal possibilities in the small project I mentioned above, some solutions will start with a singular focus and then grow to encompass multiple opportunities which, when taken together, identify possible direction. Go, or No Go, becomes a handy thought-exercise, allowing some semblance of choice to rescue you in your confused state. Go if there's more ahead that way. If there isn't much, it's a no-go. Actively identifying constraints and opportunities should be first on your mind as you walk, photograph, sketch, and measure. Having allowed for initial impressions to establish in your mind, reach out, sketching, and discussing initial findings alongside the people who know the place better than you. Be a humble tourist, embodying gratitude and alert for the lessons to be learned there, with them.

People

Myth, Story, Culture, Heritage

Talk to the people with a vested interest in the long-term sustainability of the site. Break bread, share a meal. Assume rightly that they will teach you something about the site. Ask open-ended questions. Listen carefully. Think before you speak. Ask follow-up questions. Do your best to prompt a story. Listen to everyone there, not just the self-elected vocal minority. Your job is to discover how people know the site, what it means to them, how they use it, and how it shapes them in turn. Your aim is to understand their perspectives and help them develop a vision for how they hope to see it in the future. Foster conversations with empathy. Hold as best you can a prospective, opportunistic, productive and open mind. Take notes that highlight and outline the main points of what's said. Restrain your imagination if you can while you remain open to the stories and words of others. Listen deeply and intently to discern important connections and relationships. If you're listening carefully and people feel they're being heard, you'll be building mutual trust, rapport, and respect. Your conversation will be most productive from an equal footing, with the designer and stakeholders together on level ground, each contributing to a shared vision.

Be open, understanding, patient, and receptive. Explore the heritage, mixing of cultures, and social values of those who know the place best. Take a genuine and keen interest in their history. The people you serve as a designer perpetuate these histories through their agency and knowledge of the patterns and processes at work on, in, and around their sites. You are a visitor, but as a designer, you are also at times, potentially their agent of change and their mediator in determining the "highest and best use" of their land. You will leave once the work is done, and while you might return to administer construction or conduct post-occupancy evaluations, they will remain and continue the legacy. Your role is that of a sort of counselor, or trusted advisor. You assist in framing, articulating, and giving form to their goals and priorities, and you are responsible for the way the work starts and how the landscape is staged to potentially come together. Having established professional rapport, you should summarize and share back the important discoveries you made. Sometimes, your fresh eyes and your skills in visual communication will be just the thing they've been waiting for. Consider the power of representation as a vehicle to break through and record the stories and ideals of those in your care. Each project is a new story, embedded like a middle chapter in a much longer history.

Principles

Attitudes, Values, Beliefs, Guiding Tenets

A reasonable and competent designer can take a clear position on the key issues, while remaining grounded in utility, beauty, and meaning. Determining principles that govern action is a critical step in decision-making, and does not always come easy. I recommend you start as you would with any written work, like a paper or thesis, by defining key terms. Actually define them, exploring the etymology of the words themselves, linking that lineage to today, and all while considering how that foundational vocabulary can enable the creation of a persuasive argument for a potential design proposition.

According to Oxford Dictionaries, a principle is: "a fundamental truth or proposition that serves as the foundation for a system of belief or behavior or for a chain of reasoning." In design, principles are at their simplest, a sort of roadmap of critical phrases that guides your concept. They're a written articulation of what you hope to achieve. Consider topical and prescient words or phrases that identify meaningful values attributable to the work. Write them down and edit them as required. The Biomimicry Guild offers great examples. "Increased resource efficiency, maximum output with minimal input, closed-loop systems, balanced bio-and-technosphere," these phrases suggest core tenets of an idea and they allude to direction and intent. Principles simultaneously suggest opportunities and boundaries. You'll also find inspiration in the Sustainable Sites guidelines, for example: "Conserve aquatic ecosystems, design stormwater features as functional amenities, redevelop degraded sites." These are clarion calls, and invitations to learn and develop concepts with ecological best practices in mind. Yours might pursue other scenarios, but regardless, principles cannot be easily measured and tested, nor immediately deployed or verified. Instead, they simply galvanize priorities and help in forming plans of action. The outcome of a set of well-articulated principles is a value-driven roadmap that can lead to a meaningful concept.

Your argument will become more persuasive as you build evidence upon situational information related to the site and its stakeholders. As you listen to people and read the site, you will garner the components required to abstract and organize a thoughtful, and innovative proposition. Write out your design principles as if you were making a vision or mission statement. These words focus your process, informing direction, identifying goal posts, discarding anything superfluous, and consequently framing a strong starting position for the development of a framework.

If you find it difficult to generate principles, or with writing out your thoughts in general, I recommend you search for things that you're excited about. There will be ideas and technologies, inspirations and exemplars that are so interesting you simply have to study and write about them. First find your motivation. Easy-writing follows.

Framing

Structure, Organization, Rational Diagramming

Further research is a given. But what to do with all that information? Did you map too much? Do you recognize the scale of the problem? What are your Principles? You'll need to discard some content quickly, while keeping hold of the most useful, relevant, potentially interesting, provocative, or unique conceptual essence. You do not want too much data. You are looking for just the right amount to make your point. Prioritize key discoveries into a clear and legible structure. This is often best illustrated with a series of simple incremental diagrams. Identify a practical datum; an organizing geometry [in plan view], to tie the various features together. With a logical framework diagram drafted – essentially a distilled graphic of your analysis and site reconnaissance – you can critique elements of a given program, testing against exemplars or precedents, and other discoveries from research and other prior steps. Employ a Framing strategy that carefully eliminates possibilities by identifying clear constraints. Boundaries, hazardous, or otherwise no-go areas. Consider the utility of tools such as a SWOT analysis, along with other matrices and rubrics that offer a means to organize and prioritize information and key terms. Bridge your written principles into this work.

In my studios, we use a simple decision-making tool that lists and identifies indispensable vocabulary for six critical factors of site design. Write out this line in the X-axis: Ecology, Culture, Element, Material, Operation, and Time. Under each of these columns in the Y-axis, list rows of the relevant terms, and be exhaustive, list everything you can imagine falling under these core topics related to the site design. Then with everything listed, a page full, select one keyword or phrase per column to focus on in your concept development. There should be a clear and simple throughline to connect these to your analytical, representational, and conceptual work. Your jury will be impressed you considered so much information, and even more so to see you've made some rational and useful decisions. HOK's Problem Seeking goes further with a helpful tool they call the Information Index, which assesses critical programming concerns in five steps: (1) Establish Goals, (2) Collect and Analyze Facts, (3) Uncover and Test Concepts, (4) Determine Needs, and (5) State the Problem. Draw these headers out horizontally in X, then write four rows in Y, 1 Function, 2 Form, 3 Economy, and 4 Time.

All four considerations interact at each step. For example, in the first step when goals are investigated, function goals, form goals, economic goals, and time goals should emerge. With each of these having three subcategories, the process includes asking twelve pertinent questions regarding goals alone. Since the first three steps constitute the main search for information, three times twelve provides the basis for thirty-six pertinent questions.

From this matrix and other similar tools, you can determine useful correlations and connections between the needs of the project and your aims as its designer. It's difficult to overstate the value of an organized matrix of findings from this decision-making phase in communicating the foundations of your process.

Right-sizing the elements of the program is next, as you'll need to justify the scale and scope of the intervention, for a host of reasons ranging from economic to ethical. The professional and outward-serving designation of landscape architecture mandates our work address the health, safety, and welfare of the general public. While there is an art to finding and framing a problem, or making a landscape more broadly, ours is not solely a visual or even ameliorative practice, but rather a combinatory artform that fuses artful meaning with rigorous interrogation and practical engineering. I would encourage you to draw as much emphasis on data-gathering and data-filtering as possible, doing so through clear decision-making, and strong, articulate, methods of visual communication. There are myriad examples to test out for yourself.

A frame, or rather a framework, is required at some stage of the process. A grid, a membrane, skeleton, scaffolding, registration, or construction lines are all potentially valuable instruments that enable you to defensibly situate and grow the physical features of your concept. Resulting from the analysis of key site features, frameworks emerge from existing conditions as integrated, responsive, and flexible armatures. They are less effective when superimposed *a-priori.* View your and your colleague's research and analysis through this frame by ordering, arranging, and classifying the different elements of the design under your consideration. The frame is not the design, just as the scaffolding is not the building itself. But without it, the concept cannot rise above a superficial surface level. Each tier in the gridwork allows for more information to be layered and managed.

While remaining connected to the surrounding and adjacent systems at work, individual foci, activities, programs, etc., along with their sequencing, procession, and hierarchies of scale come into greater resolution and legibility. A good framework brings the whole concept together and focuses energy on what is most critical. It provides a mesh to situate landscape structures, plantings, and water features within a network of pathways and spaces. A framework also suggests a rational arrangement and proportioning of those designed features. Framing sets you up for forming, so be sure to eliminate clutter and distractions, clearing a path for experimentation with a properly sized set of materials, formal geometries, and temporal concerns.

Forming

Sculpture, Composition, Dimension, Resolution

You can start making anything, at any time, with any materials you wish. Provided you're not breaking any laws, you can just go for it. Pick something up, if it's yours go ahead, and figure it out. Cut it open, rotate, flip, stretch, or break it in any way you like. Something might happen. Did you pick up a pencil? Good, start drawing. Paper? Start folding. Dowels and glue? Start cutting and gluing. If you've been paying attention, on-site, with its people, you've learned how things work, you've established principles, and started to frame opportunities. As you proceed through the steps in this outline, make a concerted effort to give conceptual form to elements and characteristics of these experiences through diverse representational media. The more you experiment with design communication techniques, the more likely you are to learn that certain materials and approaches allow for different and varying degrees of discovery. You may not know what form an idea will take until you try to make it. And you might not even know what is possible until you get your hands on the material in question. You might carve a form out of or into the land, you might build a component upward. The idea might be hanging off a cliff. Having made the first prototype, react to it. Viewing it from every angle, consider its validity against your vision for the project.

As you iterate, layer after layer, making, reviewing, and reacting, the subject of your models and drawings inevitably becomes more vivid and precise. I recommend you start from an open position, gain traction, and then build iteratively as you go. Make a flurry of design investments early on, quickly, while remaining dedicated to seeing an optimized hybrid version pay off through further revision. Manufacture these early formations to stack on each other progressively, with a through-line and narrative in mind. This approach imbues a deeper meaning in the formal iterations themselves, imparting the values of their author, synthesizing new and important connections, and bridging research into design. In *Making Thinking*, Stephen Temple argues that "designing happens not simply from an inspired moment but as a result of rigorous transformative interactions between thinking and making in which concepts are discovered, transformed, and realized in concrete form." Like other beginning design educators, he offers a rational constructionist methodology, or

> a form of learning that builds connections between thinking and making, building connections between the abstractness of ideas and the concreteness of lived experience. The constructionist approach is an outgrowth of developmental learning theories that hold that ideas are not merely passively absorbed, but are constructed in the mind of the learner.

The strength of following this direction lies in the cumulative dis-coveries which occur with each new action. The response each iteration receives will continue to guide your formal decisions. You might go forward, or backward, but as you continue ahead inevitably, each idea and decision builds on the last, and over a short span of time, form accumulates.

By the Forming stage, it is ideal to be able to say the following with some degree of certainty: You're sincere about a premise. You can justify your initial deductions and decisions, communicating them through systematic, analytical, and layered visuals. Your research is nearly complete, relevant data has been reduced, and you count yourself among the people who understand the conditions and opportunities of the site. You've remained critical yet open to external stimuli throughout and you're now giving a degree of form and proportion to the otherwise intangible dialog. If instead, you find yourself here before Site, People, Principles, or Framing have been considered, you'll likely be drawing on too many eons of inspiration. I would ask you to give form to terrain, structures, and plantings without *a-priori* assumptions. Drink from the endless well of knowledge and ingenuity, yes, but in small sips, and over a deliberate, methodical, and judicious course. If you try to understand too much, too quickly, unguided by a framework or principles, suddenly encumbered by building codes and restrictive ordinances, you may just as soon become overwhelmed and worse, disinterested. This phenomenon is colloquially known as "analysis paralysis," and it befalls us all at some point, in some form, despite our best efforts. This perception can largely be avoided though, through careful attention to the process and proper amounts of weight assigned to the most critical factors throughout.

I find precedents and case-studies the most applicable in the Forming stage. While it's enjoyable and even useful to wander around for inspiration early on, to me, the use of case studies, precedents, or exemplars is most beneficial when a framework is complete, and most relevant when prompted by a scenario or a situation present and under study. Centuries of landworks and infrastructures, myriad objects, artifacts, and architectures; innumerable muses pose too many cultural and social evolutions to address with any seriousness. The body of seminal work in landscape architecture alone presents too many sources to consider, let alone address meaningfully. You have to be selective, and your concept is strongest if it grows from a clear and specific idea you've articulated as the result of an analytical and deductive process, in my estimation, lest you be overwhelmed by creative possibility. If your aim is to make something for its own sake, this essay might not be very helpful to you. If however, you're attempting to uncover some deeper meaning or issue to be resolved, if you're following a path that is leading you through meaningful connections and previously unforeseen discoveries, please consider the following.

Forming has to do with shaping materials to suit a program and determining strategies for longevity and performance. By shaping materials to suit a program, I am suggesting that you consider the materials in your hands as a means of realizing a concept. The representational media is worthy of scrutiny, in and of itself, but it is also best seen as an extension of the subject in physical-full-scale. A program offers useful information, and a framework provides practical dimensions and accordance for optimization. As you begin forming gathering spaces, sequences and networks of circulation, you will need one to discern sizes and proportions for elements of your design. This is an excellent cue to search for specific exemplars. How big or small is something, and how is it functioning somewhere else? Dimension and draw visual notes from precedents and experiments in analog and with three-dimensional scale models as a starting point. What are the dimensions of an element that works really well in its landscape, a low seating wall, and a stairway integrated into a hillside? Draft it to scale and incorporate it into your library. What are the proportions of the street to the surrounding building heights? How do the volumes and negative spaces shape their respective programs, and vice versa? Make scale models, plans, sections, and diagrams of the precedents, doing whatever you can to understand their sacred geometries. More detail comes as you incorporate, integrate, and synthesize a concept; connecting and revealing patterns from a site and your interpretations of these foundational discoveries.

Determining strategies for longevity and performance refers to sustainability and its deliberate pursuit. To sustain, a landscape requires a host of factors to work in harmony with one another. There needs to exist a balance between capacity and consumption; the ability of a place to support its population, and its population's ability to support it in turn. Consider this while you're analyzing the site, thinking and reflecting, and later while you're working on advancing a particular proposition. Forming the physical surface of a landscape is an act that is tied directly to the fundamental natural patterns and processes of an ecosystem, and thus to its inherent ability to adapt over time. Here, I'm referring to the topic of resilience. A term that describes the ability of a given system to respond or bounce back and achieve a normal degree of stasis after a disturbance. With that in mind, how will you conceive of a path through the shifting dunes, or by a meandering river? They have moved since the last time you looked. How might you model the changing tidal zone to anticipate rising sea levels? How can the media in your hands and the means by which you use them help you bring these and other important questions into the light?

When focused and intentional, true material experimentation fosters direct contact between concepts and a means of validating them. By choosing representational media that closely reflects the characteristics and properties of full-scale materials in the field, you produce a simulated measurable environment, and potentially an immersive psychological response. Textures, volumes, and spatial definition manifest as each element is incorporated, evaluated, and revised. You can increase or decrease scale, or even in the passage of time to gain perspective. You can inject as much variation in your methods as time permits. Forming refers to reality, to eventual full-scale construction, and therefore engages in tectonics; structures, components, their joinery, fastening, and the means of connecting dimensional or a-dimensional units together to reasonable standards. Tectonics is defined as "the science or art of construction, both in relation to use and artistic design." It refers to "the activity of making the materially requisite construction that answers certain needs, and by extension to the activity that raises this construction to an art form." This is a crucially important connection to consider, between the forming of artifacts and the formation of a process. Both feed reciprocally into the other.

Due to my training, I think of forming somewhat simultaneously in terms of landform, structures, and plants. I know this is reductive, but it represents a good pre-condition for an effective approach. I learned this as a first-semester student in Joseph S. R. Volpe's foundation studio, and I've partially adopted it in my own teaching. Volpe takes students through these three principle elements of a designed landscape incrementally, building one on the next in pursuit of a combinatory environment that integrates all its parts into a complex whole. When landform, structure, and plants are combined and arranged thoughtfully, nodes, corridors, and gateways form to integrate with the site, and with each other, giving definition to the elements, their connections and uses, and composing a sequence of experience. This design process is resolved by the introduction of clear geometries of space, be they circular, rectilinear, biomorphic, or geomorphic, and deliberate, even semi-precise degrees of enclosure, so as to define or codify the intended program. Spatial definition is a vast spectrum, from well-articulated volumes of space or connection to vague edges, partial definitions, or those which encompass the broader expanse. Therefore, the precision of this craft demands specificity and industry standards of excellence.

I recognize it looms large and intimidating – an encyclopedic tome that sits on your shelf – but within the highly detailed technical graphics, you'll find the narrative in Time Saver Standards for Landscape Architects stands the test of time. As the book indicates, "grading of a site should be thought of as a systematic process that begins with the analysis and understanding of the existing site and ends with an overall detailed grading plan." As a designer, you're asked to "determine how existing landforms would affect proposed use areas, such as building locations, roads, parking areas, walkways, plazas, and lawn areas." And, the reference suggests you do this by working through each of these design problems/opportunities, in order:

> Define general use areas, set building floor areas by spot elevations, and diagram drainage flow using slope arrows pointing along the direction of flow. This will help in the following procedures: 1. Developing a general landform concept. 2.

Locating swales and surface water flow. 3. Locating drainage receptacles. 4. Calculating water runoff for various areas. And 5. Defining an area that could be altered (raised or lowered) with limited Impact on drainage or existing trees. This area could be used to help balance any surplus cut or fill.

These are practical instructions, particularly in defining the role of landform through the site's existing conditions and proposed uses. They offer a best-practices lane for you to follow. But perhaps most importantly, as a designer, these standards allow for an incredible amount of interpretation. Each site, each group of people, each set of principles, and every unique framework will offer some veiled room for improvisation. Each can also infer or demand a specific solution.

Landscape structures – pads, landings, paved spaces, the hard edges, walls, curbs, joints – and plantings – groundcover, shrubs, canopy trees, the soft edges; plants as floor, wall, and ceiling – come next in my process. Both are designed with the terrain, integrated to highlight the advantages of the site, and resolve certain issues, be they circulatory, spatial, technological, programmatic, or otherwise, their deliberate combination and layering, aiming to define and enhance the overall experience of a place. When well-integrated with landform, landscape structures seem to emerge from the site, fusing hard and soft together, shaping cues for movement or rest or play, rather than appearing awkwardly placed or carelessly inserted. Landscape structures usually perform best when they respond to the unique qualities and characteristics of a physical place. These expensive and semi-permanent interventions require anchors to and foundations on the ground. The same ground that has been there long before your design process started. As individual or mono-functional objects, they underperform. But as interconnected and conglomerated features possessing a complimentary style, gesture, or materiality, landscape structures are the familiar hardscape of daily life – the sidewalk, the front stoop, the riverside seating wall or the ramp – and all are designed to varying degrees of optimization, all around us.

Consider how they form to define space and shape experience through gathering, movement, and procession. How some improve safety or promote wellness, like a shade structure that helps cool a space in midday, presenting a comfortable respite and a contrast to a less desirable condition. How might a wide tree-lined pedestrian corridor invite movement? Maybe it arcs in a gentle bend to draw the eye? Or is it a straight vector that intersects with a landmark, or opens toward the horizon, drawing a longer view and sharper sense of orientation to the environment beyond? How does a staircase invite ascension above the ground below? How does that elevated prospect change the view? To experience the landscape is to move through it in three dimensions. And unless you're walking through unmanaged forest or desert, it's more likely than not you're traversing over intentional structures designed by landscape architects or other engineers of the land. Similarly, plants and landforms suggest natural harmonies with one another. Grades and slopes in the topography indicate microclimates fit for particular species and plant communities. Plants reciprocate, with somewhat predictable habits, and patterns, and their root structures can act in stabilizing slopes and forecasting where erosion and deposition are likely to occur.

The most remarkable thing about plants is how they develop over time.

> Every year they add height and girth in a flush of new growth. They are forever expanding, from the bottom to the top and from the inside to the outside, a tree that is not expanding is a tree that is dying.

In forming with plants, consider their desired, established maximal condition, and visualize the stages of the growth that will lead them to that future state. Plants are nearly always immature when installed in a landscape, and some take a very long time to mature. I subscribe to an intaglio or subtractive approach, looking for opportunities to fill whole areas or zones on a map. I would almost always advocate for removing as few existing trees as possible unless there is a particularly egregious specimen. With the critical root zone of as many existing plants as possible indicated, I then identify the different topographic zones for suitable palates of plant material. I try to completely fill a design; a landscape, using a grid based on the important registrations from the site framework. With the zones filled in and assumptions about the growth of those plants in mind, I'll look for areas that preclude plantings – inherited boundaries, existing subgrade infrastructure, other hazards or safety concerns, and other important elements in the design. A sensible overlay of the desired information and a thoughtful analysis is required to delineate massings and structure plant communities.

From there, the design work goes into schematic production. The concept is stripped to its essence. The layers of research and analysis come together to create a site plan, a high-quality model, and various other measurable and replicable outputs. Experimentation is mostly set aside for efficiency and standard formulae. The better, the more legible, and the more organized the record of the creative beginnings, the more that conceptual spirit will be captured in the work ahead. Beyond schematic design, the work will largely be clarified and validated through revision, reduction, and negotiation between the design team and stakeholders. Design development will further articulate the work, and the construction documents and specifications will provide instructions to a contractor and provide legal documentation to ensure the work is built while protecting the designer, owner, and contractor from liability. While in practice conceptualization might sometimes only represent a small portion of the design process, it nevertheless represents a pivotal moment and set of associated actions that set the project on its course. Do your very best to be innovative and prospective, while communicating how your concept is the consequence of a rigorous and creative process.

Conclusion

Managing one's time has been complicated in recent years by an overwhelming amount of instant, free, highly entertaining, passive content. Put it all away. Stop scrolling literally and figuratively through an algorithm designed to steal your time. Instead, tune your vibrations back into yourself, into nature, to your own heartbeat. Listen to the sounds of the waves, any waves. Breathe, and meditate. Practice gratitude for your heartbeat, for the gift of life. Turn off the distractions, and let your mind focus. These may seem cliche, but let that thought go too. If silence is too intimidating at first, play the piano, or a game of chess, do a crossword puzzle and exercise your brain a little. Swim. Hike. Be in nature. The silence will help. You'll need to understand how to use the tools and techniques in your skillset, for yourself. And you'll have to spend some quiet time thinking about these things. You'll want to give shape to your ideas through thoughtful and careful deliberation of the facts presented in a given project. Let your mind rest between working sessions. In my estimation, forming a concept requires a lot of effort and concentration. Data-gathering and filtering, sketching, drawing, and modeling, all while thinking small-to-large-to-small, aiming to simplify complexity and gain a level of working understanding. There's too much to think about, but nevertheless, a design concept is shaped by its whole process. The drawings and diagrams, the informal conversations, shared principles, as well as an ability to compromise, demonstrate patience, empathy, and to apply your imagination, ingenuity, and hard work. Above all, make some time for yourself to reflect.

Speaking of time, notions of end-client, or end-goal are complicated by landscape's longevity. With that, along with the looming question, of when is the end in mind, the pursuit of sustainability – a balance of resources and willingness to maintain them – should be a goal of every designer, for every project. Sustainability is, in fact, inevitable, by definition, if humanity is to survive. While nothing is assured, what is clear is that some actions will more than likely accelerate its pace, while others will continue to resist adapting to change. Future reforms will be required if ecological and economic balance is ever to manifest. Your work can contribute positively toward this great human effort. Dispense with the myth of genius and the savior complex and do good work in your community. As you build on previous experience, your community grows.

I recommend the use of these lenses, in sequence – Site, People, Principles, Framing, and Forming – to generate as accurate a "model" of the existing landscape as you can. Gather the right amount of information, visualize them along with the integration of your strategies, and make beautiful and imaginative images to drive the conversation. Give the dialog physical form, through research and design, through the myriad possibilities in experimentation and representation, imbuing in your work the unique values and aspirations that make it your own.

Index

Note: *Italic* page numbers refer to figures.

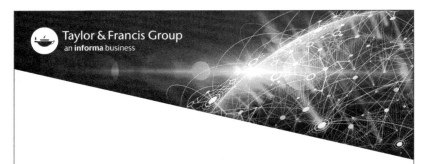